NOVA SCOTIA FOLK ART

AN ILLUSTRATED GUIDE

RAY CRONIN

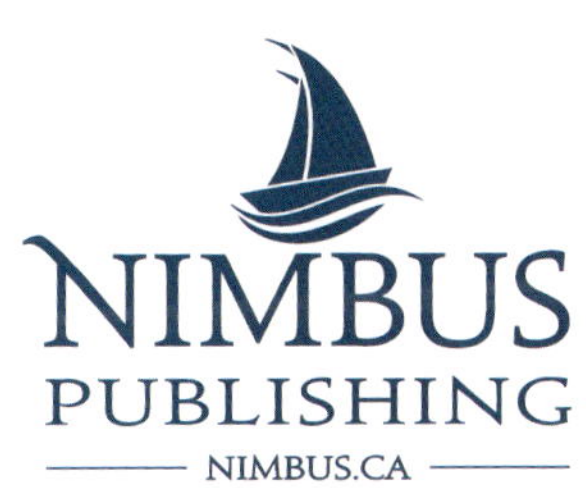

Nimbus Publishing Limited
3660 Strawberry Hill Street, Halifax, NS, B3K 5A9
(902) 455-4286 nimbus.ca

Nimbus Publishing is based in Kjipuktuk, Mi'kma'ki, the traditional territory of the Mi'kmaq People.

Printed and bound in China
NB1440

All images courtesy AGNS
Photography: Michael Tompkins and RAW Photography for AGNS
Produced in cooperation with the Art Gallery of Nova Scotia
The author has made all reasonable attempts to obtain permission to reproduce the images within. The publisher assumes no responsibility or liability for any errors or omissions.

Editor: Angela Mombourquette
Design: Jenn Embree

Library and Archives Canada Cataloguing in Publication

Title: Nova Scotia folk art : an illustrated guide / Ray Cronin.
Names: Cronin, Ray, 1964- author.
Description: Includes bibliographical references and index.
Identifiers: Canadiana (print) 2023058571X | Canadiana (ebook) 20230585736 |
ISBN 9781771088343 (softcover) | ISBN 9781771088350 (HTML)
Subjects: LCSH: Folk art—Nova Scotia. | LCSH: Folk artists—Nova Scotia.
Classification: LCC NK842.N6 C76 2024 | DDC 745.09716—dc23

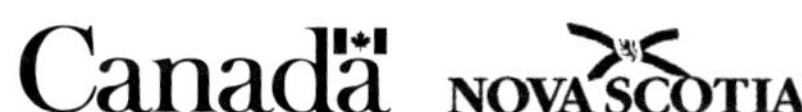

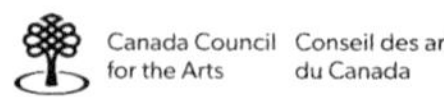

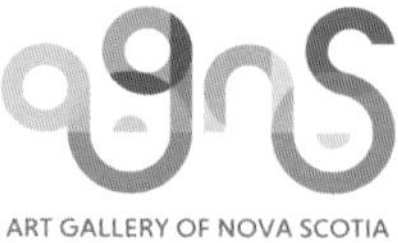

Nimbus Publishing acknowledges the financial support for its publishing activities from the Government of Canada, the Canada Council for the Arts, and from the Province of Nova Scotia. We are pleased to work in partnership with the Province of Nova Scotia to develop and promote our creative industries for the benefit of all Nova Scotians.

TABLE OF CONTENTS

CLASSIC OR FIRST-WAVE ARTISTS

SECOND-WAVE ARTISTS

THIRD-WAVE ARTISTS

FOREWORD

THE ART GALLERY OF NOVA SCOTIA IS PLEASED TO PARTNER WITH Nimbus Publishing to celebrate the rich and varied history of folk art in Nova Scotia. From the 1976 formative nationally touring exhibition *Folk Art of Nova Scotia*, the Art Gallery of Nova Scotia has been proud of its role in promoting, sharing, exhibiting, and acquiring the special work being made by folk artists here in this province.

For anyone who has asked themselves "what is folk art?" this book helps answer the question with an overview of regional variations in folk art across the breadth of the province and the waves of creation it has seen and continues to see. Ray Cronin, in his former role as senior curator at the Art Gallery of Nova Scotia, enjoyed the vibrant conversation folk art elicited and debate over what that term meant and has evolved to mean. In this publication he critically examines the art form and helps navigate the blurry line between the historical figures of the genre and the living artists working in the contemporary art realm.

The Art Gallery of Nova Scotia is inextricably tied to the fabrication of the genre of Nova Scotia Folk Art. Established in 1975, the first curator and director of the Gallery, Bernard Riordon, was one of a dedicated group of collectors and curators who wanted to bring the work of classic folk art to a broader audience. Twenty percent of acquisitions made by the Gallery in the first five years were folk art and include superlative examples from the classic artists of Nova Scotia Folk Art, which the AGNS helped define. While the Gallery is best known for being the home of the Maud Lewis House, that structure was acquired well after this first wave of collecting (and was restored many years after that), but two of Maud Lewis's paintings were among the first works acquired, along with pieces by Charlie Ray Atkinson, Samuel Bolivar, Ralph Boutilier, Evelyn Dickie, Collins Eisenhauer, and so many more.

Continuing the format utilized in the catalogue associated with the Art Gallery of Nova Scotia's 1976 exhibition of Nova Scotia Folk Art, Ray Cronin explores each artist and their work, providing context to their unique creations and distinct voices. This publication is filled with images of works by iconic

Nova Scotia folk artists, many from the Gallery's collection. It is so exciting to see the scope of the works and marvel at the ingenuity of each artist as well as the humour and subtlety that has helped define what is considered Nova Scotia Folk Art, and which has expanded considerably since that first publication. The AGNS is exceptionally proud to champion this beguiling, charismatic art form.

I want to commend Ray Cronin for this important work, helping to update the narrative around folk art and celebrate a brand of art truly unique to Nova Scotia. I also want to recognize the work of the Art Gallery of Nova Scotia's collections team, namely Shannon Parker, Laufer Curator of Collections, Troy Wagner, Assistant Registrar, and our technical team, Don Van Buskirk, Frank Lively, and James Norton, who worked carefully with the team at Nimbus and with Ray to make these wonderful works of art accessible.

Sarah Moore Fillmore, Chief Executive Officer, Art Gallery of Nova Scotia
NOVEMBER 2023

INTRODUCTION

"BEHIND THOSE WEATHERED DOORS"

FOLK ART IS NOT UNIQUE TO NOVA SCOTIA OR EVEN TO CANADA. IT HAS flourished wherever there are traditions of what we have come to call "fine art," the sophisticated counterpoint to folk art's supposed naïveté. In Nova Scotia, however, contemporary folk art has become a distinct style, related to but distinct from the weather vanes, ship's models, crooked knives, samplers, rugs, and other items historically produced by mostly rural people for mostly domestic use. Those objects, most of which are merely utilitarian, some of which are exquisite, are examples of what has been traditionally known as folk art—that is, as expressions of folk traditions. But in Nova Scotia a different form of expression evolved in the twentieth century, one which focussed more on the "artist" than on the "folk," and which stressed individual creativity over collective utility.

There may be many folk artists in Canada, but really there is only one integrated folk art scene—that of Nova Scotia. Art historian Erin Morton, in her book *For Folk's Sake: Art and Economy in Twentieth-Century Nova Scotia*, documents the evolution of folk art in Nova Scotia as a creation of cultural elites—galleries, critics, and collectors. As she writes, "The concept of folk art could not exist in its current form had art institutions not conjured it up to begin with."[1] This book then, will look at that process of "conjuring," at the exhibitions, collections, and festivals that allowed a group of Nova Scotia artists to move their creations from the roadside to the museum, and in so doing to create its own genre: Nova Scotia Folk Art.

Nova Scotia Folk Art is a contemporary art rather than a traditional one, and it has had, roughly, three phases, which I, among others, call "classic" or "first wave," "second wave," and "third wave." As artist and educator Harold Pearse correctly points out, "Nova Scotia Folk Art comes in waves,"[2] and those waves are still coming ashore.

Classic folk art is the work of artists who did not think of themselves as artists, who made art that they never considered to be art at all. They made objects for their own amusement, or for the amusement of their family and friends, and to make a little extra money selling souvenirs to tourists. There were no festivals, no folk art galleries, and no touring exhibitions when they started, just a sign by the side of the road, a painted house, or colourful sculptures in the yard to attract the attention of passers-by. In the 1970s these artists were "discovered" by a dedicated group of collectors and curators who brought their work to wider attention. Bernard Riordon, the first curator and director of the Art Gallery of Nova Scotia (AGNS) was one. So were Halifax artist and art professor Gerald Ferguson, Bridgewater antique dealer Murray Stewart, and Dalhousie Art Gallery curator Bruce Ferguson. But no one had more to do with the discovery, and in some way the creation, of Nova Scotia Folk Art than artist, collector, and art and antique dealer Chris Huntington.

Through his tireless promotion of folk art and artists, through his Wild Goose Chase Gallery in Blockhouse, through his annual auctions, and through his work with the AGNS and the Canadian Museum of History to build collections of Nova Scotia Folk Art, he sought out and brought to light the treasures that he knew were behind Nova Scotians' "weathered doors."[3]

The second phase of Nova Scotia Folk Art consists of a generation of artists who started making work after witnessing the burst of attention paid to folk art in the 1970s and early 1980s. This group was directly influenced by classic folk artists, who were often their neighbours or family members. These second-wave artists were self-aware—they were making folk art to sell, primarily at another innovation of Huntington's: the Nova Scotia Folk Art Festival, which had its first iteration in Blockhouse in 1988 and has been held yearly ever since.

The second-wave artists worked in a context where there was excitement about Nova Scotia Folk Art, and what seemed to be an ever-growing market, with ever-increasing media attention, more and more venues for exhibition and sales, and enthusiastic collectors.

The third phase saw a large increase in the number of artists, and what some bemoan as a drop in the overall originality and creativity. For many, Nova Scotia Folk Art had become a style, and many newer artists were emulating older ones. However, as with any art form, there are always the ones who rise to the top; the artists who make work for art galleries and for the most discerning collectors. These artists may work in a primitive or folk style, but they themselves are not naive, nor are they unaware of the impact of their work and its function as art. Many don't call themselves folk artists anymore, but all, at some point in their careers,

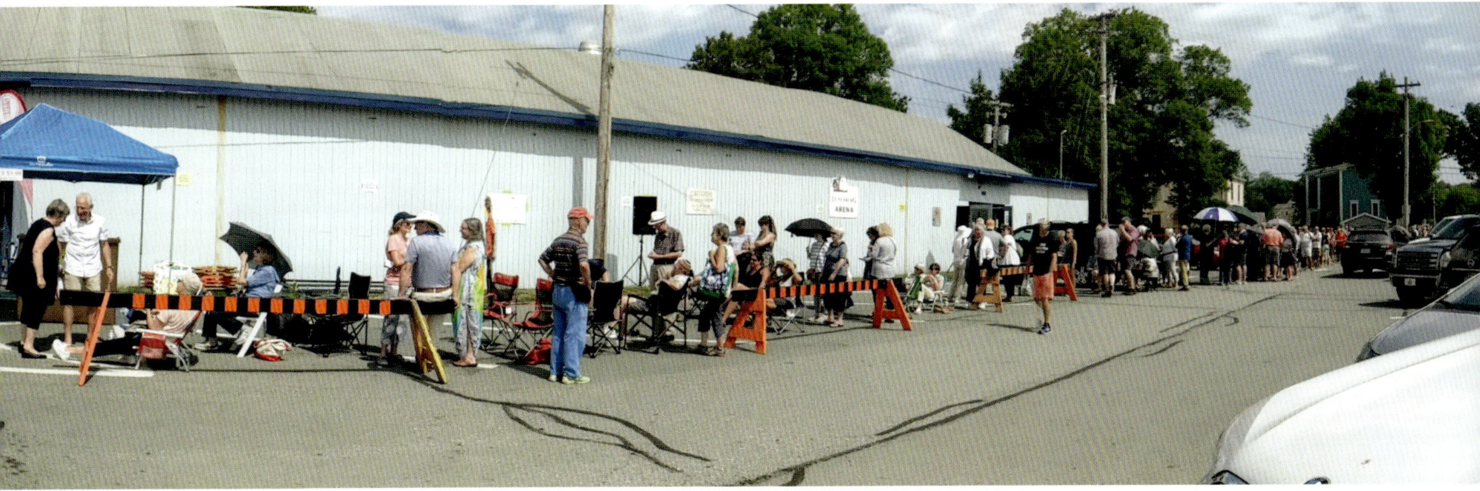

People lining up for the Nova Scotia Folk Art Festival.

(NOVA SCOTIA FOLK ART FESTIVAL SOCIETY)

self-identified as folk artists. The attention has lagged, and there are fewer galleries and shops to show their work, but collectors still start lining up hours before the opening of the annual Nova Scotia Folk Art Festival in Lunenburg, competing to snap up the cream of the show in the first minutes after the doors open at noon.

Because this book is about the genre "Nova Scotia Folk Art," it does not include the traditional decorative arts—works that I believe are properly included with the fine crafts, such as ceramics, weaving, and jewellery. Nor will you see Chéticamp rug-hooking here, or traditional or contemporary Mi'kmaw baskets or quillwork, African Nova Scotian basketry, or examples of metal or woodworking that fit into other categories. These exclusions reflect only the limits of the scope of this book, and the specificities of the genre under discussion. Traditional folk art has always been about objects; often the maker is unknown. In Nova Scotia we have seen the shift in focus from object to artist; the makers, and their stories, are central to the appeal. In the end, I make no attempt to define folk art globally, but rather look at it as a local phenomenon, one that has grown here as the result of a unique combination of circumstances and opportunities.

THE ORIGINS OF NOVA SCOTIA FOLK ART

Before we can get into how Nova Scotia Folk Art evolved, we need some clarity on the overall genre. What is folk art, anyway?

According to *The Oxford Dictionary of Art*, folk art includes "objects and decorations made in a traditional fashion by craftsmen without formal training."[4]

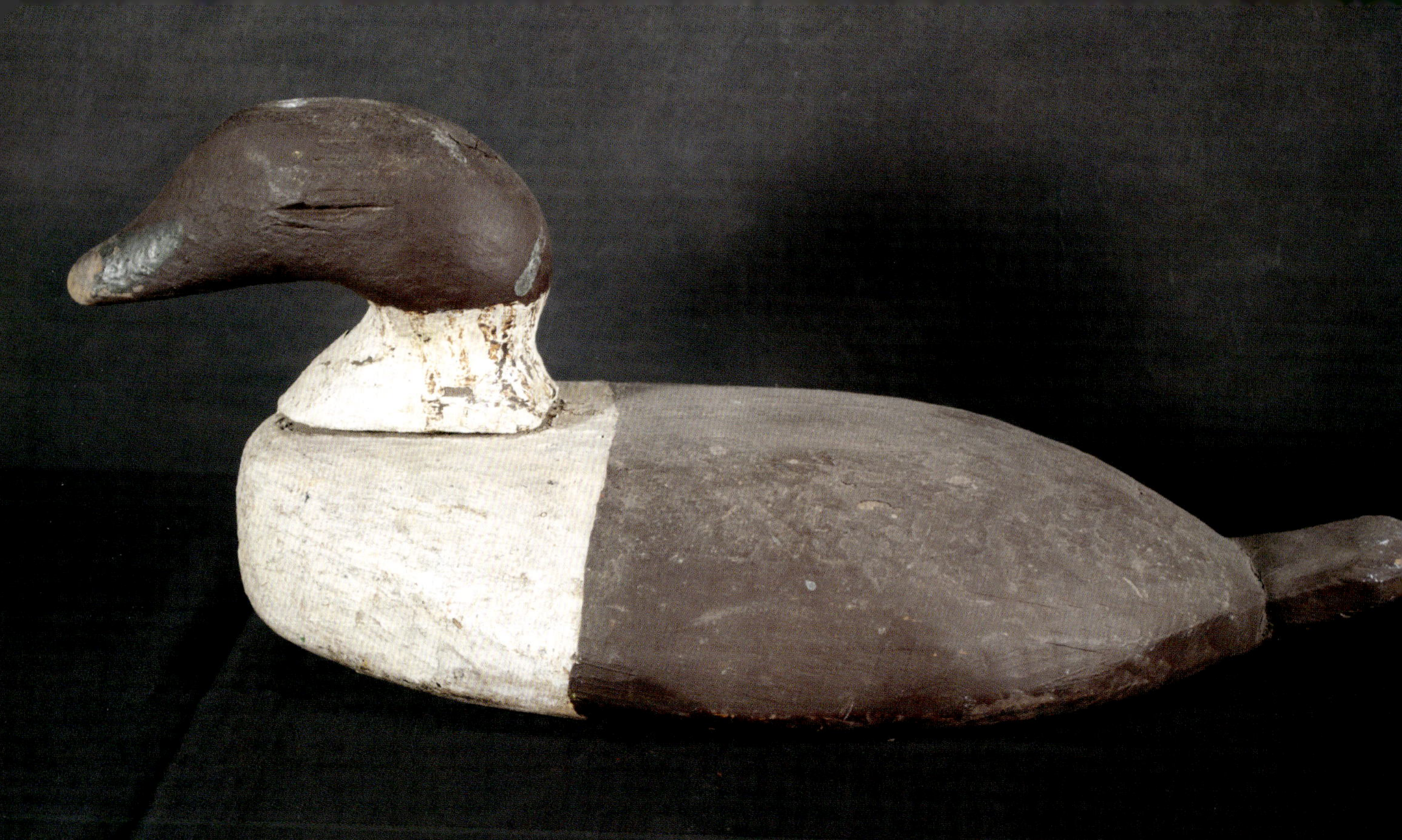

Decoy,
Artist Unknown
(AGNS)

That seems clear enough, and it certainly is apt when one is discussing such forms of folk art as butter moulds, weather vanes, duck decoys, crooked knives, ship models, game boards, samplers and so on. These objects, long collected by individuals and institutions alike, reflect traditions that have been passed down in families and communities for generations.

The dictionary goes on to say that "folk art is little subject to fashion and changing taste. Its methods are handed down in the home from generation to generation, and traditional designs and patterns persist with little alteration."[5] That is, a trivet made by the local blacksmith would be in a local style he would have learned from his predecessor—often his father, uncle, or older brother. A sailor's scrimshaw carving on whalebone would have reflected the carvings he would have seen by older sailors from his community—whether that community is defined as the ship he sailed on, or the village where he lived when he wasn't at sea. And all dairy farmers had a pattern, carved into the wooden moulds that went with the family farm, that would be pressed into their butter.

As a definition this is fine, as far as it goes. But what about something like a painting by Maud Lewis or Joe Norris? Do Maud's black cats or Joe's seagulls reflect the way paintings were always made in their communities, passed down from generation to generation? Of course not. And one need only make repeat visits to the Nova Scotia Folk Art Festival in Lunenburg to see how individual artists innovate in terms of their techniques and subject matter to know that here, at least, we are not dealing with something "little subject to fashion and changing taste." Obviously, the definition is lacking.

In the introduction to *Folk Art of Nova Scotia*, the catalogue to the first touring exhibition organized by the then-new Art Gallery of Nova Scotia, curator Bernard Riordon writes that "the problem of defining 'folk art' rose regularly throughout the planning and production stages of the exhibition. It was felt that perhaps words such as 'naïve' or 'primitive' would more fully describe the exhibition that we were presenting."[6] Here is *The Oxford Dictionary of Art* again, on the term "naïve art": "Term applied to painting produced in sophisticated societies but lacking conventional expertise in representational skills."[7] What's more, they helpfully suggest that "naïve artists are not necessarily untrained or amateurs. Sophisticated artists may also deliberately affect a naïve style."[8] That is a better definition, and it certainly has room for the works of Lewis and Norris. However, throughout the later 1970s and 1980s curators in Canada hesitated to brand the work of untrained (or less trained) artists as "naïve"—shying away from the implied judgement in the term. After all, while "uneducated" and "naïve" are not necessarily synonyms, they are often used in just that manner. "Naïve," it was thought, was patronizing.

The **Canadian Museum of Civilization** began in May 1856 as part of the Geological Survey of Canada. The museum later became **the National Museum of Canada** and then the **National Museum of Man**. In 1986, it became the **Canadian Museum of Civilization**. In 2012 it became known as the **Canadian Museum of History**.

Whatever its name, though, from the 1970s on folk art was a major focus for Canadian museums and art galleries, primarily driven by the AGNS and the then–National Museum of Man (now the Canadian Museum of History). In addition to *Folk Art of Nova Scotia*, which toured the country from 1976 to 1978, there were other survey exhibitions such as *A People's Art*, organized by the National Gallery of Canada in 1973; *From the Heart: Folk Art in Canada*, mounted by the National Museum of Man in 1983; *Spirit of Nova Scotia: Traditional Decorative Folk Art 1780–1930*, organized and toured by the AGNS; and *This Other Eden: Canadian Folk Art Outdoors*, mounted by the renamed Canadian Museum of Civilization (now the Canadian Museum of History) that toured through the early 2000s. The AGNS also mounted numerous group exhibitions that did not tour, and held large touring retrospectives of Maud Lewis (1997–1998) and Joe Norris (2000–2001). Most, but not all, of these exhibitions were of what has come to be known as "contemporary" folk art—that is, work by identifiable artists made in the twentieth century. In Canada, at least, the term "folk art" still comprises both the traditional and the contemporary: folk, naïve, and primitive expressions alike.

But the AGNS's exhibition in 1976 of Nova Scotia Folk Art had another effect. In order to differentiate their project from *A People's Art*, the National Gallery's exhibition of "primitive, naïve, provincial and folk painting in Canada," the curators chose to exhibit only works from the twentieth century, and primarily works by individuals who were making objects for display. There were only a few traditional items in this exhibition, added for context. The show was built up around what would have once been called naïve art—paintings, drawings, sculptures, and textile works that, according to the curators, were art. They were "individual statements which display the creative features of spontaneity, simplicity, and in some cases, humour."[9] The cover of the catalogue featured a photograph of four nearly life-sized sculptures by Collins Eisenhauer of contemporary politicians. These were hardly the product of methods "handed down in the home from generation to generation." Instead, they were, as Riordon wrote, "individual statements," the "unique creations" of "a group of imaginative individuals."[10] That exhibition, which featured the work of twenty-one Nova Scotia folk artists (all but four of them living when the show was first mounted), was a departure for the folk art genre in Canada. For the first time, an exhibition focussed not on handicrafts but almost exclusively on works made for aesthetic purposes—as art, not as functional objects.

In 1976, folk art was a relatively recent interest of the fledgling AGNS, which had only been incorporated in 1975. Recent, but strategic, as folk art was an area that was demonstrably Nova Scotian and which could be marketed both internally and externally to help the AGNS in its desire to create a permanent building for itself (in 1975 the AGNS occupied the old site of the Nova Scotia College of Art and Design, in a building owned by Dalhousie University that would soon be turned to Dal's own purposes). As Riordon told Erin Morton, the decision early on to focus on folk art was a calculated one, because such a focus only required "a small amount of resources and money to develop it."[11] The AGNS was ready to buy. But it needed a seller.

As central as Bernard Riordon is to the history of folk art in Nova Scotia, the most important figure by far is Chris Huntington. An artist and antique dealer from Maine, Huntington and his then-wife Ellen had decided to move to Nova Scotia in 1974. They sold their antique business and, in an auction that made front-page news in the United States, their large collection of

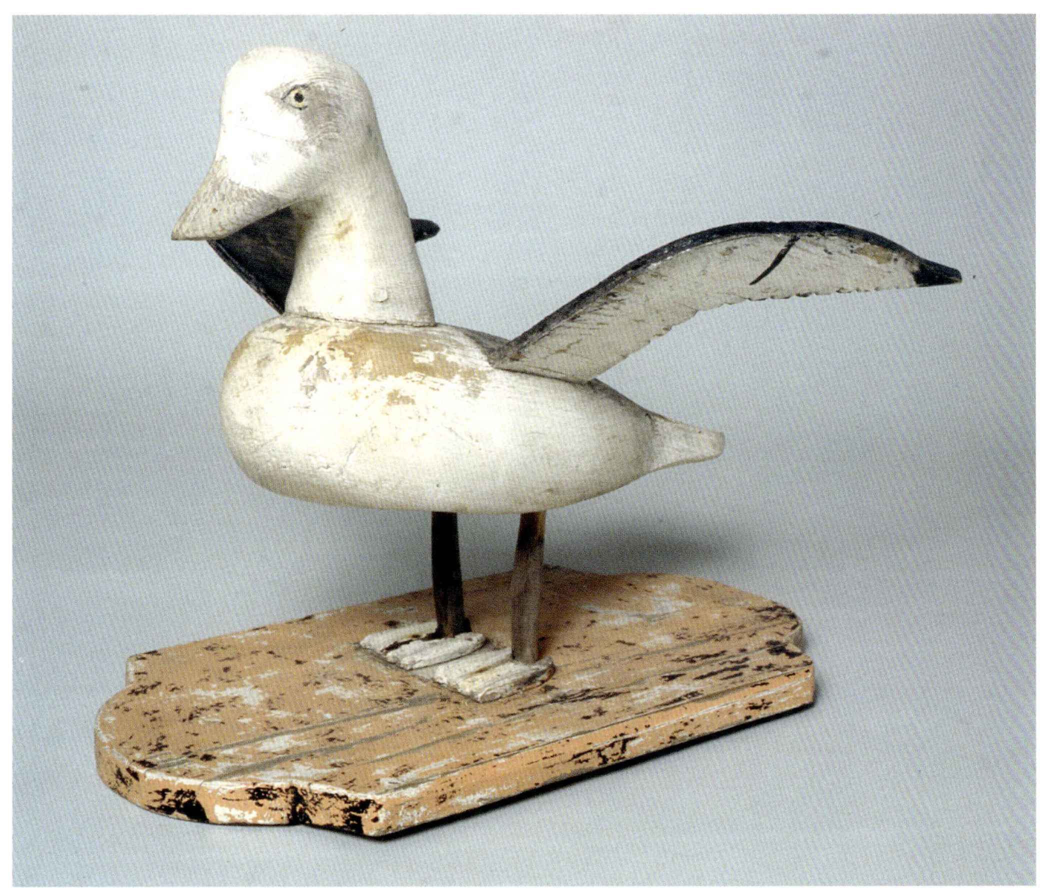

Seagull,
Charles Atkinson

(AGNS)

New England antiques and folk art. Huntington's intention in moving to Queens County was to concentrate on his own painting. However, soon after moving he began to see examples of contemporary folk art that he simply couldn't resist. He and Ellen had already been familiar with Collins Eisenhauer, through the efforts of Nova Scotia antique dealer Murray Stewart. But at their new home of Eagle Head they found that their neighbour, Charlie Tanner, made distinctive lawn decorations and, on being asked if had anything else, had shown Huntington a quirky carving that was eventually included in the *Folk Art of Nova Scotia* exhibition.

Huntington struck a deal with Tanner—he would buy all the carvings Tanner could produce. Then Huntington began scouring the province, following leads or just knocking on the doors of houses that displayed intriguing lawn decorations, birdhouses, or anything else that suggested there might be something interesting going on. He was driven by one big question: "How many more Charlie Tanners were there out there behind those weathered doors?"[12]

Plenty, as it turned out. The story of Nova Scotia Folk Art in the 1970s is one of discovery, and the discoverer's name that keeps coming up is Chris Huntington.

Charlie Atkinson, Samuel Bollivar, Ralph Boutilier, Ellison Eagles, Sidney Howard, Clarence "Bubby" Mooers, Joe Norris, Charlie Tanner, and Harry Wile were all "discovered," or at least brought to greater public attention, by the efforts of Chris Huntington. He also introduced these artists, and many more, to the idea of being fairly paid for their work. When he was rummaging in Ralph Boutilier's basement, for instance, and found his now-iconic blue jay sculpture, Boutilier offered to sell it for $50 because it didn't work. Huntington gave him $100.

Huntington soon became the "go-to" person for contemporary Nova Scotia Folk Art. When the AGNS determined to do an exhibition to travel the country, he and Ellen were logical members of the show's selection committee. They were joined by Murray Stewart, artist and NSCAD Professor Gerald Ferguson, and Dalhousie Art Gallery curator Bruce Ferguson (no relation). There were nineteen lenders to the project, but over 60 percent of the work included was from Chris or Ellen Huntington's collections (the only artists in the exhibition whose work had not been collected by the Huntingtons were Maud Lewis, Joe Sleep, Evelyn Dickie, and Fred Trask). The show travelled to six Canadian cities, including a stop at the National Gallery of Canada. In 1977 Huntington sold much of the work he had loaned to the exhibition to the National Museum of Man and the Art Gallery of Nova Scotia, establishing the core Nova Scotia Folk Art collections for both institutions (Huntington has also made significant gifts of folk art to the AGNS).

The artists in *Folk Art of Nova Scotia* were similar in that they were mostly elderly, mostly little-educated, and mostly rural. Few of them had much schooling beyond elementary, and all of them had worked hard all their lives in working-class occupations. They made their art with no expectation of fame or profit. They worked in relative isolation and obscurity and few of them even knew that there were other people making the kinds of things they were—that is, until Huntington and the AGNS shone a spotlight on them.

There was an element of having mounted this exhibition in the nick of time. Of the fifteen living artists in the exhibition, ten were deceased by 1982, and others had stopped making work for health reasons. But there was a growing national and international interest in folk art. Chris Huntington started putting advertisements in local papers seeking folk artists, and one of the things he began to notice was a growing number of artists who started making work directly as a result of the attention paid to the 1976 exhibition. No longer making objects for their own amusement, this second wave of folk artists was seeking a market. And they found one.

Through the early 1980s the interest in Nova Scotia Folk Art kept growing. The National Museum of Man's touring exhibition in 1983, *From the Heart*, included several Nova Scotian artists, including Charlie Atkinson, Ralph Boutilier, Collins Eisenhauer, Albert Lohnes, Clarence "Bubby" Mooers, Joe Norris, and Joe Sleep. Interestingly, Maud Lewis was not included—her star had not yet begun to rise. The AGNS mounted six survey exhibitions of folk art throughout the 1980s, as well as solo shows by artists such as Charlie Tanner, Joe Sleep, and Ellen Gould Sullivan.

The second generation of folk artists was coming to the fore, including artists such as Eddie Mandaggio, Wes Hubley, Harold "Dick" Tutty, Murray Gallant, and the Naugler Brothers: Bradford, Leo, and Ransford. Toronto commercial art galleries such as Mira Godard and Wynick/Tuck were mounting exhibitions of Nova Scotia folk art and selling out, and there were more and more venues for folk artists to sell their work opening up in Nova Scotia, including the Houston North Gallery in Lunenburg that had originally focussed mostly on Inuit art. In addition, Chris Huntington had opened his Wild Goose Chase Gallery in Blockhouse, outside Lunenburg.

The next big step in the evolution of Nova Scotia Folk Art was to come in 1989. Huntington decided that a festival celebrating folk art, coupled with an auction of antiques and art, would be a good project for his new gallery. Halifax's SoHo Kitchen (with co-owner and aspiring folk artist Kyle Jackson) came on board as co-sponsors of the "First Annual Nova Scotia Folk Art Festival and Picnic,"

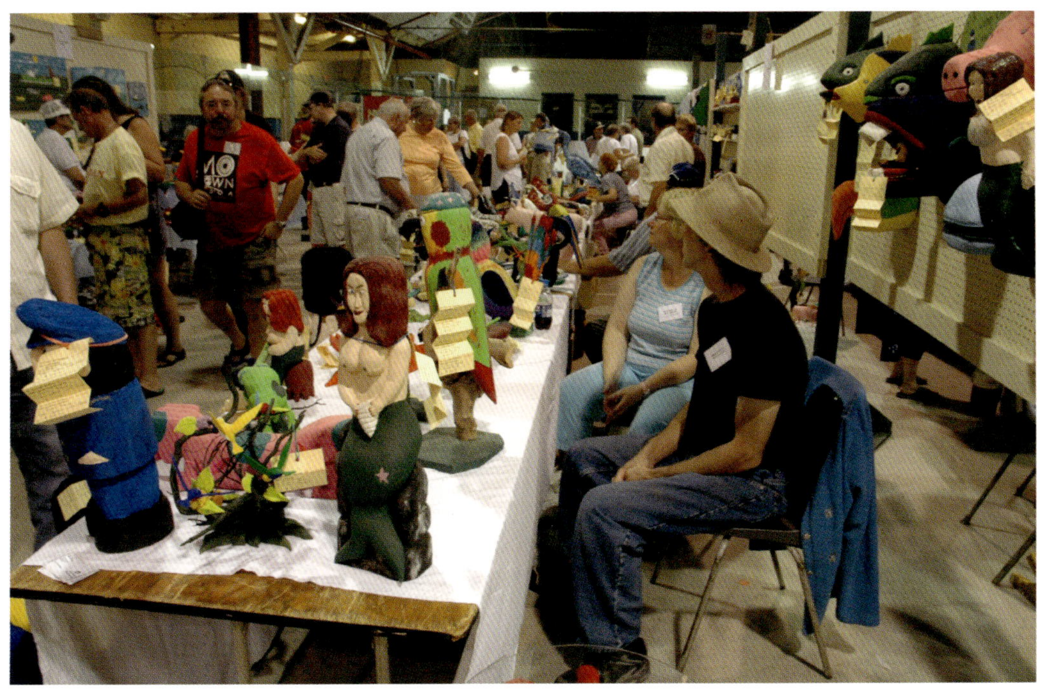

Crowds at the current-day Nova Scotia Folk Art Festival.

(NOVA SCOTIA FOLK ART FESTIVAL SOCIETY)

and Huntington also enlisted the aid of two other friends, the artists and gallery owners Lorne Reid and David Stephens of Chéticamp. Nineteen artists showed their work in that first festival, including Jackson, Stephens, and Reid. The organizers took no commission on sales; instead the 40 percent commission was donated to the AGNS for its folk art acquisition budget.

The festival introduced a new generation of folk artists to the public, as only two of the exhibitors—Sidney Howard and Clarence Mooers—were part of the first wave of Nova Scotia folk artists. New to the public were artists such as Eddie Mandaggio, Leo Naugler, Bradford Naugler, Garnet McPhail, and Walter Cook. And while the festival has undergone many changes, it has run every year since, now with over fifty exhibitors each year and thousands of visitors. In 1992, for the fourth iteration of the festival, the location was moved indoors to the Lunenburg Community Arena, where it has remained ever since.

More than anything else, the success of the Nova Scotia Folk Art Festival, since 2002 managed by the non-profit Lunenburg Heritage Society, was the factor that ensured that "Nova Scotia Folk Art" became a recognized and enduring art style. Each year new artists are featured, and while the overall quality

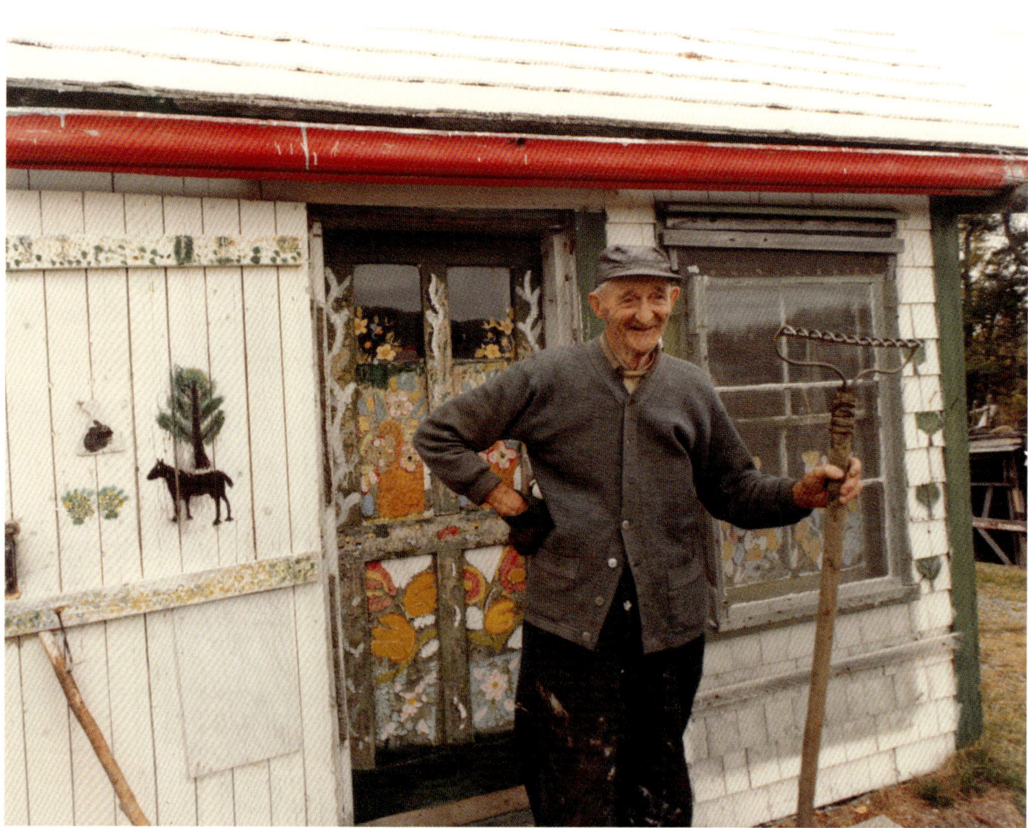

Everett Lewis outside his home—the famous painted house.

(AGNS)

has suffered from those early years, with a certain preponderance of "cottage craft" stylings, there remain many serious artists working in a folk art style who show at the festival every year, including such artists as Bradford Naugler, Barry Colpitts, and Laura Kenney.

The 1980s were notable in Nova Scotia Folk Art for another reason—the opening of a permanent home for the Art Gallery of Nova Scotia. That home included a large permanent collection display of Nova Scotia Folk Art, but it did not include the one object that had been the major reason for the success of the gallery's building plans: Maud Lewis's painted house.

The province of Nova Scotia acquired Maud Lewis's painted house in 1984, with the promise that it would be restored and put on view. That promise was a major spur for the plan to build a new home for the gallery on the Halifax waterfront, as the proposed building would feature the house as a central attraction. Unfortunately, the plan for a building on the waterfront at that time was killed by political factors. The land on the waterfront went to a private developer, and an abandoned historical building across the street from the provincial legislature was designated as the site for a new art gallery.

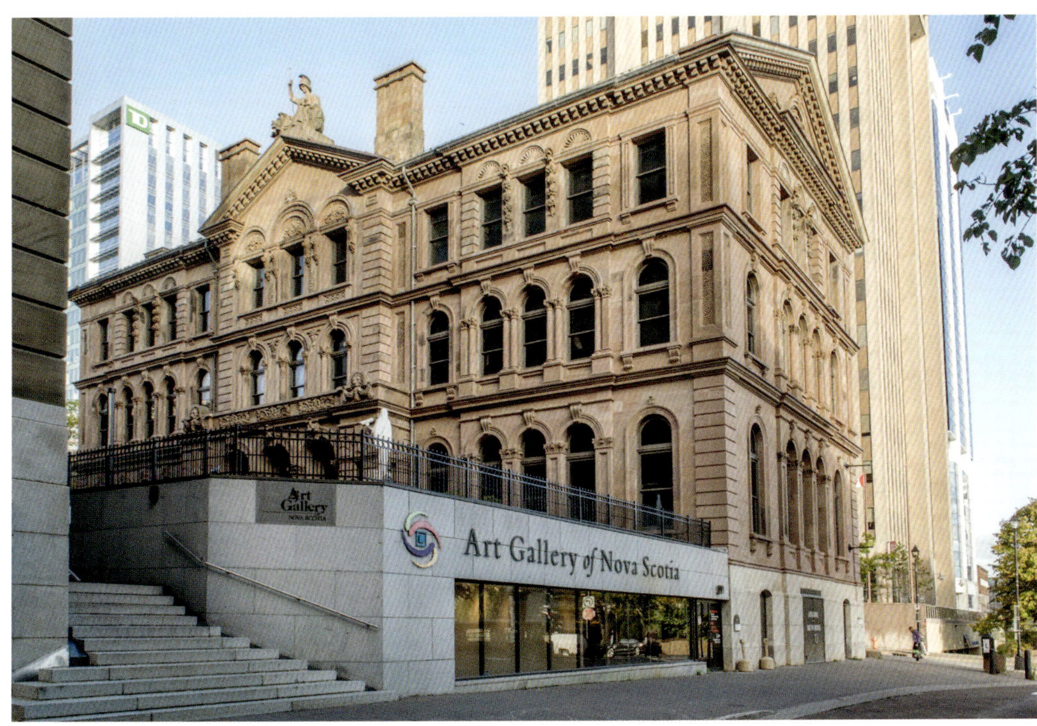

The exterior of the Art Gallery of Nova Scotia.

(AGNS)

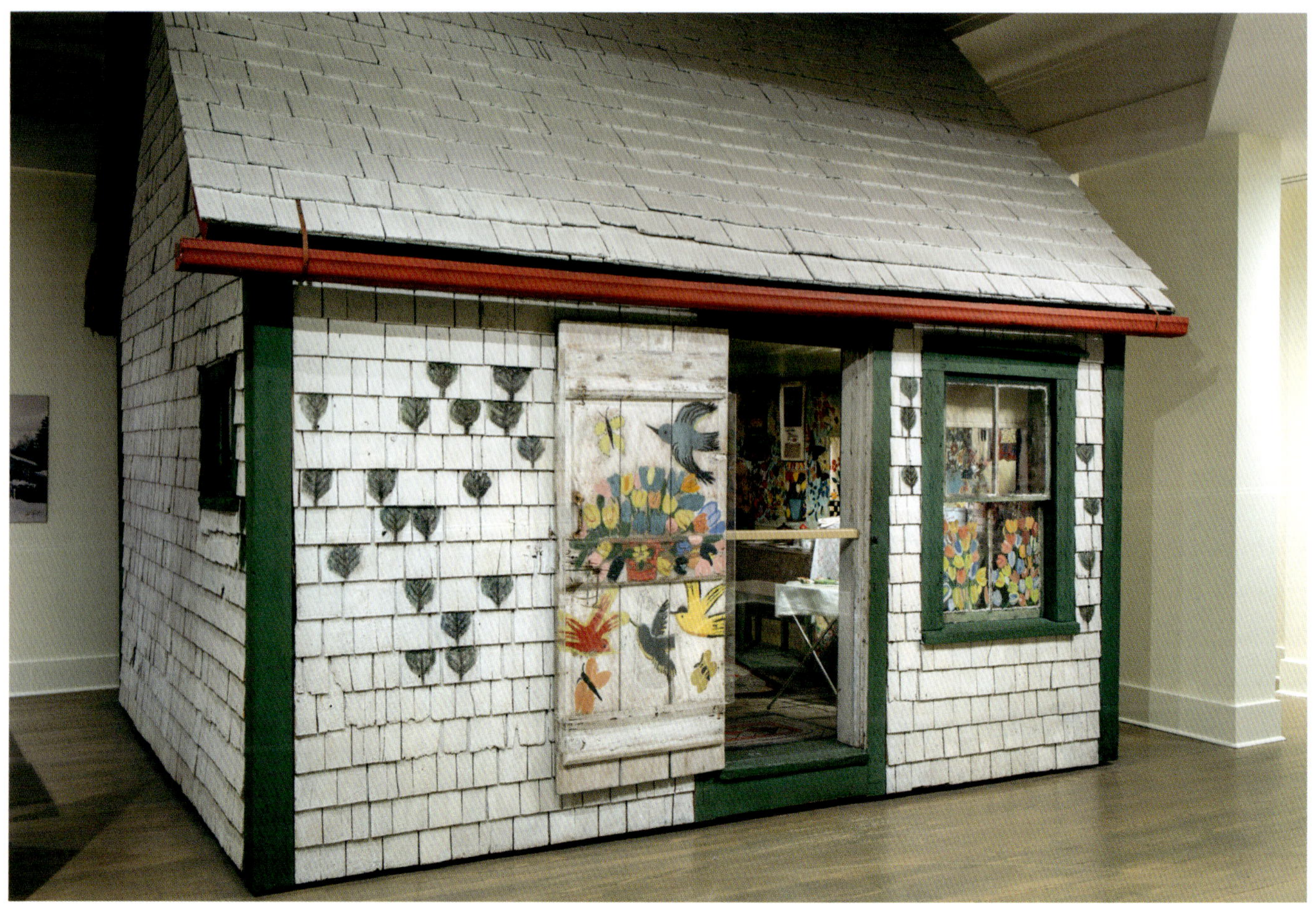

Maud Lewis's painted house, installed at the Art Gallery of Nova Scotia.

(AGNS)

The new Art Gallery of Nova Scotia opened to the public in 1988, without the space for Maud's house.

Ironically, it would take a decade for Maud's house to find a space in the building she was so central to helping build.

Maud's time came in 1997 with the opening of the Phase Two expansion of the AGNS, where the gallery acquired two floors and part of the basement of the Provincial Building located across the Ondaatje Court from the AGNS.

The Scotiabank Maud Lewis Gallery, which was supported by the Bank of Nova Scotia and the Craig Foundation, provided a permanent display space for the Maud Lewis house, and for an exhibition of her work. Shortly thereafter, a nationally touring exhibition of Maud's paintings, whose lead sponsor was also Scotiabank, toured the country to large audiences and critical acclaim. Maud Lewis has rarely been out of the spotlight since, with numerous books, plays, and even a feature film dedicated to her life and art.

With the creation of the Maud Lewis Gallery, the AGNS now had two permanent folk art displays. Riordon soon began planning for another major retrospective, this one of the paintings and painted furniture of Lower Prospect's Joe Norris. It, too, was both a popular and a critical success. But the AGNS's focus on folk art was beginning to draw critical attention. In 1997 the AGNS held a symposium entitled "Folk Art: Is it All Over?" No firm conclusions were drawn, but the discussion was shifted away from the traditional notion of "folk" toward folk art just being a kind of art. As Chris Huntington wrote afterward, "To call folk art just that, is, in itself, demeaning. ...[I]t is, after all, Art with a capital A, first and foremost."[13]

However, through the 1990s Nova Scotia Folk Art was suffering from its own success. Huntington severed relations with the Nova Scotia Folk Art Festival in 1992. In 1993 he made large donations of folk art to the AGNS and to the DesBrisay Museum in Bridgewater, and then closed his gallery and held a major auction to sell off much of his remaining holdings. He publicly proclaimed that his commercial days were over. In 1995 Houston North Gallery in Lunenburg, one of the major dealers of folk art, stopped handling any folk art except for the classic genre—works by deceased artists such as Joe Norris, Collins Eisenhauer, and Ralph Boutilier. In 1997 the AGNS mounted the exhibition *A Life of Its Own: Chris Huntington and the Resurgence of Nova Scotia Folk Art 1975–1995*, an exhibition that certainly had a retrospective feel.

As Scott Higgins (a freelance writer and also a folk artist) noted in an article in 1999, "new artists began appearing who had no previous tradition of making art." He continued: "Now the artistry was being created solely for the market, and most of it had the same 'look.'"[14] Huntington and Houston, at least, agreed. Even the AGNS, with its focus on major solo shows by deceased, classic-era folk artists Maud Lewis and Joe Norris, seemed to be signalling that folk art was becoming a thing of the past.

Except that Nova Scotian artists kept making folk art. Certainly, the majority of work being made in the last twenty years isn't of the standard of work by Joe Norris or Collins Eisenhauer, but that is the same as saying that most painting today isn't at the level of that of Alex Colville. And of course it isn't—most of the painting of his day wasn't up to his level either. There is always more mediocre work than good work, no matter when it is being made, and great work is even more rare. Folk art was popular, and its emergence as a style meant that more and more people could make work that evoked the look and feel of the classic era of folk art. That just meant that collectors, critics, and curators had to be more discerning.

What is clear, however, is that contemporary Nova Scotia Folk Art has lost some of its momentum. It is no longer as prominent in galleries or museums

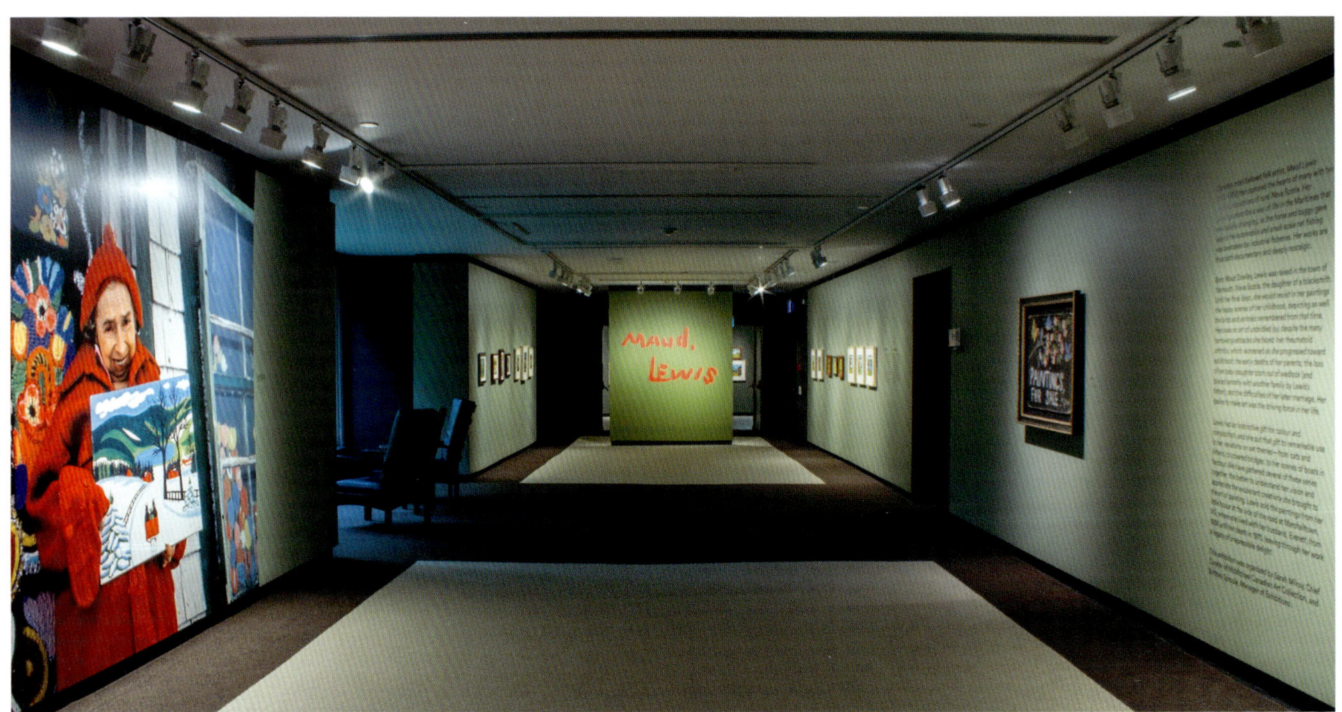

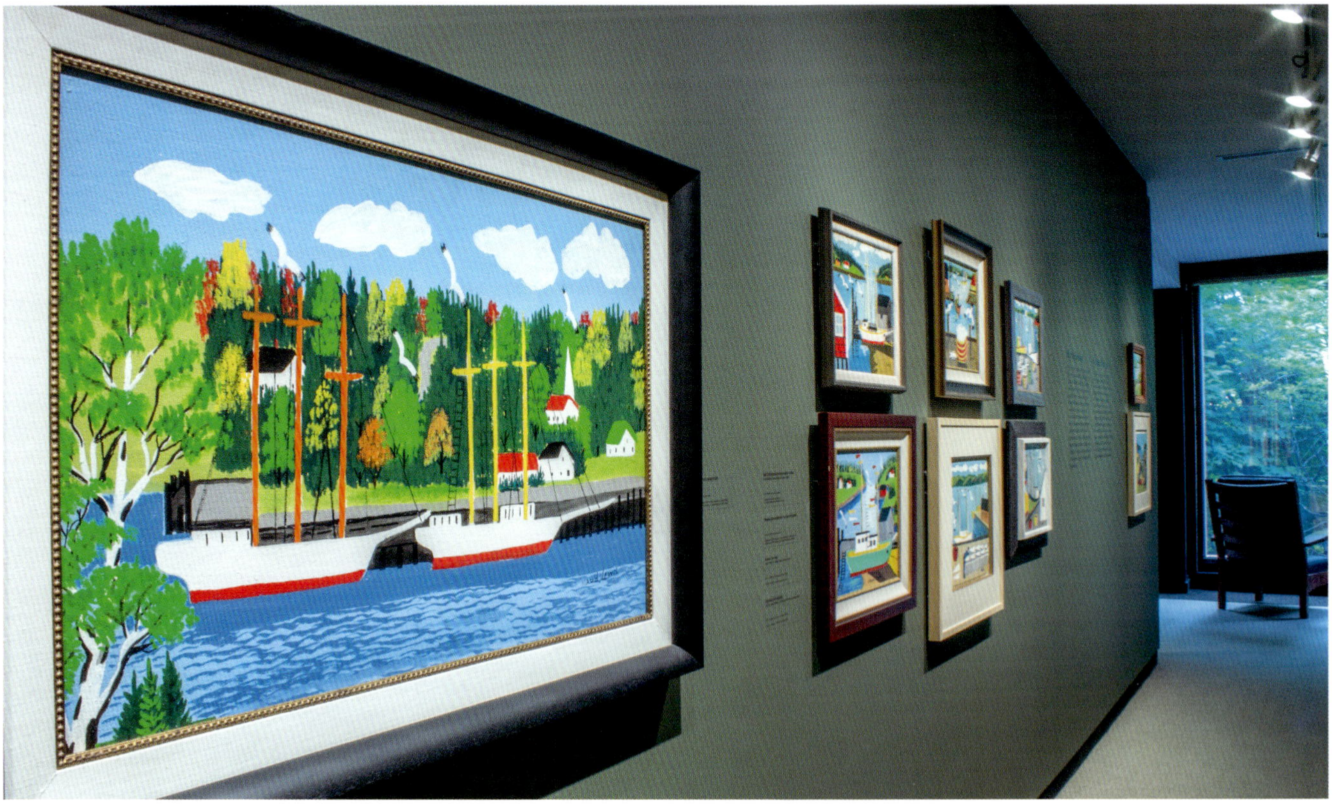

The Maud Lewis show at the McMichael Gallery in Kleinberg, ON, 2019.

(MCMICHAEL CANADIAN ART COLLECTION)

(for instance, at the AGNS, "the house that Maud built," folk art has been moved into a smaller space, swapping places with the gallery's Indigenous art exhibition). There are fewer serious galleries where one can purchase new work. Gone are the days when Mira Godard—who represented Alex Colville among many other famous artists—would mount an exhibition of the work of Joe Norris, Scott Higgins, or Eddie Mandaggio. But the Canadian Museum of History has just acquired a major work by Barry Colpitts. Work by Laura Kenney and David Stephens was included in a survey of contemporary Nova Scotia fine art at the AGNS a few years ago, and Bradford Naugler continues to make first-rate carvings. He is joined now at the festival by his son, Craig.

In the summer of 2019 Maud Lewis was exhibited with six contemporary Nova Scotia artists in China, and she was also the subject of a major solo show at the McMichael Canadian Art Collection in Ontario.

Her work has never been more valuable or more high profile.

So is folk art over? No—hardly.

But it has evolved. Once considered different from fine art, the best folk art is now being judged as art. That is a higher standard, one that fewer makers will live up to—but that's the same for every form of culture, whether that's music, literature, or fine art. High standards don't stop people from making things, but they do hold up models for excellence.

There are classic Nova Scotia folk artists who undoubtedly deserve the kind of attention paid to Maud Lewis—Ralph Boutilier, Harold Cromwell, and Collins Eisenhauer, to name but a few—but until that happens their work can be seen in the AGNS's folk art galleries. There may be less excitement about folk art now, but I don't think there is any less being made.

As Bradford Naugler said in 1997 when asked by the *Halifax Daily News* if folk art was all over: "Yeah, it's all over. All over Nova Scotia."[15]

A NOTE FROM THE AUTHOR

ALL THREE WAVES OF NOVA SCOTIA FOLK ART ARE REPRESENTED IN THE following sections. The first-wave, or "classic," artists all started making folk art before the seminal exhibition of Nova Scotia Folk Art in 1976. Most of the artists included in that exhibition are featured here.

The second wave is made up of artists who were directly influenced by the first wave, and who were collected by institutions in the later 1970s and '80s. Many of the second-wave artists were included in the first three iterations of the Nova Scotia Folk Art Festival.

I have chosen the fourth Nova Scotia Folk Art Festival as the demarcation point of the second and third waves of folk artists, because it was at that point that Chris Huntington stopped his involvement and the festival moved from Blockhouse to Lunenburg. While still juried, the Festival became more democratic in its ensuing years, with a broader selection of exhibitors.

These waves are not rigid, but fluid, and the second- and third-wave categories in particular are open to interpretation.

One important element of third-wave folk artists though, is that they are working fully in an environment where Nova Scotia Folk Art is a style of contemporary art—not a separate category from fine art, as classic-era folk was considered, and not the evolving category that second-wave artists worked under.

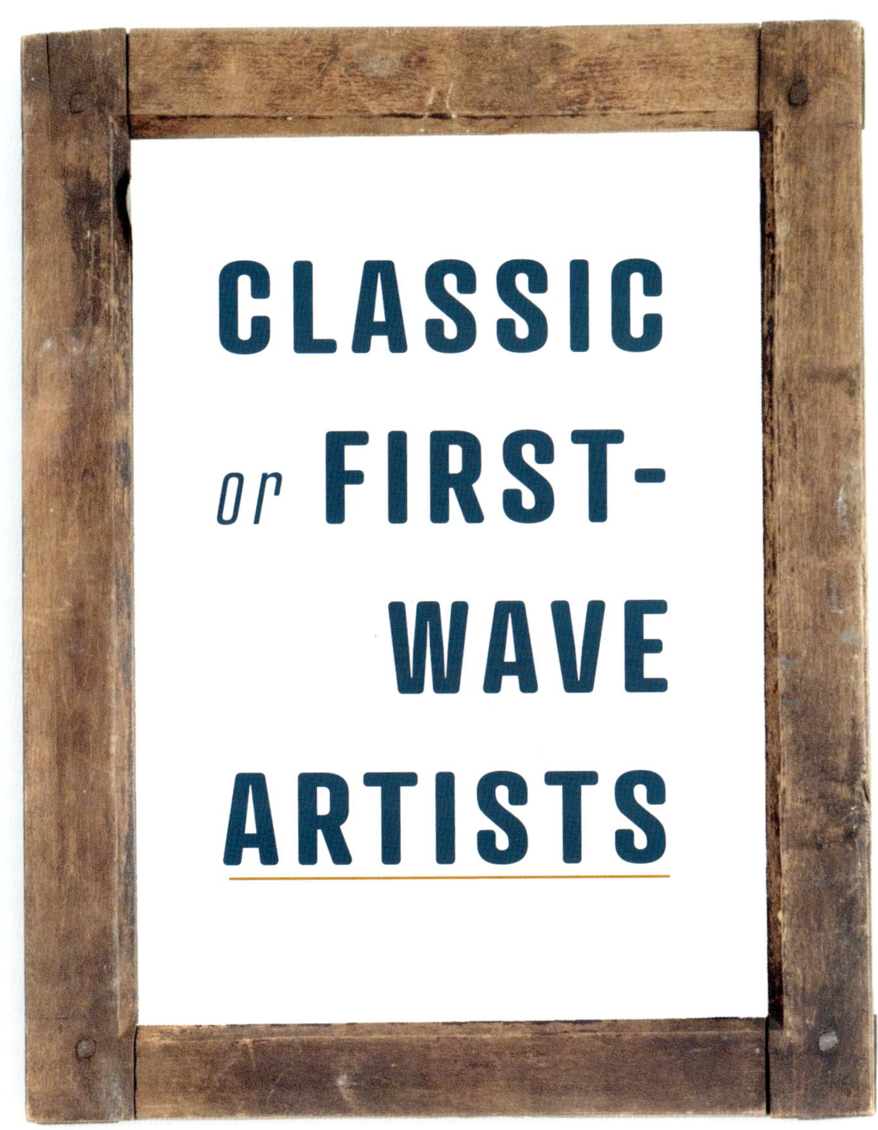
CLASSIC
or FIRST-
WAVE
ARTISTS

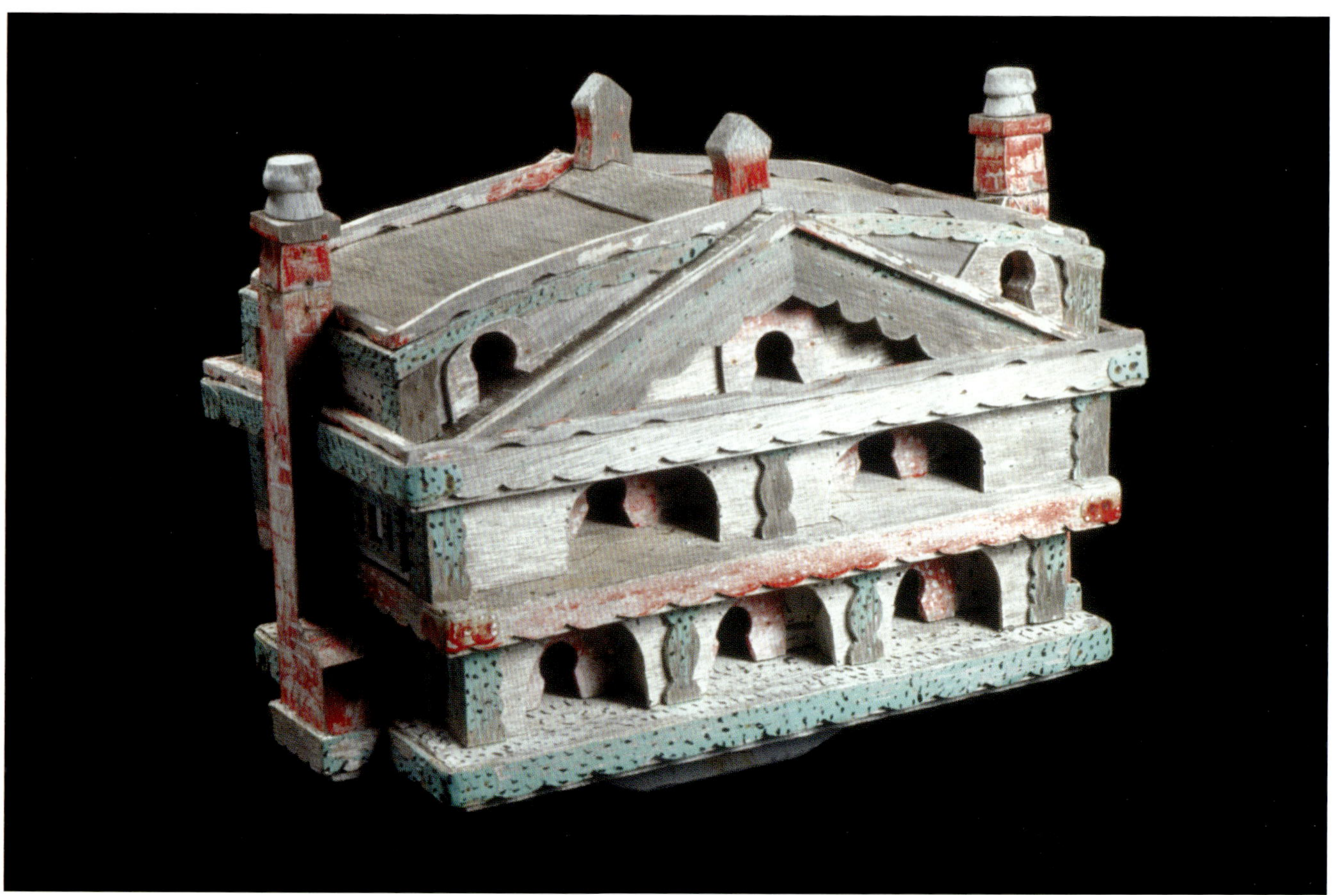

Impressionist Castle,
Charles Atkinson

(CANADIAN MUSEUM OF HISTORY, 78-188, CD1997-0345-055)

CHARLES ATKINSON

(CAPE SABLE ISLAND, SHELBURNE COUNTY)

1904–1977

CHARLES "CHARLIE" ATKINSON WAS BORN AT SOUTH SIDE, CAPE SABLE Island, in Shelburne County. Cape Sable Island is one of the southernmost parts of Nova Scotia, accessed by a causeway from Barrington Passage on the mainland. For most of Charlie Atkinson's life, however, it was only accessible by boat. Atkinson worked as a fisher and boatbuilder, and throughout his life he was a woodcarver. He first made useful items such as bird decoys, and tools such as wheelbarrows and sleds. "I just picked it up," he said. "Didn't have much learnin', you know, just what came to my head."[16]

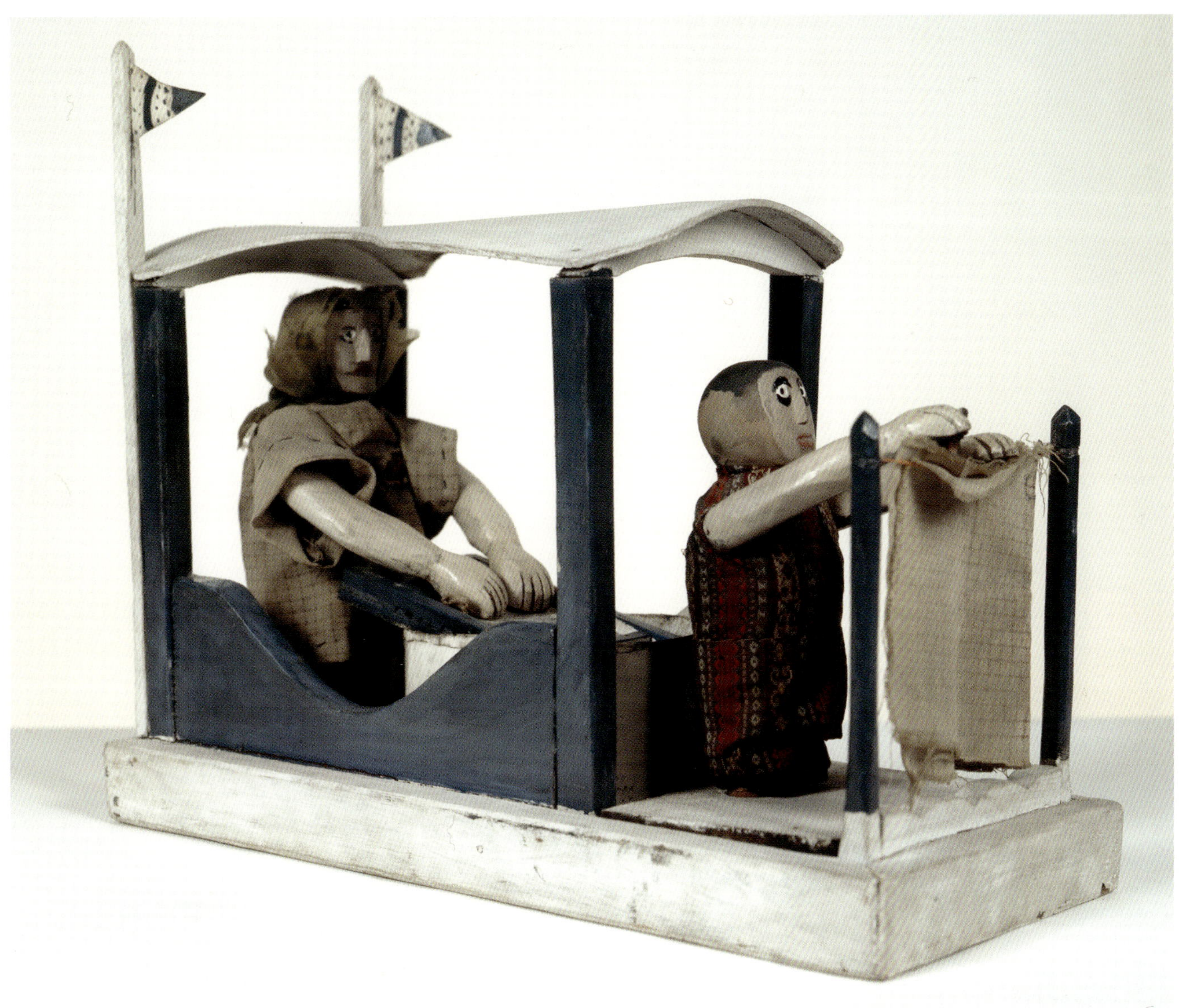

Washer Woman, Charles Atkinson

(AGNS)

By the mid-1960s he had arrived at what has become his signature style—painted objects with bright spots that would influence a whole other generation of Nova Scotia folk artists. Two of his birdhouses are in the collection of the Canadian Museum of History. One, fancifully named *Impressionist Castle* by the museum curators, is also pictured in a photo of the house next door to Atkinson's home on Cape Sable Island, which was included in the catalogue for *Folk Art of Nova Scotia*, though the birdhouse itself was not included in the exhibition. *Impressionist Castle* (1970-75) is an impressive three-story house with arches and chimneys on each side—a mansion for the birds. *Spotted Birdhouse*, also in the Canadian Museum of History's collection, features three small carved birds and Atkinson's exuberant spotted painting. That work was included in the

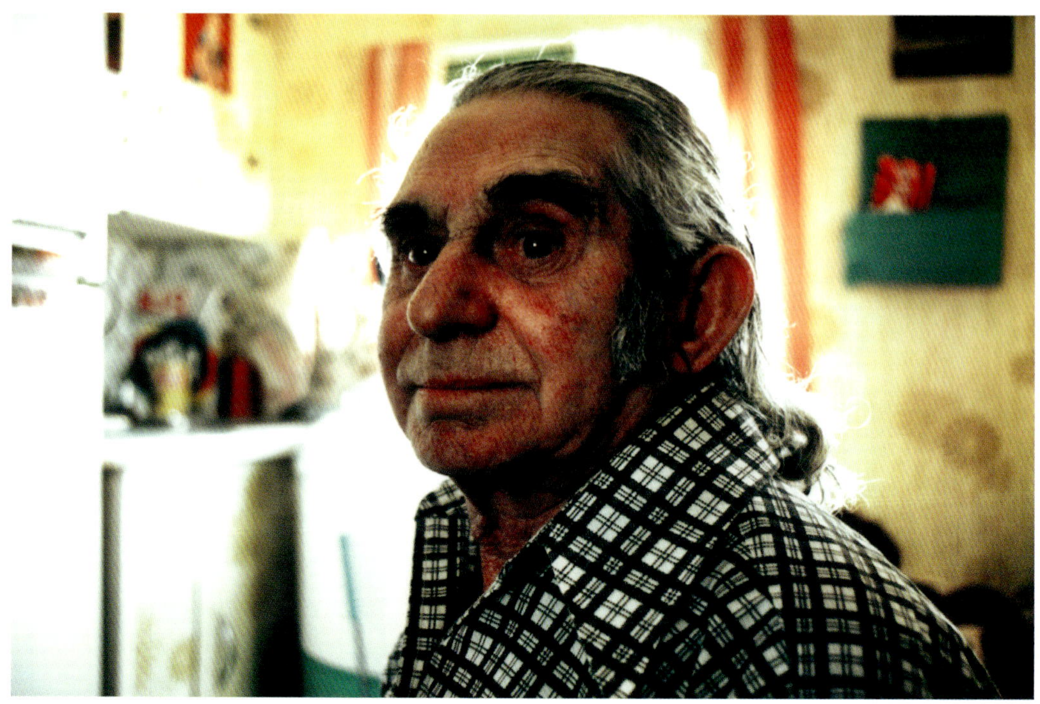

Charles Atkinson

(AGNS)

museum's touring show *From the Heart: Folk Art in Canada*. Atkinson's *Church*, from 1966, another birdhouse, is in the collection of the AGNS. Atkinson also made whirligigs to decorate his yard; one of these, *Farmer Sawing*, is in the collection of the AGNS.

Some of the Nova Scotia folk artists who were brought to the public's attention by the *Folk Art of Nova Scotia* exhibition were able to make modest livings from the increased interest in their work. Atkinson, unfortunately, suffered a stroke before the exhibition, which crippled his hand, making carving impossible. In fact, it was by mere chance that his work was preserved at all. In 1975, unable to make work anymore, he put all of his remaining objects up for sale as a group. Alerted by two antique pickers, Chris Huntington sought out Atkinson and purchased the lot. The works by Atkinson in the collections of the Canadian Museum of History and the Art Gallery of Nova Scotia were part of that purchase.

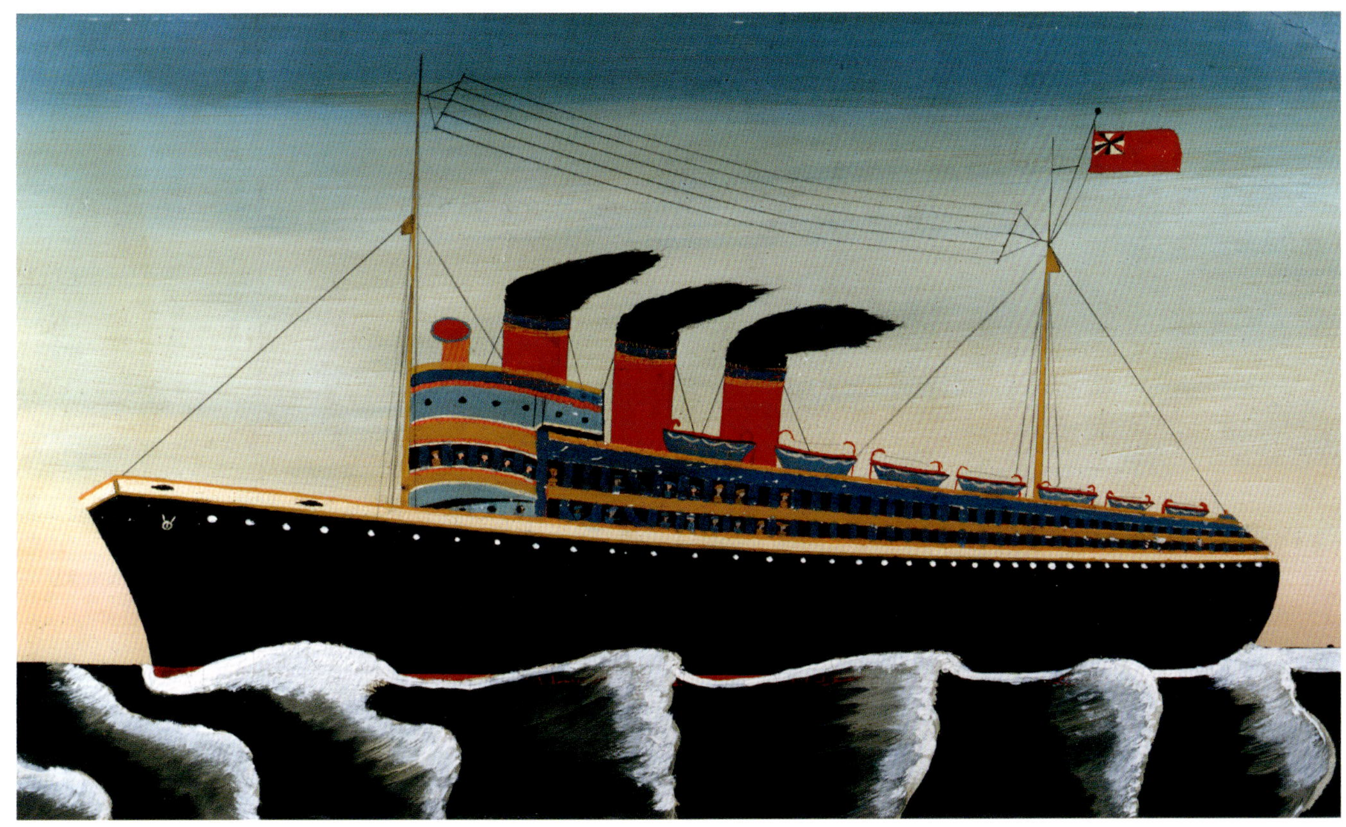

Ocean Liner, Samuel Bollivar

(AGNS)

SAMUEL BOLLIVAR

(DAYSPRING, LUNENBURG COUNTY)

1884–1977

SAMUEL BOLLIVAR ONLY MADE A FEW PAINTINGS IN HIS LIFETIME: approximately a dozen works made with oil paint on paper. A former fisher and shipyard worker, Bollivar retired from the Halifax shipyard and moved back to Dayspring in Lunenburg County. He painted as a hobby, giving some works to family members, hanging one on his front porch, and displaying the few others in his back shed, where he liked to sit and rest. Chris Huntington, driving by one day, saw a painting hanging on the porch and stopped. He was able to purchase it from Bollivar, and on a return visit bought the rest of the paintings the artist had. This proved to be timely as Bollivar had stopped painting due

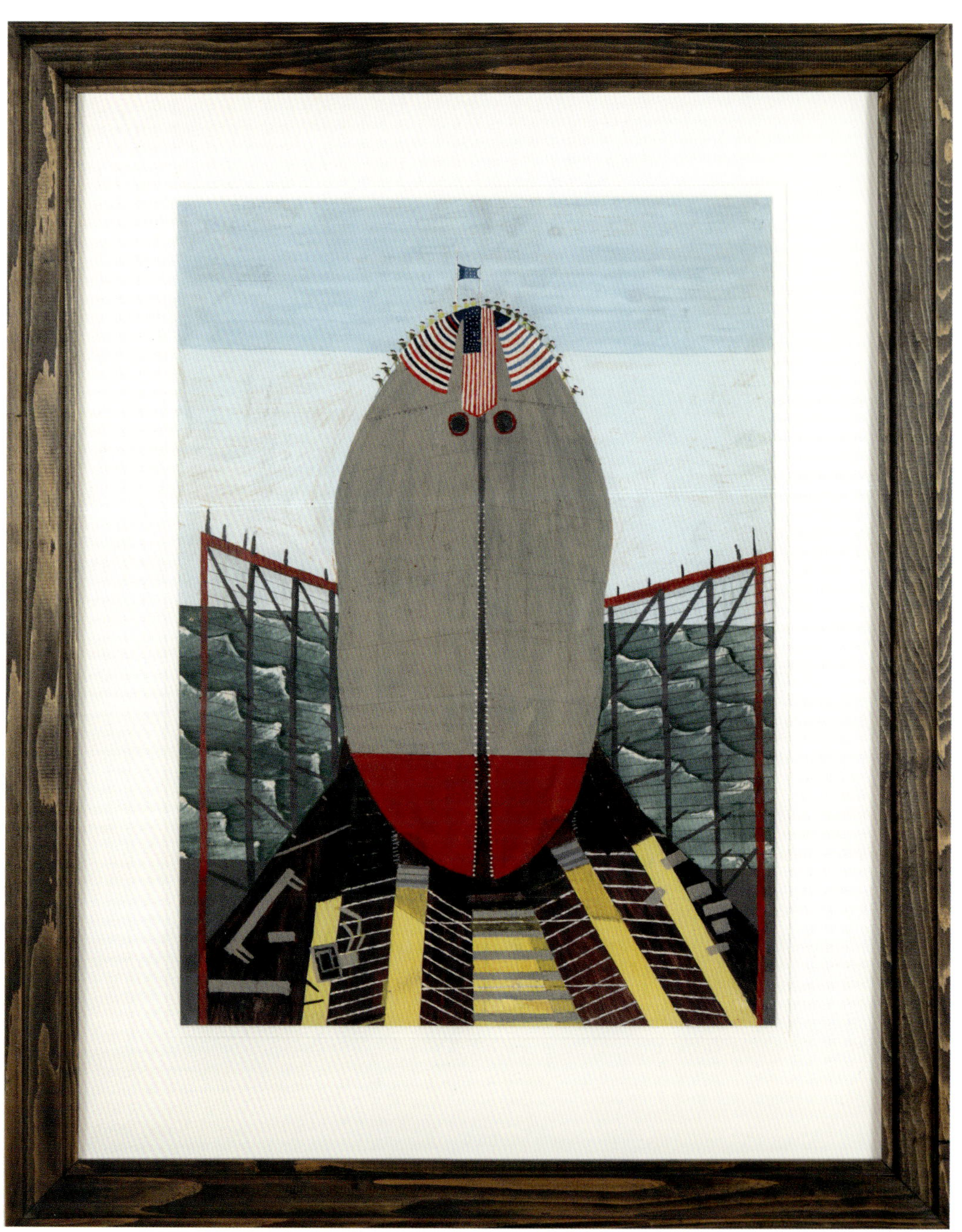

Valley Forge, Samuel Bollivar

(RAW PHOTOGRAPHY FOR AGNS)

to his deteriorating eyesight. Bollivar told the Art Gallery of Nova Scotia in 1976 that he wished he had been encouraged earlier, feeling that he could have made hundreds of paintings.[17]

His work was included in the *Folk Art of Nova Scotia* exhibition and in *Nova Scotia Folk Art*, which toured Great Britain in 1989–90. Two of those works, *Valley Forge* and *Ocean Liner* (both from 1967), are now in the permanent collection of the AGNS. *Ocean Liner* and other works by Bollivar follow the traditional

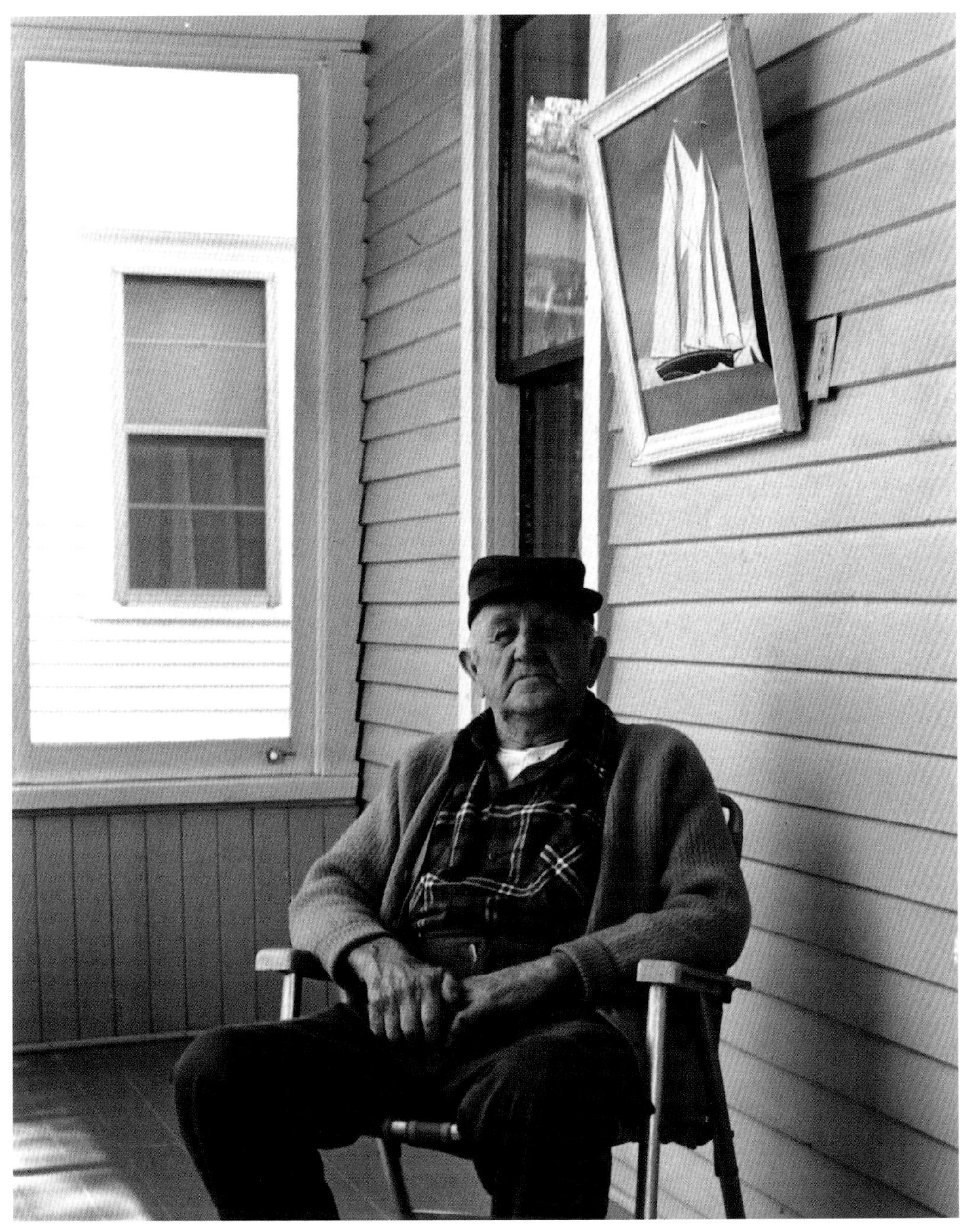

Samuel Bollivar

(AGNS)

format of the ship portrait. *Valley Forge* is particularly striking—it is a view of a ship being launched off a slip at the shipyard, but from the point of view of a worker on the slip, rather than from an onlooker's perspective. Although Bollivar had certainly seen such sights in his career, many of his paintings were based on images garnered from popular media. As his wife related to the AGNS in 1985, "He copied subjects from published sources, which occupied him even before he worked at the Halifax shipyards from 1943 to 1954."[18]

RALPH BOUTILIER

(MILTON, QUEENS COUNTY)

1906–1989

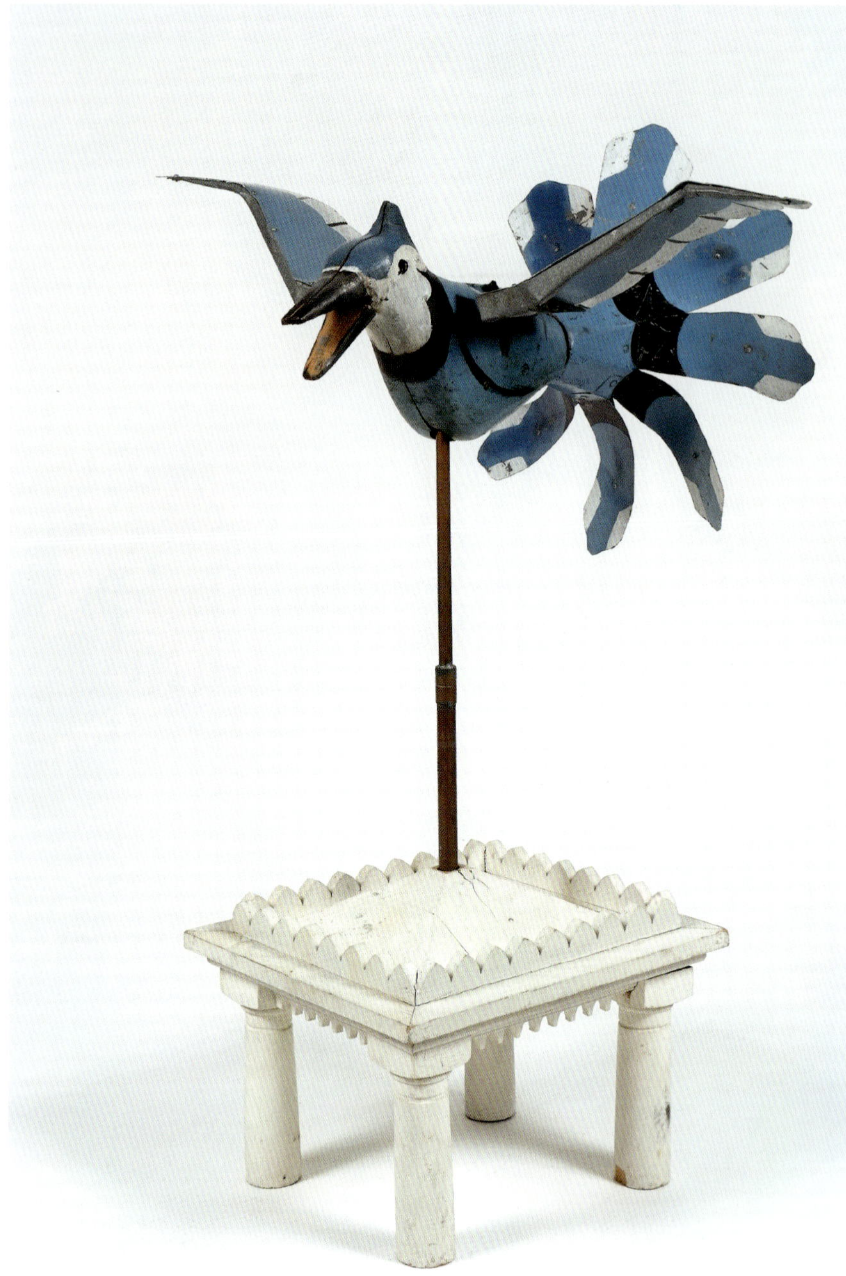

Blue Jay, Ralph Boutilier (AGNS)

"I AM LUCKY IN THIS WAY TO know my own talent, to bring it out, to know that there was something hidden which is coming out now. I am a good worker yet. I am past seventy. I still have a good arm, a good body to work."[19] —Ralph Boutilier

Ralph Boutilier was born at Boutilers Point, and eventually settled in the nearby village of Milton. He painted for years, but it was his sculptures that would make him one of our best-known folk artists, dubbed by his peers the "dean" of Nova Scotia Folk Art. In his youth Boutilier worked for his father, a tugboat captain who hauled logs from Ingramport to St. Margarets Bay. From there he went to sea, but soon settled on land, working various jobs such as sign painter, carpenter, barber, electrician, and boatbuilder. From 1936 on he began to make paintings as a hobby, eventually selling them to tourists around St. Margarets Bay. "I was really enjoying myself," he remembered. "My God, I couldn't wait until I got home [to] sit down and start painting."[20]

He told the AGNS in 1976 that he started making whirligigs in 1968. The first, a blue jay, had been abandoned in Boutilier's basement when

Chris Huntington first saw it. "I put it out in the wind, and it didn't stand up," Boutilier said, "so I throwed it in the basement and never thought no more of that."[21] The story was actually even more interesting that that. Boutilier was a tinkerer and machinist who had designed and made most of his woodworking equipment. He probably didn't remember that the source for the blue jay was actually an article in *Popular Mechanics* from 1957—complete with the mechanical specifications to make the jay's wings flap in the wind. He was hardly the first, and certainly not the last, of Nova Scotia's folk artists to be influenced as much by popular culture as they were by local memories and stories.

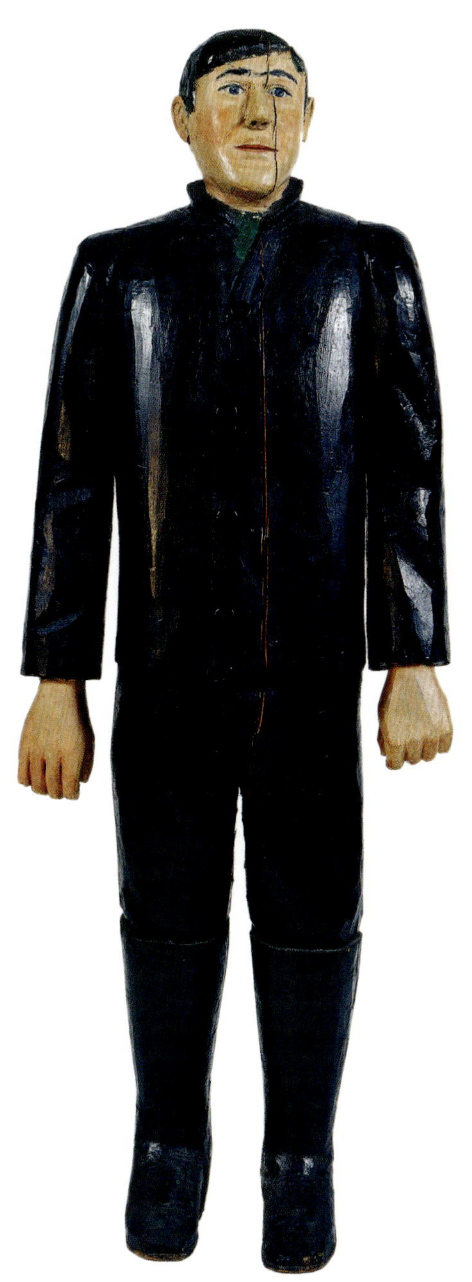

Fisherman, Ralph Boutilier

(AGNS)

Around the time he was working on the blue jay, Boutilier started carving figures for friends and neighbours, and he created what is one of the masterpieces of the Nova Scotia Folk Art genre: *Fisherman*, now in the collection of the AGNS. This near–life-sized figure of a fisherman is depicted clad in a slicker and rubber boots, standing in a relaxed pose with his hands at his side. Boutilier put more realism into his carvings than did most of his peers, and the face of this figure is particularly strong, with a pensive look that is quite engaging. Boutilier put his decades of experience painting to good use in colouring his sculptures, which can be seen in the treatment of his *Fisherman*'s face and in the plumage of his whirligig birds.

He stopped carving for about five years until he decided to revisit the bird whirligigs. He wanted to make versions of birds that were closer to life-sized, which meant larger birds than the blue jay he had made several years earlier.

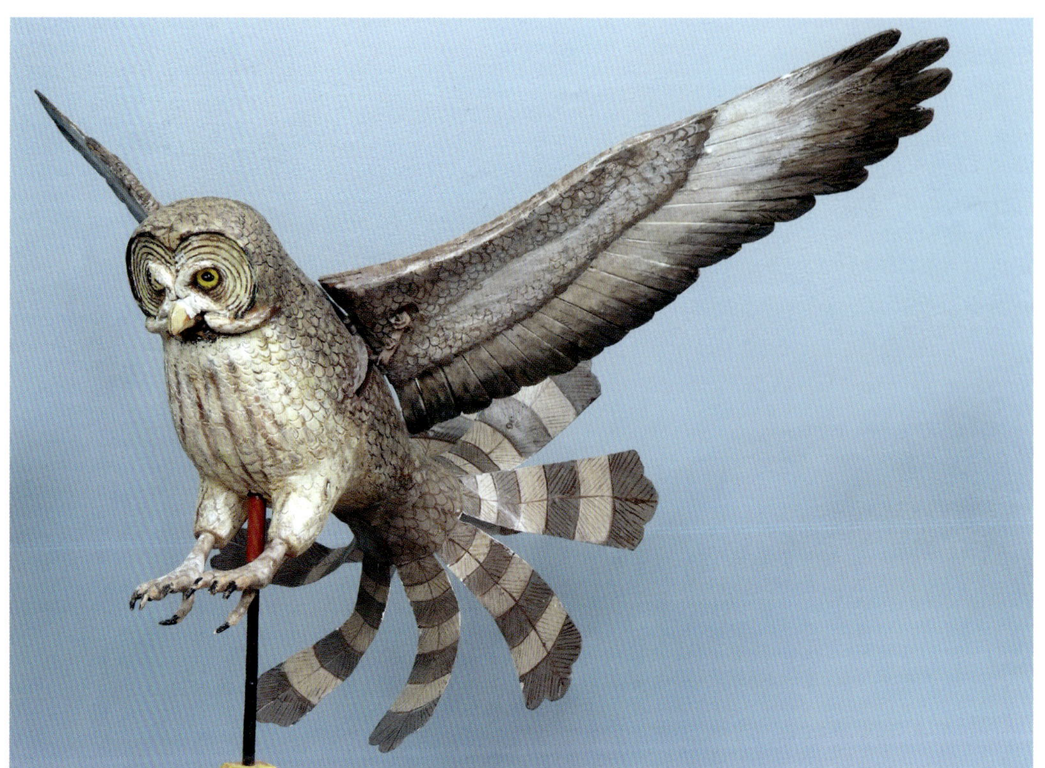

Great Horned Owl, Ralph Boutilier

(AGNS)

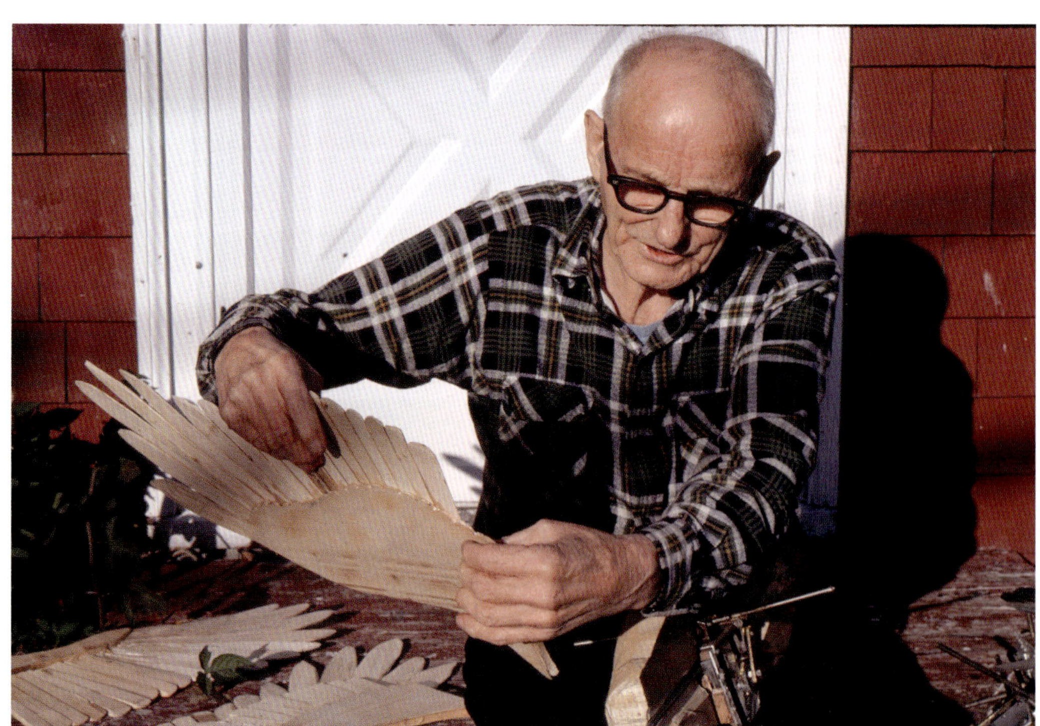

Ralph Boutilier at work

(AGNS)

The first of this new series was an eagle, and he was quite pleased with the realistic effect he was able to create. "When I put the eagle out on the lawn, I was watching it going in the wind. The first thing this eagle came over from the grove, he flew around and around it, and kept circling until he got right down close, before he knew it wasn't a real eagle."[22] He went on to make a marsh hawk, a great horned owl, and a seagull, among others. His self-portrait, *Boutilier at Work*, is one of his last large-scale figures. "I'd been carving, making men and women until the day I figured I was getting old and couldn't do much more. That's when I started making myself. I was anxious I guess."[23]

Boutilier's work was included in *Folk Art of Nova Scotia*, *From the Heart*, *Nova Scotia Folk Art*, and *A Life of Its Own*. Both the AGNS and the Canadian Museum of History have important works by the artist in their permanent collections.

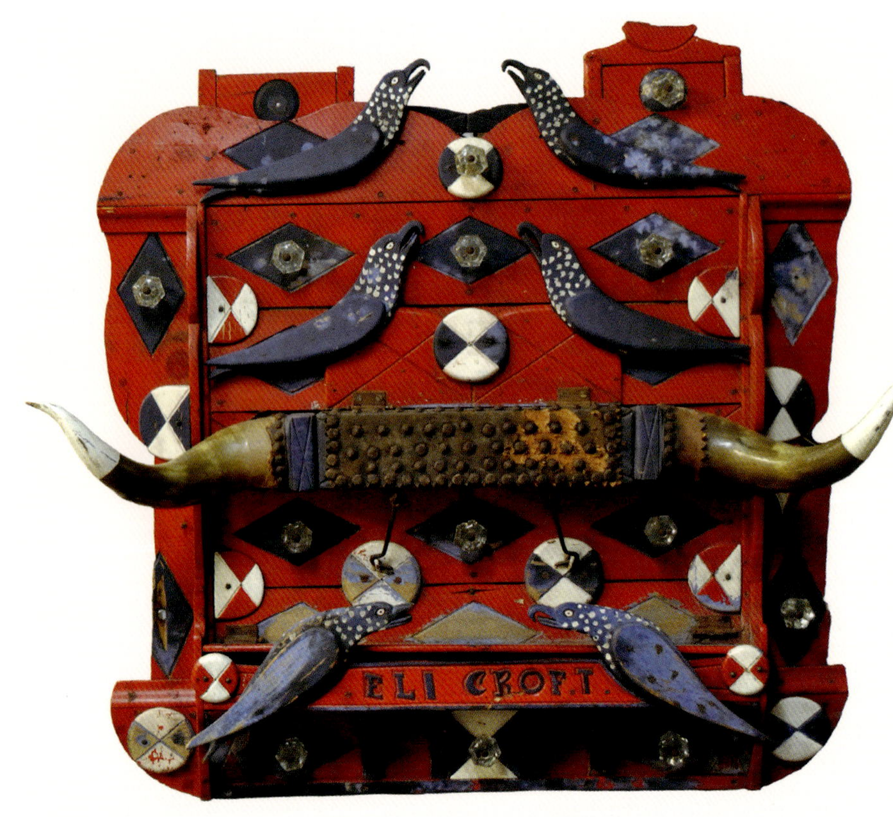

Gun Rack, Eli Croft (AGNS)

ELI CROFT

(CAMPERDOWN, LUNENBURG COUNTY)

1860–1935

UNLIKE MANY OF THE folk artists included in this book, Eli Croft never saw his work become treated as art. He was born in Lunenburg County, in the small village of Camperdown, in 1860; he died in 1935, long before folk art was recognized in Nova Scotia. Instead of making works for the tourist economy, Croft, who worked as a gold prospector and as a blacksmith, made useful objects for himself and for his neighbours. His work was discovered by Chris Huntington, who collected the few pieces that have come to be in public collections. Four pieces were included in *Folk Art of Nova Scotia*. Three of those pieces were furniture—gun racks made around moose antlers and decorated with carvings and additional designs. *Mirror and Gun Rack*, for instance, featured a framed mirror with elaborate geometric carving topped by a rack of moose antlers (to serve as the gun rack); a pair of ox horns and a carved wooden bird topped off the composition.

A gun rack in the AGNS collection is perhaps Croft's most ambitious piece, featuring his name prominently carved and a pair of ox horns to hold a rifle or shogun in a place of honour. It is decorated with numerous glass knobs from drawers, carved and painted discs, and carved and painted birds. Most of the rack is painted a brilliant red, with blues and whites predominating in the decoration. It is a powerful work.

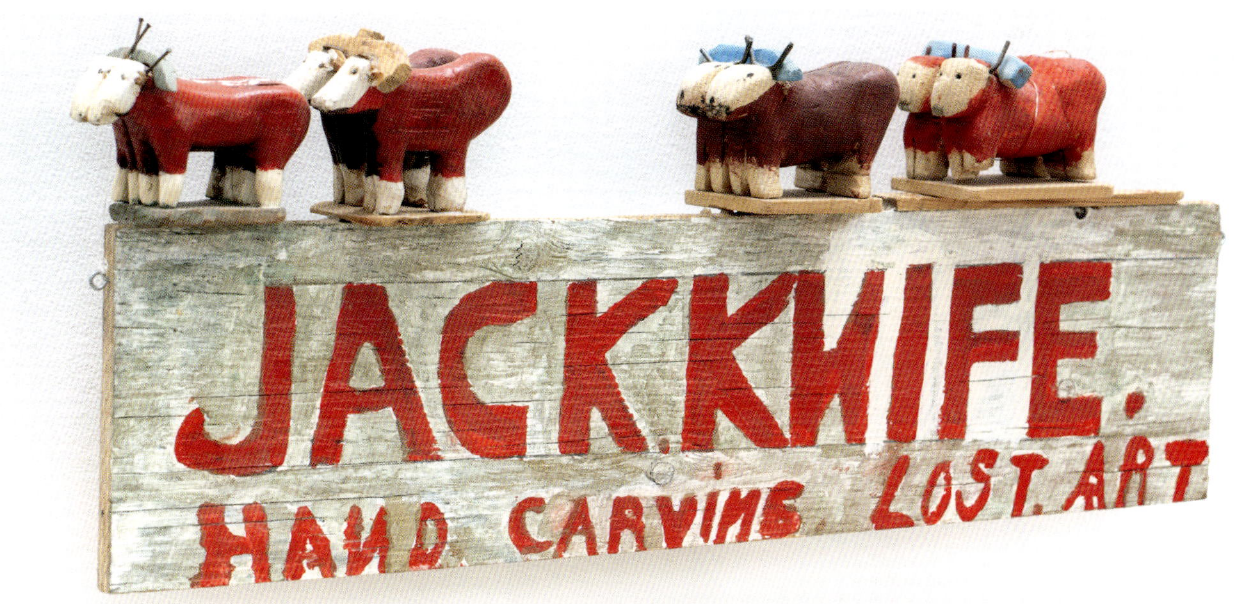

Jackknife Sign with Team of Oxen, Clayton Devine

(RAW PHOTOGRAPHY FOR AGNS)

CLAYTON DEVINE

(YARMOUTH, YARMOUTH COUNTY)

1911–1981

CLAYTON DEVINE LIVED ALL HIS LIFE IN YARMOUTH, WHERE HE WORKED as a milkman until an injury forced his retirement. He is best known for his small carvings of oxen, which he often made using simple bent nails for horns, and for his decoys. Chris Huntington bought a decoy at a flea market in the early 1970s which was, as he recalled, "signed on the bottom, 'Clayton Devine, Yarmouth, N.S.' I looked up the name in the telephone directory, called and asked, 'Do you have any more ducks?'"[24]

As with many of the first wave of Nova Scotia folk artists, he sold his small objects from his home, with a handmade sign that featured pairs of oxen at each end. He also painted, though few of those paintings have survived. Devine stopped making art in 1979 and sold everything he had left in a single lot to Chris Huntington. As Devine's nephew recalled, "As far as my aunt was concerned, he offered a very fair price for everything—and the truth is Clayton Devine's work would probably have never been known outside of Yarmouth if it hadn't been for Huntington."[25]

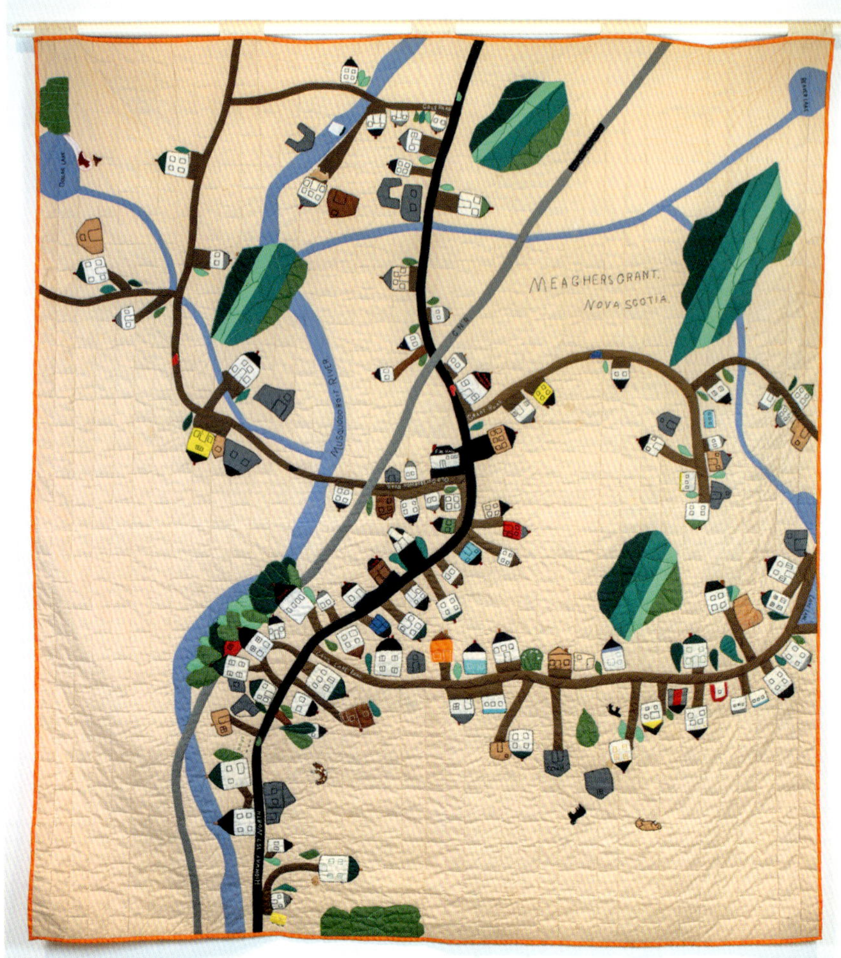

Map of Meagher's Grant, Evelyn Dickie

(RAW PHOTOGRAPHY FOR AGNS)

EVELYN DICKIE

(MEAGHERS GRANT, HALIFAX COUNTY)

1903–1993

EVELYN DICKIE WAS BORN AT Meaghers Grant in Nova Scotia's Musquodoboit Valley. After some time in the United States she returned to Meaghers Grant, where she served as the village's postmistress for thirty-three years, retiring in 1970. A traditional quilt-maker, Dickie made a remarkable quilt that was included in *Folk Art of Nova Scotia*. This work, a colourful map of Meaghers Grant, was originally collected by the painter Graham Metson (b. 1934) and then acquired by the AGNS in 1977. Dickie said that it was "accurate as far as possible—I couldn't put all the houses in."[26] A version of *Folk Art of Nova Scotia* travelled to Birmingham, Alabama, in 1979. A reviewer there described Dickie's quilt with the romanticism one often finds in responses to folk art, calling the quilt "charming" and noting how the aerial view depicted the "houses looking up like wondering children observing their first airplane."[27]

While this book has excluded traditional quilts because their makers were working in a tradition other than the style that has come to be known as "Nova Scotia Folk Art," this imaginative work, with its faithful depiction of a map—even down to the light taupe cotton background to mimic the paper—deserves its place as a defining example of the evolution of folk art from the home and into galleries and museums.

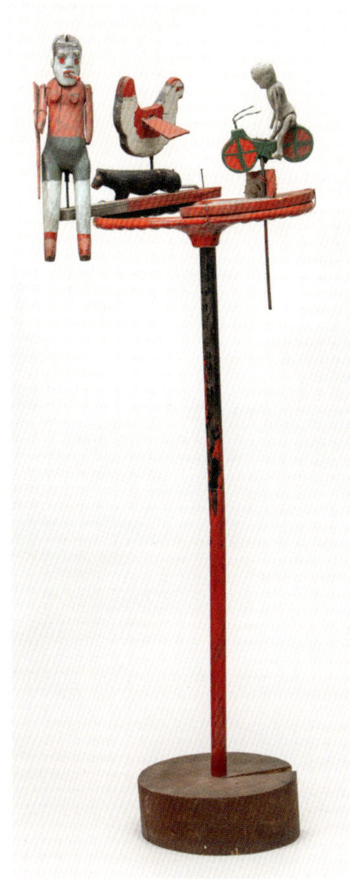

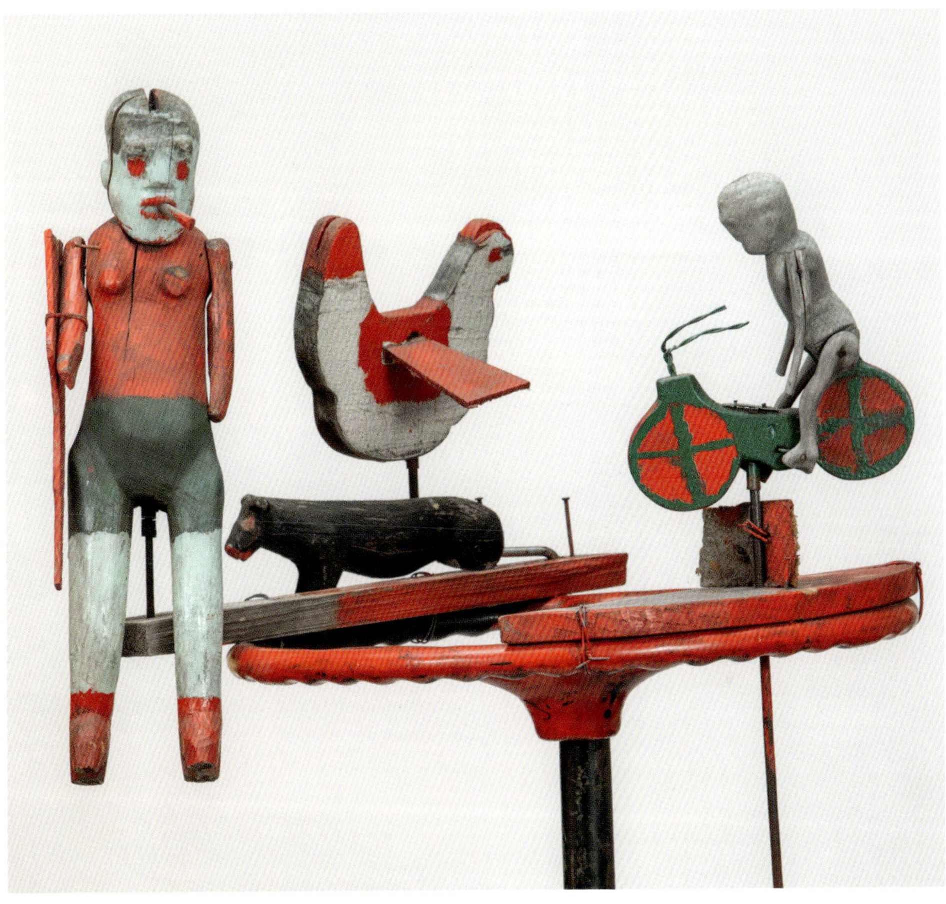

Figure Grouping on Tractor Steering Wheel, Ellison Eagles

(RAW PHOTOGRAPHY FOR AGNS)

ELLISON EAGLES

(NORTH RIVER, LUNENBURG COUNTY)

1912–1976

ELLISON EAGLES WAS ACTIVE AS A FOLK ARTIST IN THE 1970S, MOSTLY making decorations for his own small house in North River. A lumberman, he worked in camps as a saw-filer, cook, and blacksmith. He had made the odd figure out of stumps with his axe, and some of his lawn decorations were collected by Chris Huntington in the 1970s.

Two of Eagles's lawn sculptures were included in *Folk Art of Nova Scotia*: *Black Figure* and *Figure Grouping on Tractor Steering Wheel*. Eagles's rudimentary *Black Figure* has round, staring eyes and white lips, reflective of the makeup

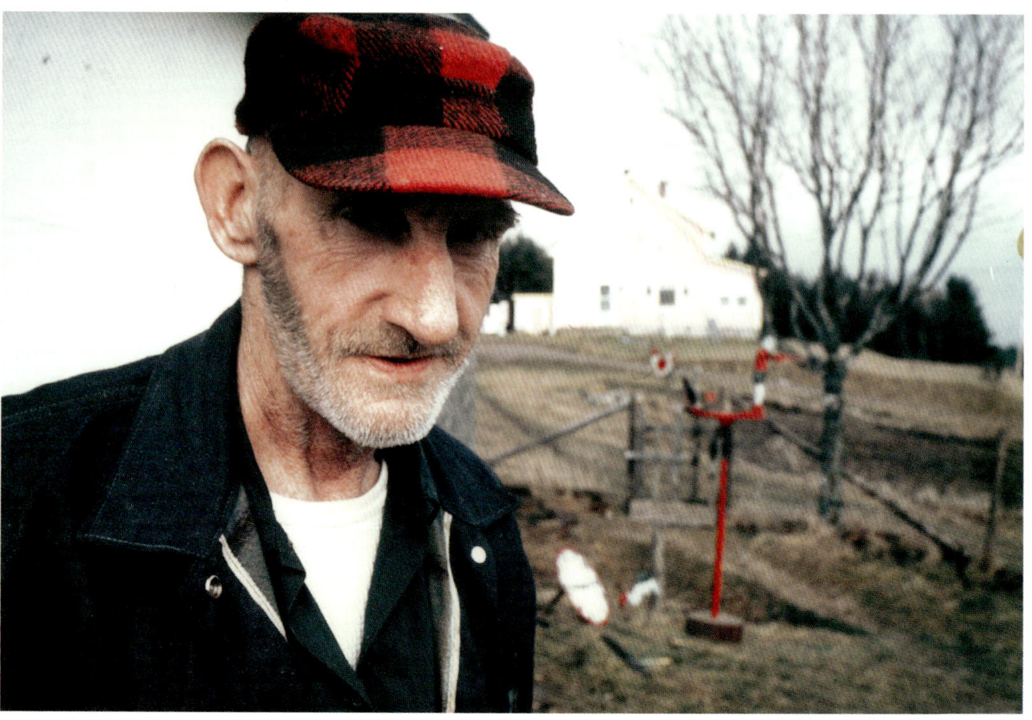

Ellison Eagles
(AGNS)

used by white performers in minstrel shows. The *Black Figure* sculpture may have been a version of a popular—and now acknowledged as racist—lawn ornament of the time: the Black jockey. It also may have been part of a tradition of sculptures of Black dancing figures, often used in ship decoration. The AGNS has a remarkable example of this type of work by James Hertle from 1855. A piece from 1975, also in the AGNS collection, is a similar size and features the free-swinging arms of the earlier figure, but *Standing Boy* is more refined and lacks the racism inherent in the Black figure.

Figure Grouping on Tractor Steering Wheel is a truly strange object, featuring a cigarette-smoking man with a rifle, a chicken, and another male figure on a bicycle or motorcycle coming face to face with a black bear. Crudely carved and painted, it nevertheless has a compelling surrealism, and a hint of the violence that can lurk behind any rural idyll. Eagles, like most of Nova Scotia's folk artists from the 1970s and earlier, came from poverty and a life of hard work and little education. Lumber camps and fishing villages could be rough places, and this work doesn't shy away from that.

COLLINS EISENHAUER (ALSO EISENER)

(UNION SQUARE, LUNENBURG COUNTY)

1898–1979

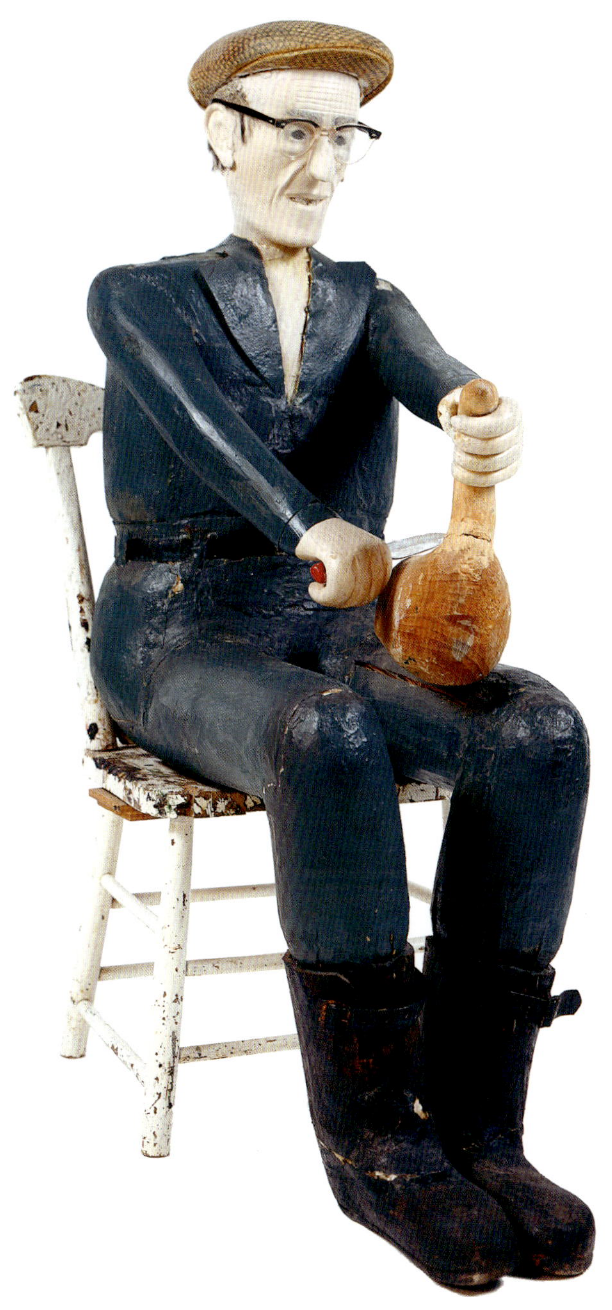

Self-Portrait, Collins Eisenhauer

(AGNS)

COLLINS EISENHAUER WAS ONE OF THE FEW Nova Scotia folk artists before 1976 who was already well-known to collectors in the province and beyond. Along with Maud Lewis, he had been the subject of attention from both the media and from the art world. Local antiques dealer and collector Murray Stewart first saw Eisenhauer's work in the early 1970s. Alerted by another dealer to an interesting yard display, Stewart drove to the nearby village of Union Square to see what he could find. "I looked around and I guess I probably near fainted," he remembered.[28] What he saw was a yard filled with carved animals and figures: men and women, dogs, cats, ducks, and geese. Over the next few years Stewart bought over one hundred carvings from Eisenhauer and resold them to collectors and antique shops throughout Ontario and the eastern United States.

A recently retired woodsman, Eisenhauer had started making sculptures to spruce up his yard. The relative notoriety created by the interest in his work set him on another path, turning him into an artist who was considered the most important folk artist in Nova Scotia history throughout the 1980s and 1990s. He still has that reputation amongst many collectors and museums—the Canadian Museum of History, for instance, which has the largest folk art collection in Canada, has forty works by Eisenhauer in its collection, but just one by Maud Lewis.

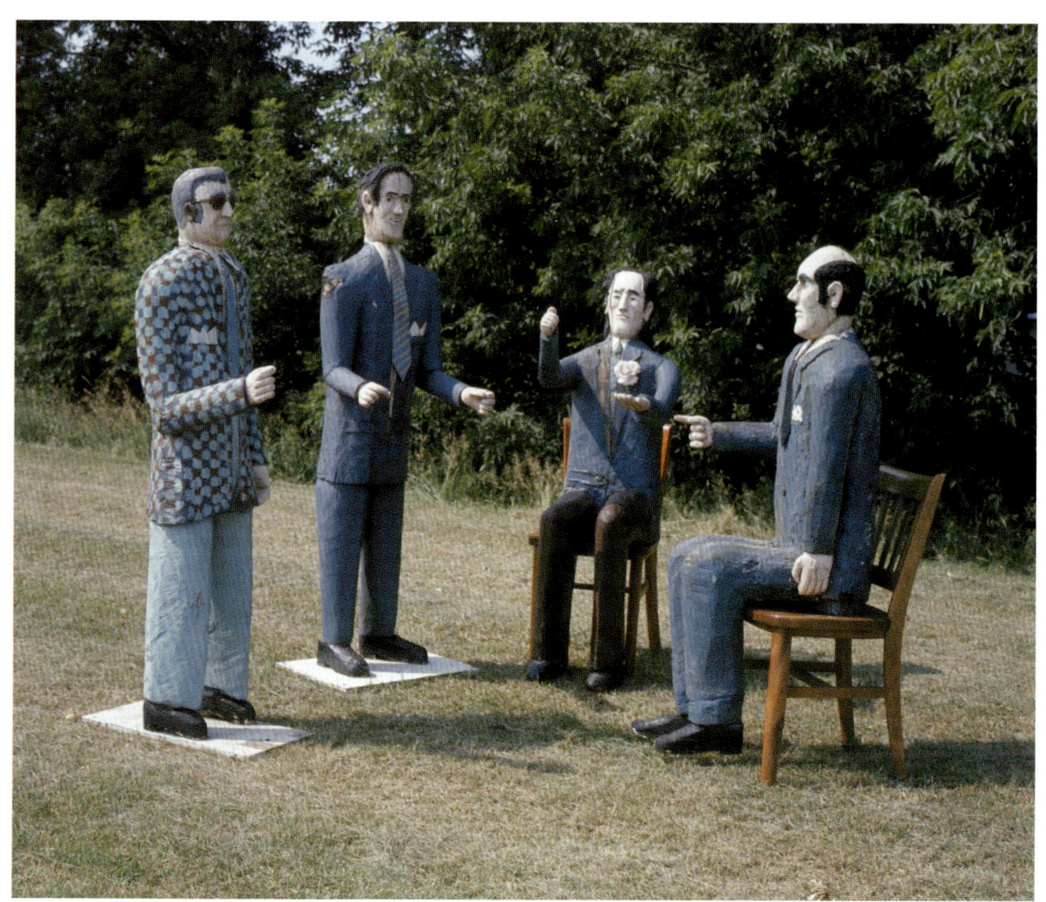

Political Figures, Collins Eisenhauer

(CANADIAN MUSEUM OF HISTORY, 75-916, CD1994-0856-019)

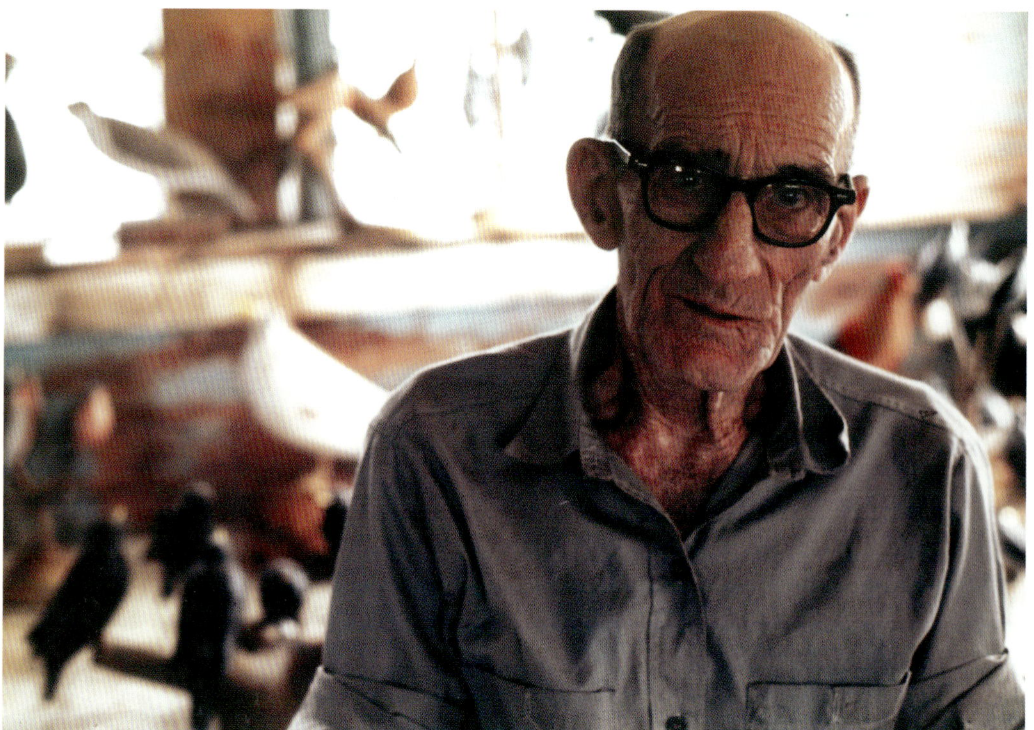

Collins Eisenhauer

(AGNS)

Folk Art of Nova Scotia included nineteen works by Eisenhauer, including his life-sized four-figure grouping, *Political Figures*. This work was made by Eisenhauer for a parade in New Germany, where he set up the politicians—which included the prime minister of the day, the leader of the opposition, the leader of the New Democratic Party, and the premier of Nova Scotia—as if they were having a political debate. "It was eight days before the election and [the judges] thought I was hitting at the politicians, but I wasn't," he ruefully told Chris Huntington. "I didn't win anything."[29]

Eisenhauer didn't take up folk art on a whim; he had been painting for his own amusement for most of his life, and when he was a child he used to make cards that his father would sell to his fellow workers in the lumber camps. But it was when he carved the figure of a policeman to hold his mailbox in 1966 that people started to notice his work. During an illness in the late 1960s he started to carve small erotic sculptures, which he described as something that was just about "having them for to look at myself."[30] Between his life-sized and near–life-sized figures, his animals—particularly his swans—and his small erotic figures, Eisenhauer was becoming the face of Nova Scotia Folk Art.

His technique was rooted in the skills he'd learned in the lumber camps. The large figures were roughed out with a chainsaw, and then smoothed out with planes and knives. He often added real elements to his sculptures to increase the verisimilitude. His self-portrait, for instance, has a real hat and glasses, and *Woman of My Dreams* (1976) sports a pair of false teeth. He carved his small figures with a jackknife. His swans were made by finding curved roots to use as the necks, which were then added to a body roughed out with a chainsaw. Most of his work was then finished up with auto-body filler to cover cracks before it was painted. His work has been included in every major group show of Nova Scotia Folk Art since 1976, but, curiously, his work has never been the subject of a solo retrospective.

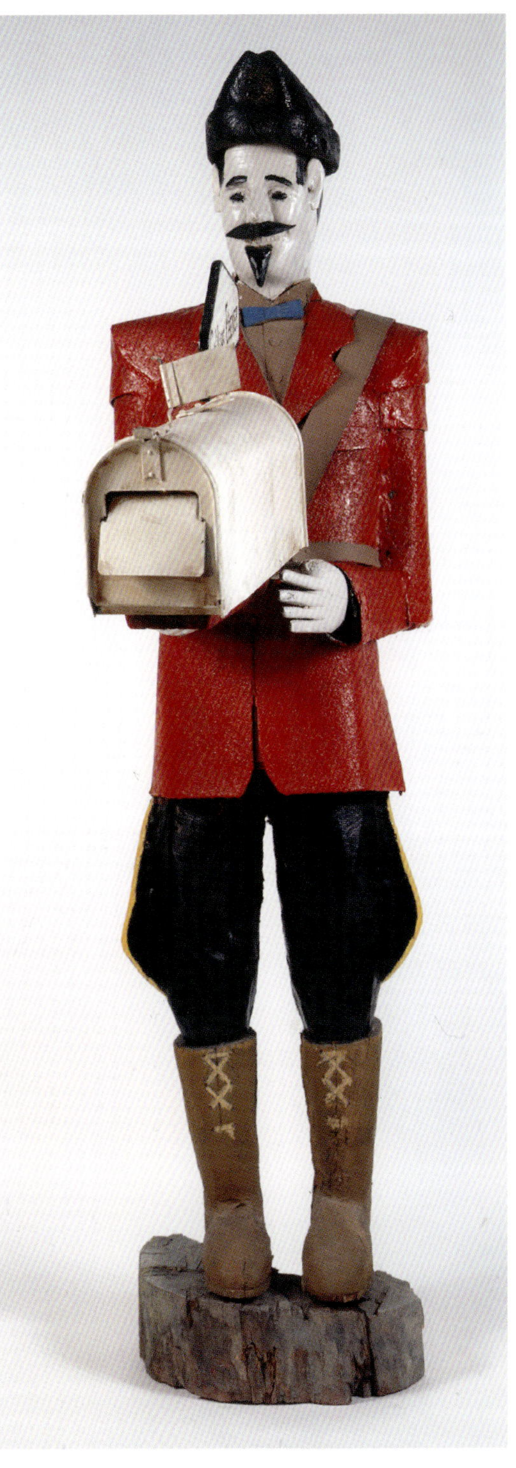

Mountie,
Collins Eisenhauer

(AGNS)

SIDNEY HOWARD

(ALBERT BRIDGE, CAPE BRETON COUNTY)

1913–1992

Figure,
Sidney Howard
(AGNS)

SIDNEY HOWARD WAS BORN IN Sydney, Cape Breton, and as a young man served in the army before getting married in 1945. After leaving the army he lived and worked in St. Catharines, Ontario. His wife died in 1952, and in 1958 Howard and his nine-year-old daughter, Louise, moved to Cape Breton. He never remarried.

Howard worked, as he described it in an interview with journalist Ted Rhodes, as "A jack of all trades and master of none."[31] In 1962 he took an image of a deer from one of his daughter's colouring books and started to make a wooden version. This was the beginning of his carving.

Howard lived on five acres of land in Albert Bridge, outside of Sydney. He didn't have a driver's licence and was dependent upon people finding him. To mark the turnoff to his house he carved six-foot figures of a man and a woman from old telephone poles. "What started me was, I bought this old place here, friends of mine couldn't find me," he told *Canadian Art*. "So I said, I better put something by the road, then they'd find me."[32]

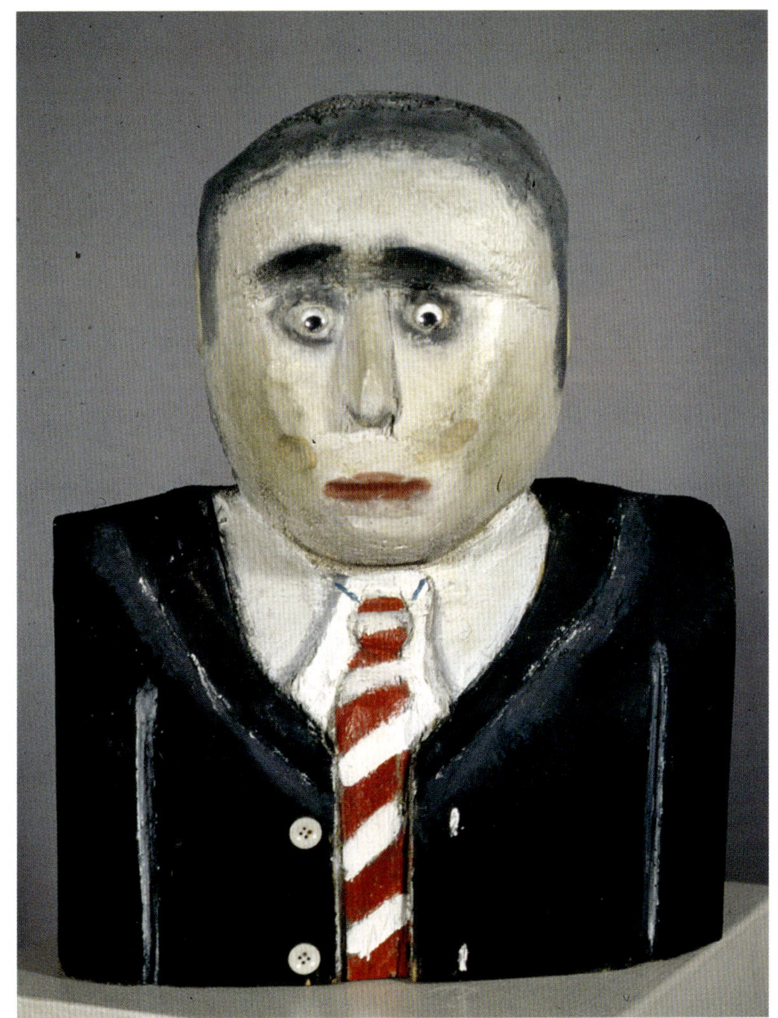

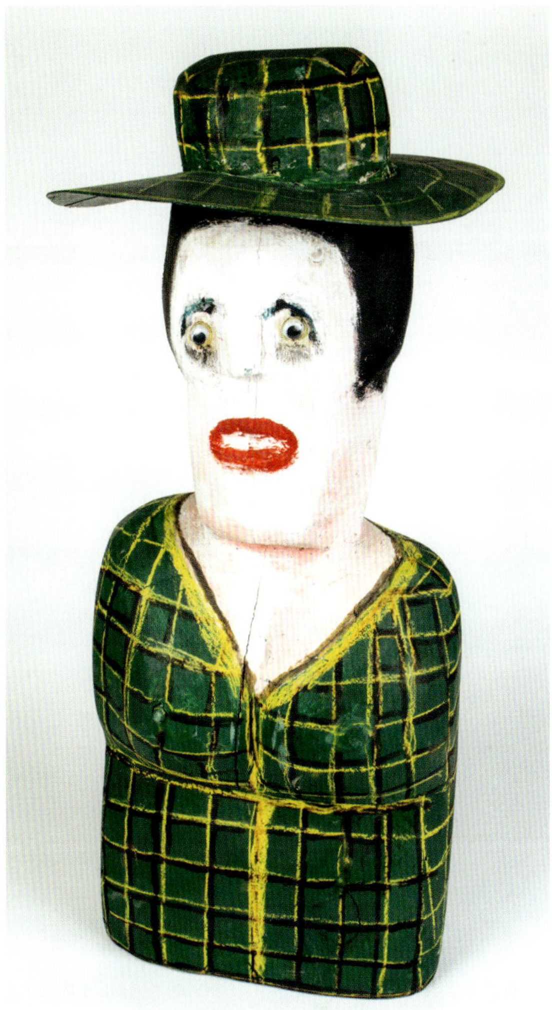

LEFT: *John Diefenbaker,* Sidney Howard

(AGNS)

RIGHT: *Rita MacNeil,* Sidney Howard

(RAW PHOTOGRAPHY FOR AGNS)

In 1975 Dalhousie Art Gallery curator Bruce Ferguson saw Howard's roadside figures and told Chris Huntington about them. Chris Huntington made the trip to Albert Bridge, on the Mira River, and ventured down the road to Howard's place. He convinced Howard to sell him some of the figures, and he kept returning for years. Soon other visitors were following these totemic figures down to the barn/studio to visit and buy Howard's carvings. Over the years, Howard would replace the figures as they were sold or stolen, and he would mix up the types of figure depicted. Among his most popular figures were the Mounties that he would carve to mark the road to his house, replacing them as they sold.

Howard's carvings were deliberately primitive, with minimal detail and plenty of evidence of the marks of making them. He didn't use auto-body filler to smooth things out; he liked the rough qualities of the axe and rasp marks (Howard didn't carve with a chainsaw but roughed his pieces out with

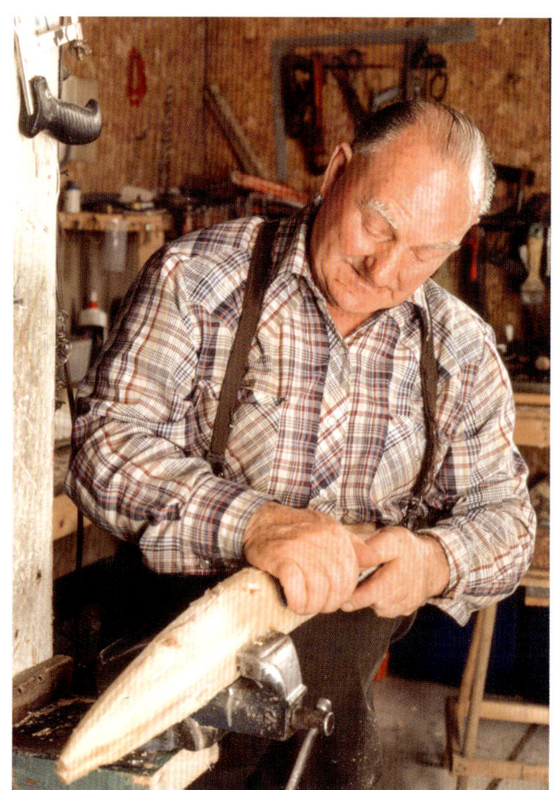

Sidney Howard

(AGNS)

an axe or hatchet). Despite, or perhaps because of, the roughness of his carvings, his work was rich with quirky character. As collector Philip Brooks wrote, "Sid's artistic magic was imparting the radiant energy, personality and quirky humour with which his creatures screamed."[33] There was something primal and elemental about Howard's carvings. One reviewer noted that his "figures are almost primitive in the other sense of the word, almost like pagan idols in their simplistic and crude carving."[34]

Howard's carving *Figure*, one of his original two roadside sculptures, was included in *Folk Art of Nova Scotia* in 1976 and in *Nova Scotia Folk Art: Canada's Cultural Heritage*, which toured Great Britain in 1989–90. His work is in the permanent collection of the Art Gallery of Nova Scotia and at the Canadian Museum of History, as well as in numerous private and corporate collections.

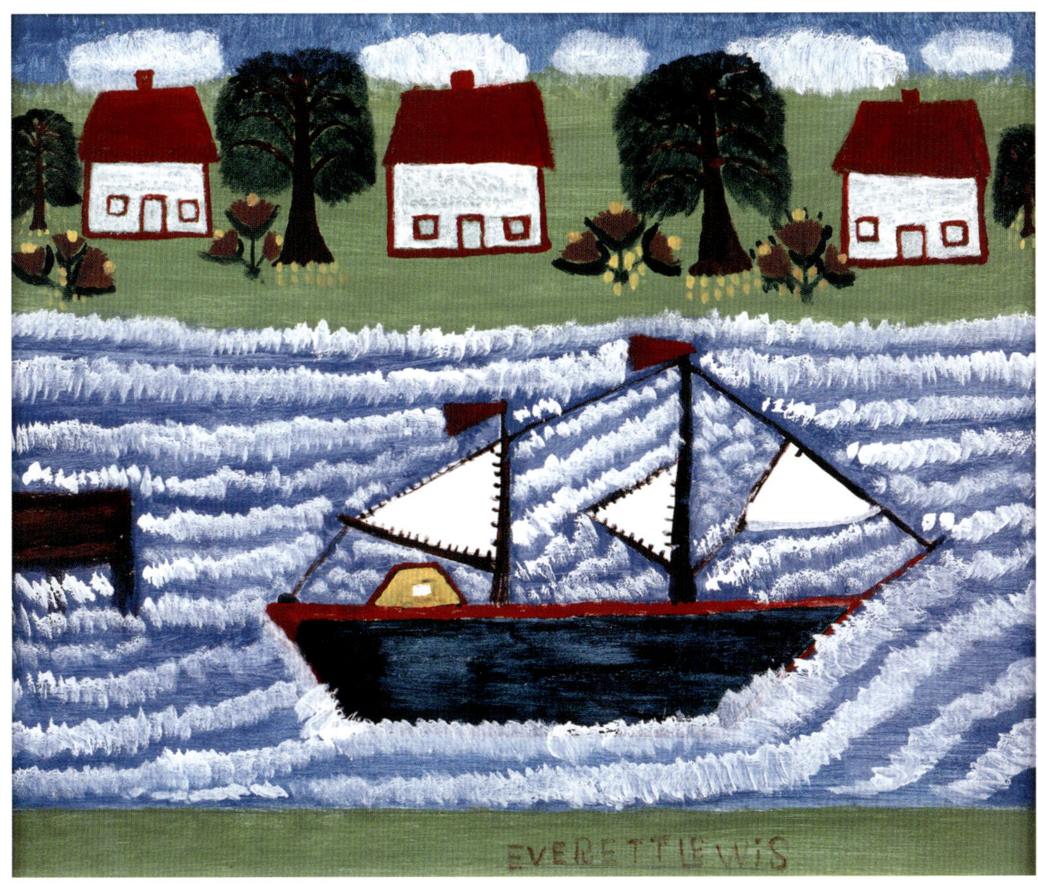

Sailboat, Everett Lewis

(AGNS)

EVERETT LEWIS

(MARSHALLTOWN, DIGBY COUNTY)

1893–1979

EVERETT LEWIS WAS RAISED ON A SO-CALLED "POOR FARM" IN Marshalltown. In his youth he worked as a farm labourer, eventually setting up as a fish peddler, selling fish he would buy at the local wharves door-to-door in Digby County. He eventually bought a small house and moved it to a piece of land he had acquired next to the poor farm. It was to this modest home, which lacked electricity and running water, that Maud Dowley moved when the two married in 1938.

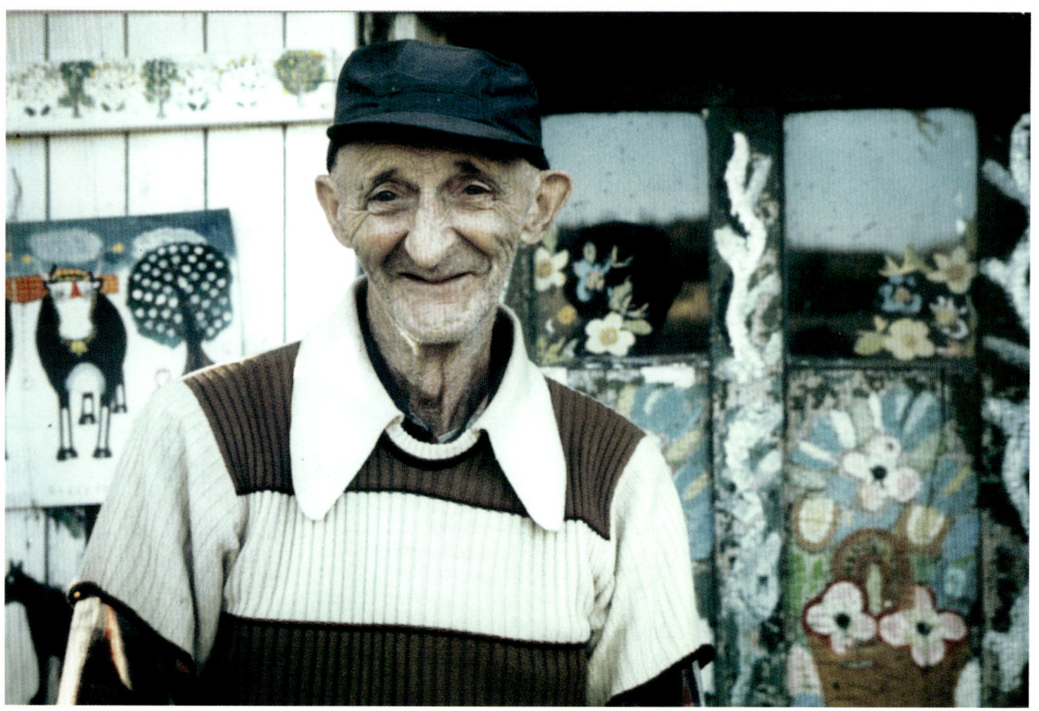

Everett Lewis
(AGNS)

Maud had been painting since her youth, when she would sell painted cards to neighbours in Yarmouth. Unable to help with the chores around the house because of crippling arthritis, she began to make paintings that Everett would sell on his fish rounds. When he took a job as a night watchman at the neighbouring poor farm, Maud began to sell her paintings from the house.

She painted on small boards that Everett cut for her from whatever scrap materials he could find. As her health worsened, Everett traced some of her most popular images—cats, oxen, sleds, deer, and more—and cut stencils out of stiff cardboard that Maud could use to ease the work of painting. Sometimes he helped her with them, filling in the colours under her direction. After Maud's death he continued to live in the painted house, even adding his own touches. The small evergreens painted on the front and sides were his work, not Maud's.

He took up painting in the early 1970s, often using the same stencils he had cut for Maud. Early on he would copy her paintings, even going so far as to copy her signature (often he would sign on the back, acknowledging that the work was "a copy of a painting by Maud Lewis by Everett Lewis"). As her stencils wore out, he made his own and developed a distinct style of his own. Everett Lewis was murdered by a burglar in 1979—a young man who had broken into the house seeking Everett's rumoured stash of money.

Three paintings by Everett were included in *Folk Art of Nova Scotia*, and his work is in the collections of the Canadian Museum of History and the AGNS.

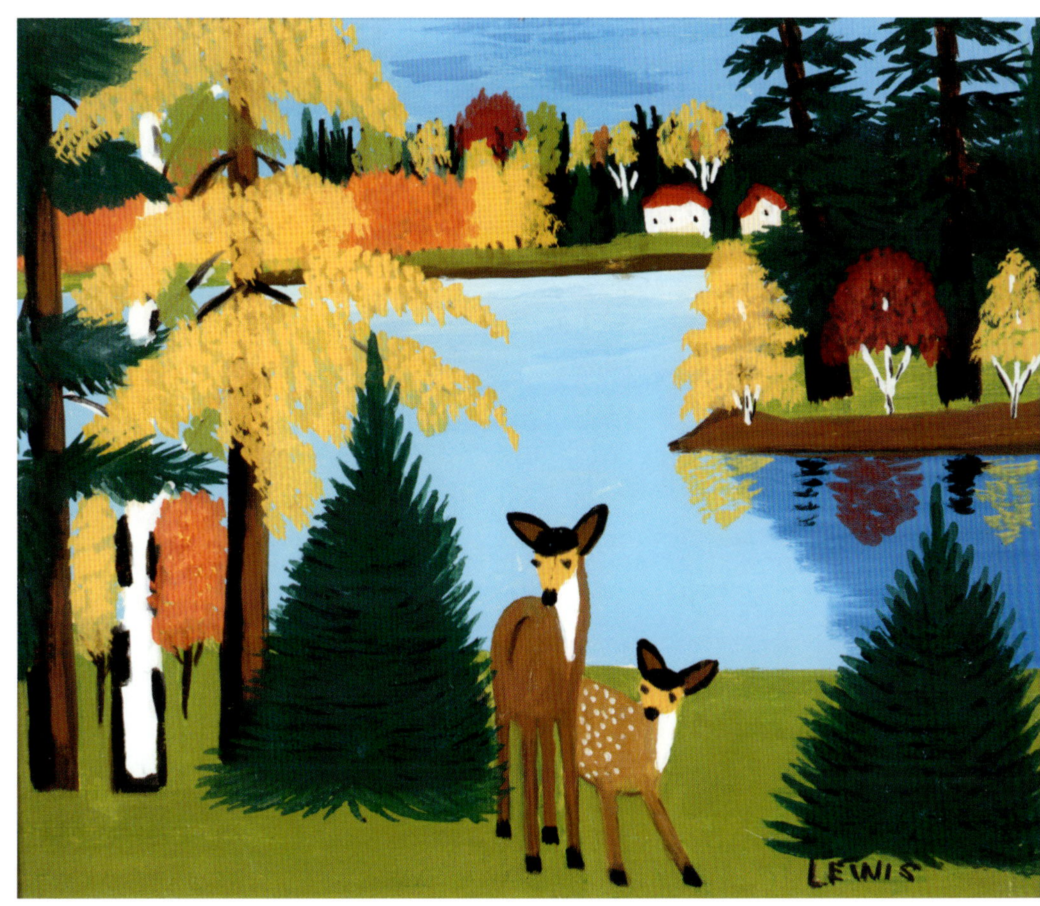

Fall Scene With Deer,
Maud Lewis

(AGNS)

MAUD LEWIS

(MARSHALLTOWN, DIGBY COUNTY)

1901–1970

MAUD LEWIS HAS BECOME THE BEST-KNOWN FOLK ARTIST IN CANADA, something she could have little imagined while she was living in her small house in Marshalltown, just outside of Digby. Works that she would have sold for a few dollars then now sell at auction for over $20,000. She never called herself an artist; painting was something she did to make much-needed money to augment the family income.

Maud Lewis's hands were curled into tight fists due to juvenile arthritis. She could barely open her hands to hold a brush. She had lifelong health problems

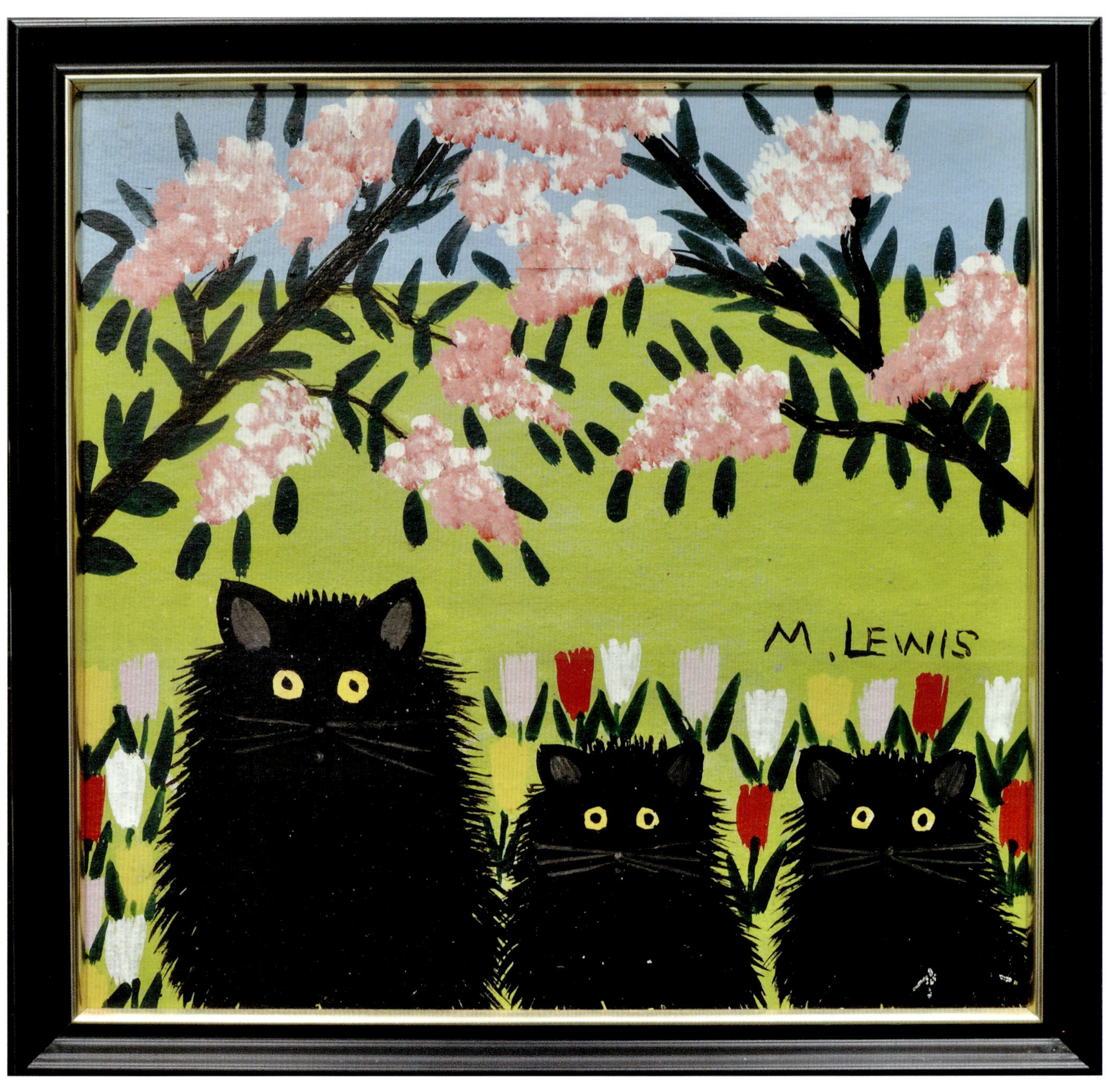

Three Black Cats, Maud Lewis (AGNS)

and lived with constant pain. Nevertheless, she painted a sunny, even joyful, world. Nostalgic and colourful, her work was popular with tourists on Nova Scotia's South Shore; a visit to Nova Scotia was not complete without stopping by "Mrs. Lewis's" roadside home to chat and buy a painting or two.

Near the end of her life, Maud Lewis was featured on a national television program and in the *Toronto Star*'s *Sunday* magazine. Her fame was just beginning to grow when she died. Her brightly painted house—she had painted

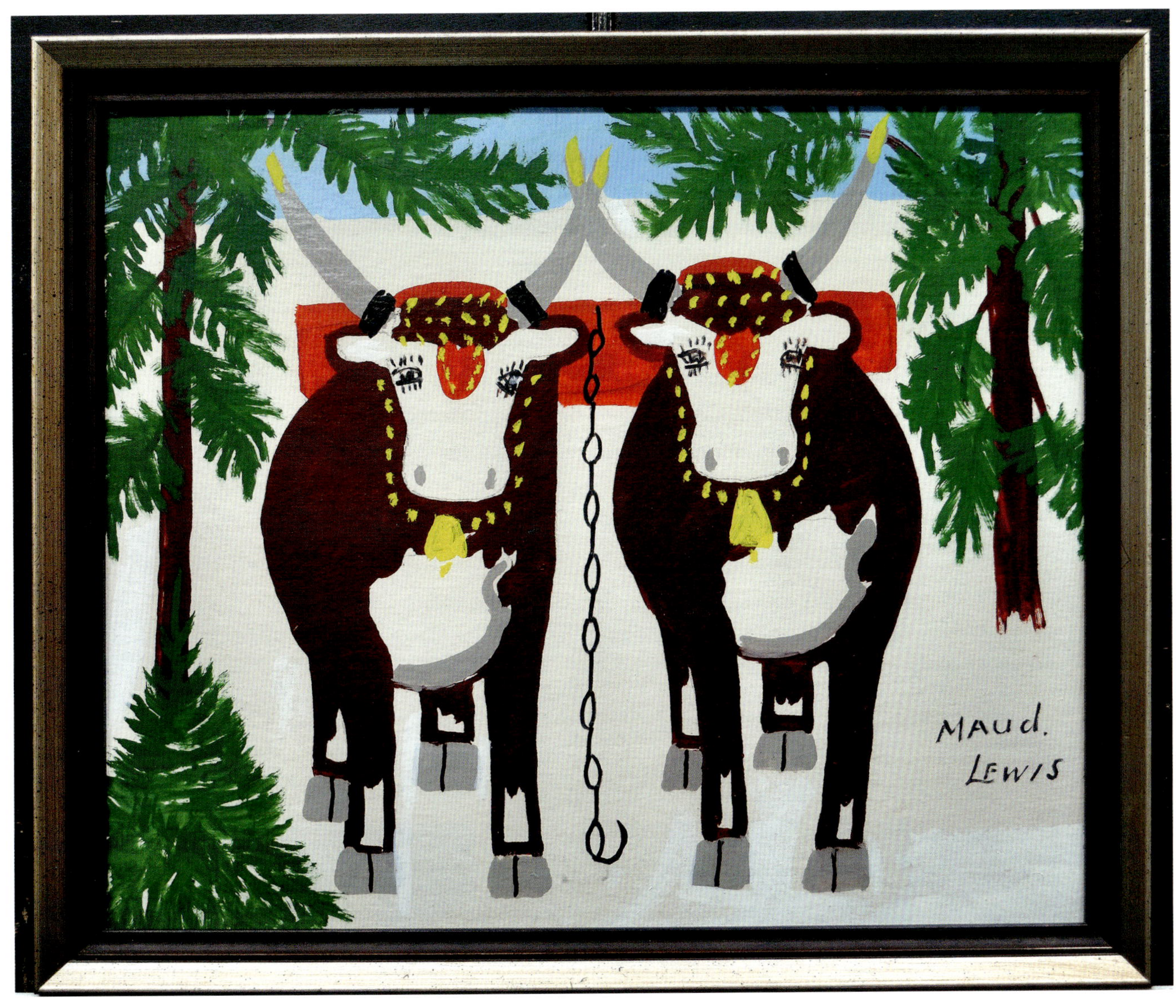

Team of Oxen in Winter, Maud Lewis

(AGNS)

nearly every inch of the house, both inside and out, with colourful images (see page 12)—soon became the centre of local efforts to save a landmark. With her husband Everett's death in 1979 the house soon fell into disrepair. Despite all their efforts, a local group was unable to raise the funds to preserve the house and it was sold to the Province of Nova Scotia and put under the care of the Art Gallery of Nova Scotia, which undertook the exhaustive restoration work it needed. The first permanent home for the AGNS, which opened in 1988, had been envisioned with a space that would hold her house, but it took ten years to raise the funds to expand the gallery and create a space for it. Finally, the house was moved inside the AGNS, where it opened to the public in 1998.

Four of Maud's paintings were included in the exhibition *Folk Art of Nova Scotia* in 1976. In 1997 the AGNS mounted a nationally touring exhibition of her work, *The Illuminated Life of Maud Lewis*. In the ensuing decades, Maud's art and her story have become ever more popular with the public in Canada and across the world. In 2019 her work was the subject of a major solo exhibition at the McMichael Canadian Art Collection in Ontario, and was part of a group exhibition of Nova Scotia Art that toured to four museums in China. *Maudie*, the acclaimed feature film starring Sally Hawkins and Ethan Hawke, told her life story to even larger audiences in 2017. Her work is included in numerous public collections, and she has become one of the most iconic Canadian artists of the twentieth century.

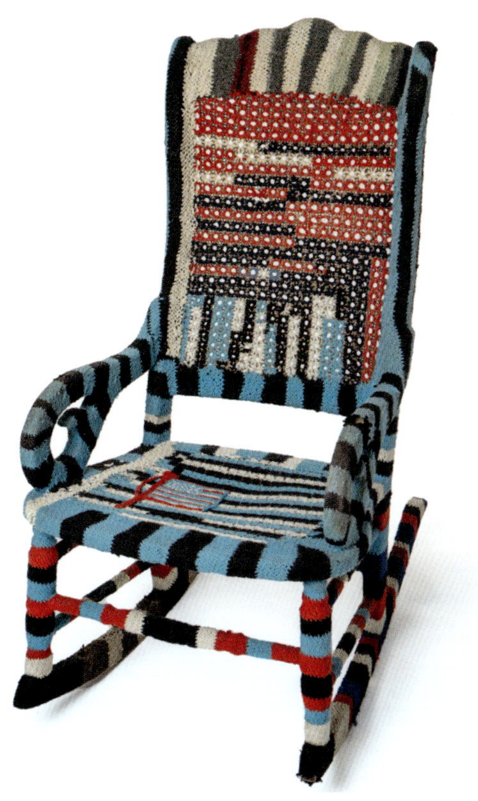

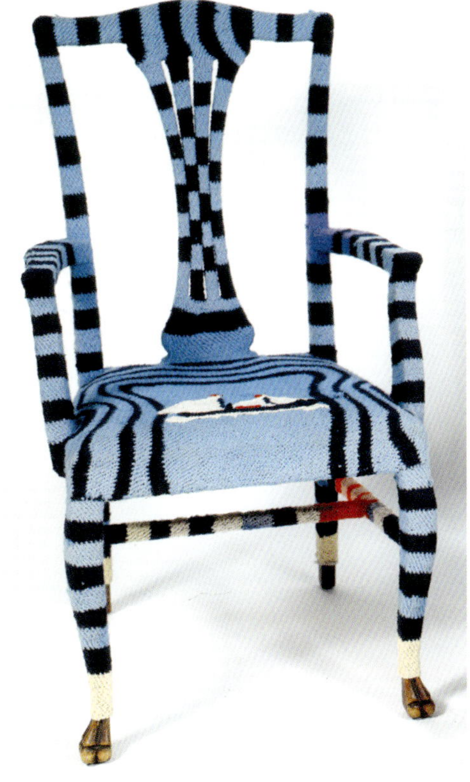

LEFT: *Red, White and Blue Rocker*, Albert Lohnes

(MICHAEL TOMPKINS FOR AGNS)

RIGHT: *Crocheted Armchair*, Albert Lohnes

(AGNS)

ALBERT LOHNES

(WEST BERLIN, QUEENS COUNTY)

1895–1977

ALBERT LOHNES WAS A SAILOR AND A FISHER WHO WORKED BOTH IN sail lofts—making and repairing sails—and on fishing schooners. He left home at thirteen and worked on the boats until he retired in 1964. His hand was injured badly when he was eighteen. While fishing in a two-man dory, a dogfish (a small species of shark) got caught up in his cod line and mangled his hand—to the point where he almost lost the hand. He left the South Shore fishery to fish out of larger boats from Gloucester, Massachusetts, and worked in that fishery until his retirement.

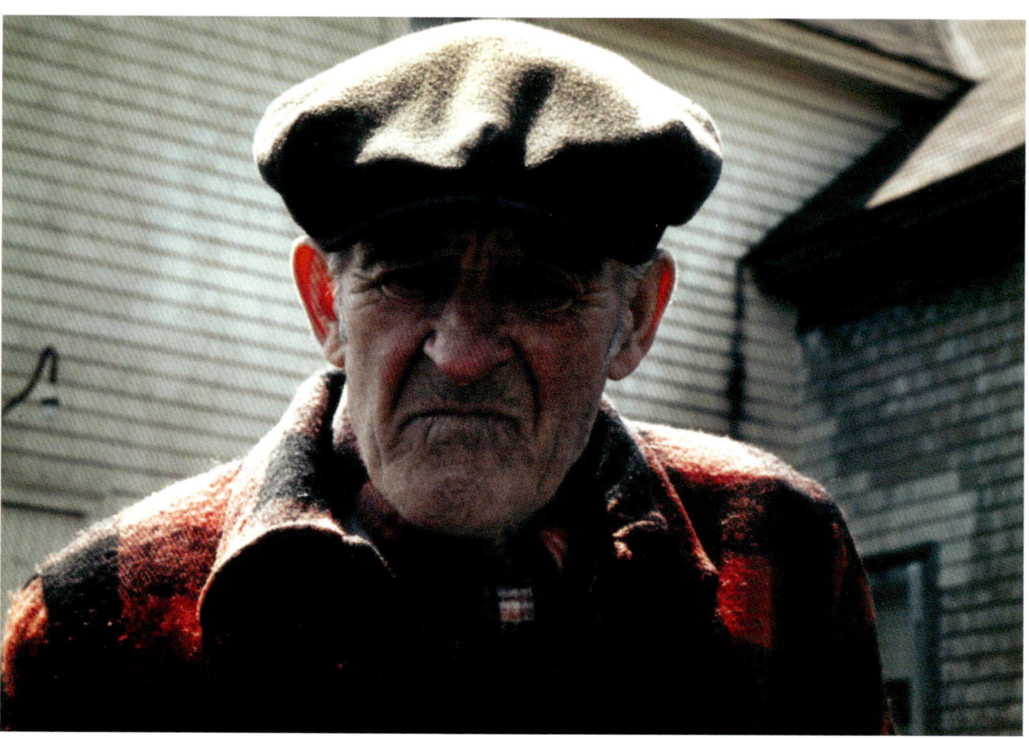

Albert Lohnes
(AGNS)

When Lohnes was around the age of thirty, the captain of one of his boats had a problem: he kept sliding around in his chair when the seas were high. Lohnes knitted a cover for the chair and rigged up a system to fix the chair to the floor. Problem solved. "Then he used to roll back and forth," Lohnes remembered, "but he couldn't slide."[35] He used red, white, and blue yarn for the covering, a design style that he would return to frequently for the rest of his life.

In the late 1960s he returned to knitting colourful coverings for chairs as something to keep him busy while he was laid up with a bad knee. "I got some yarn one day," he said, "when I couldn't do much work anymore."[36] He made sixteen known chairs in this period; most of them had a signature—"Albert Lohnes, West Berlin"—included in the knitted patterns.

His work was included in *Nova Scotia Folk Art* and *From the Heart: Folk Art in Canada*, and is in the permanent collections of the Art Gallery of Nova Scotia and the Canadian Museum of History.

CLARENCE MOOERS (ALSO MOORES)

(MILTON, QUEENS COUNTY)

1925–2002

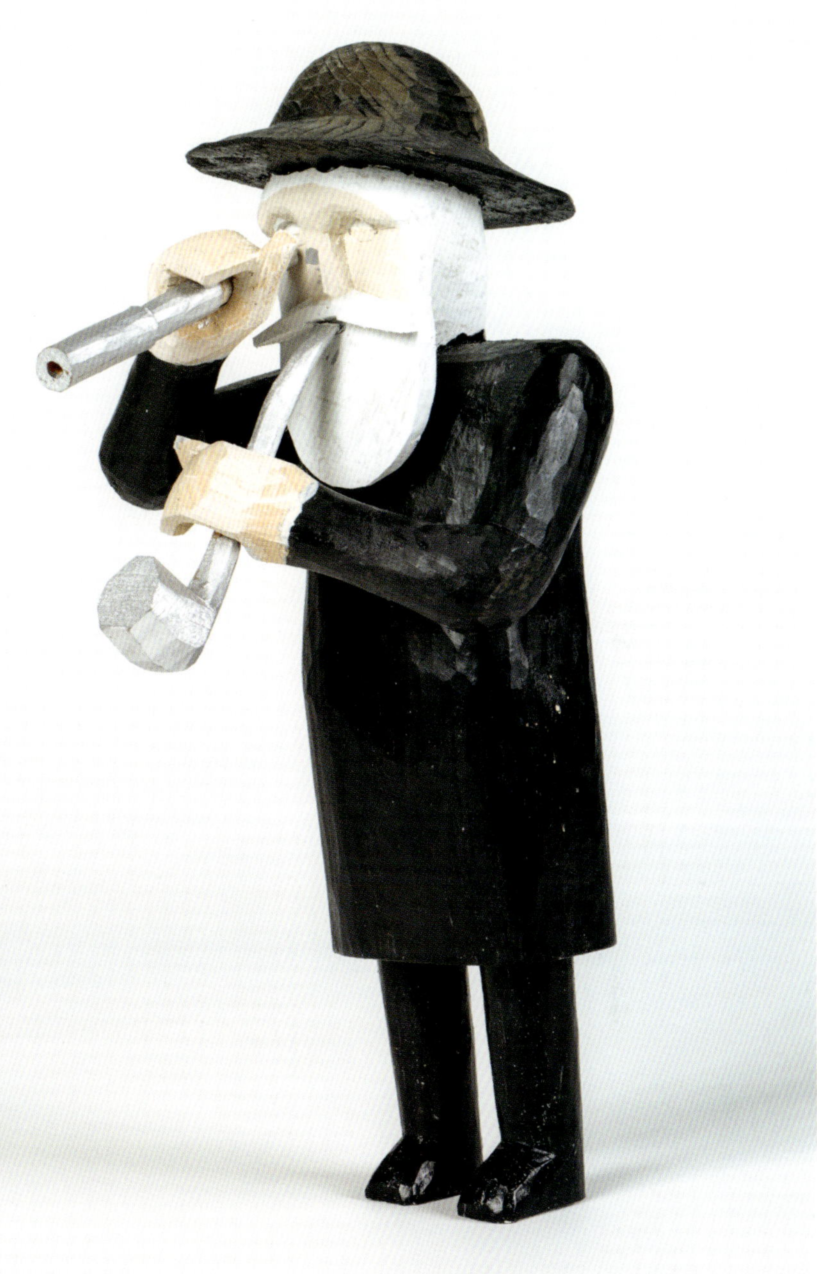

Sea Captain, Clarence Mooers

(AGNS)

CLARENCE "BUBBY" MOOERS lived his whole life in Milton, the same village in Queens County where Ralph Boutilier lived. Mooers first began carving as a boy, making decorative handles for crooked knives, a technique he learned from his father. "I made just about everything you could make," he remembered, "from a frog to a woman."[37]

A carpenter by trade, he started making larger carvings of figures and animals in 1975 to fill the time when the mill he had been working at closed. "Well, I was practically retired because I drew unemployment all the time, you couldn't get a job anywhere," he said.[38] Unlike some of his peers, such as Sidney Howard, Mooers did not carve from single logs, but instead laminated together as many as forty layers of planks to create a block of wood. His reasoning was based in his experience as a carpenter. With a log, he explained, "you run into the problem of drying the material because it will crack and so on."[39]

His first life-sized carving was *Penelope and the Poodle* (1976), which went through a series of changes. The figure started out as a man, but after discussions with Chris Huntington, Mooers changed it to a female figure, and he added a poodle at her feet. Huntington was not shy about talking with artists about how they could make works that would have more of a market, or about telling them what he felt would work better as art. He visited and revisited Mooers, and "kept going there, kept expressing interest in what he was making. And the last thing he made was really wonderful."[40] The work was included in *Folk Art of Nova Scotia* as well as *From the Heart: Folk Art in Canada*. *Penelope and the Poodle* is now in the collection of the Canadian Museum of History.

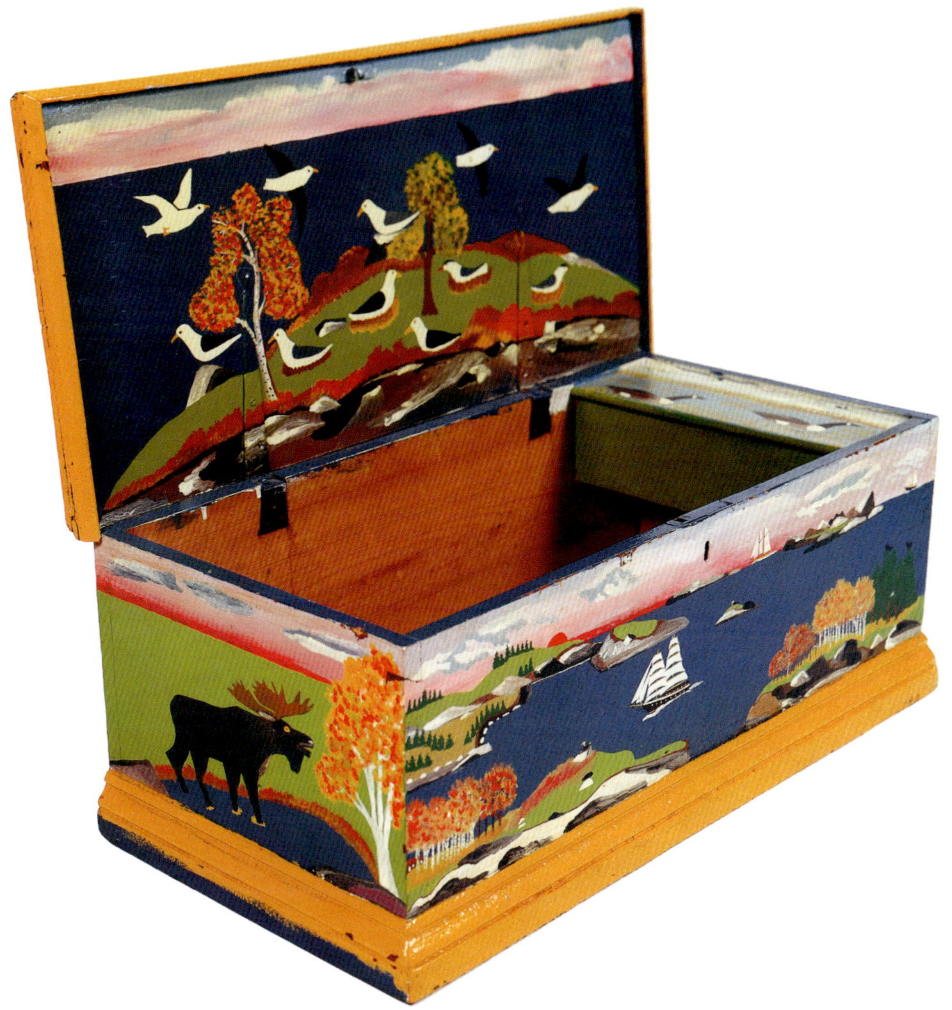

Chest,
Joseph Norris

(AGNS)

JOSEPH NORRIS

(LOWER PROSPECT, HALIFAX COUNTY)

1924–1996

ONE DAY IN 1975, CHRIS HUNTINGTON WAS DRIVING THROUGH LOWER Prospect looking for possible painting locations when he saw a weathered shack on a granite outcropping near the water. (In addition to being an antiques and art dealer, Huntington is a well-known landscape painter.) It looked like an interesting subject. What he found was an old fish shed on Joseph "Joe"

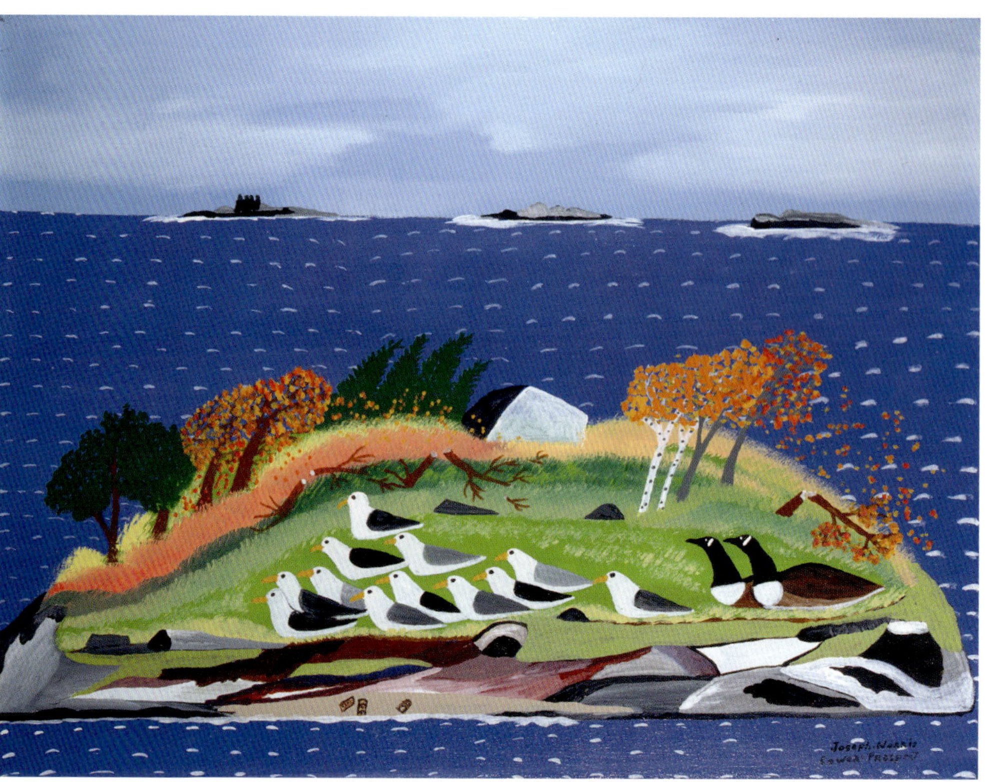

Seagulls on Island,
Joseph Norris

(AGNS)

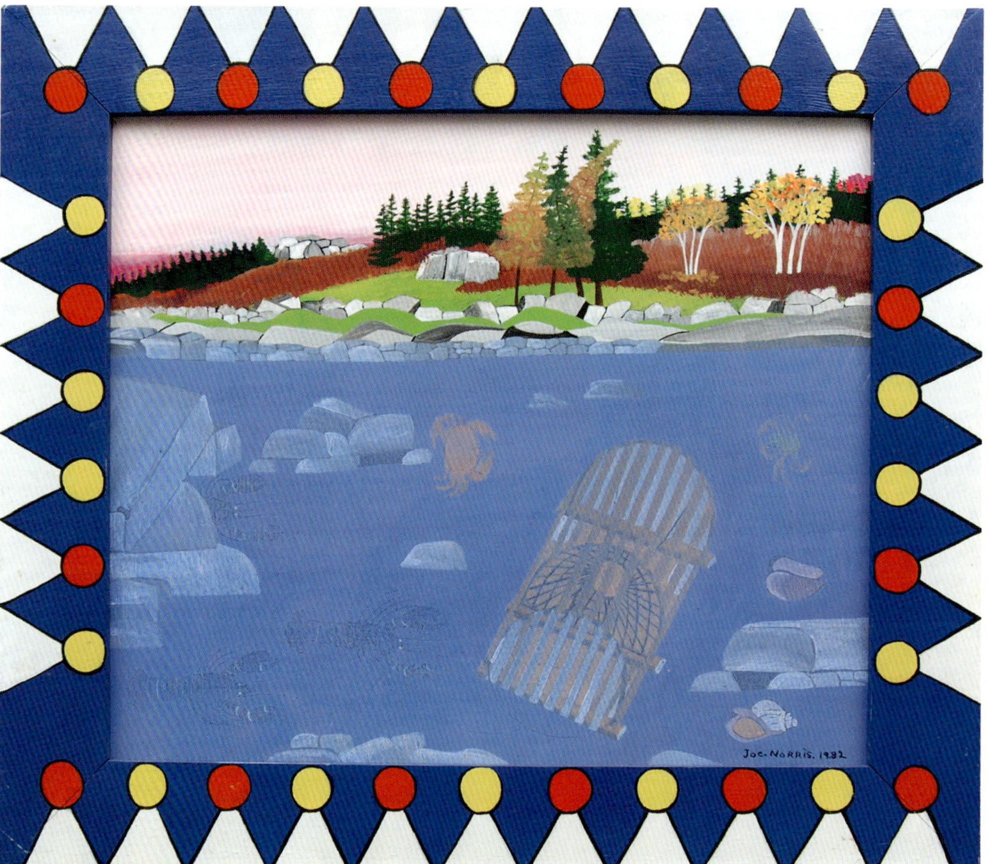

Untitled (Undersea View),
Joseph Norris

(AGNS)

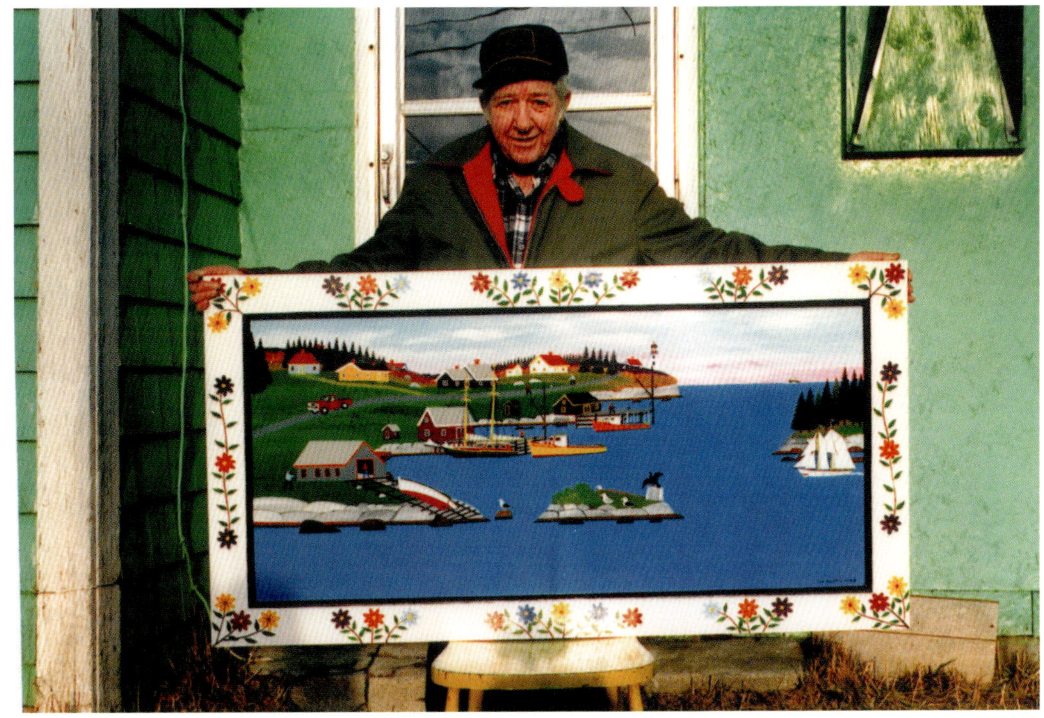

Joseph Norris

(AGNS)

Norris's property with a painting nailed to its wall. He bought that painting, and eventually hundreds more. Joe Norris had been "discovered."

Norris, a fisher who'd had to retire from the sea in 1974 at the age of forty-nine after a heart attack, painted for his own amusement. He had been encouraged to do so by the nurse who looked after him during his recovery. A tireless worker, it wasn't in him to be idle, and painting filled an important void in his life. "I had to do something, because I was used to working," he said.[41]

Huntington continued to visit, and eventually other collectors did too. In 1976, thirteen of his paintings were included in *Folk Art of Nova Scotia*, the exhibition that really launched his (and other) careers, and put "Nova Scotia Folk Art" on the art-world map.

In 1978, Bruce Ferguson, curator of the Dalhousie Art Gallery, gave Norris an exhibition, making him the first Nova Scotia folk artist to have a solo show at the public art gallery. Chris Huntington wrote for the catalogue and introduced the theme that would come to define Norris as an artist: "Joe Norris is firstly an artist; secondly, he is a folk artist."[42] Norris would always be considered the most sophisticated of the classic folk artists: an artist who made remarkable paintings with aesthetic power that went beyond their rural subject matter—and even went beyond Norris's own compelling personal story.

Norris painted seascapes, both on panels and on the popular painted furniture that he made for collectors. Seagulls, lobsters, whales, and other maritime life forms abound in his works, which feature startlingly bright colours that, at first, may seem unrealistic. Norris always claimed they were realistic, which they were. In his eulogy for Joe Norris, John Houston, Norris's art dealer in his later life, remembered: "Already, people recalling their travels will refer to a 'perfect Joe Norris sunset' they drove through."

In addition to *Folk Art of Nova Scotia* Norris's work was included in *From the Heart: Folk Art in Canada* and *Nova Scotia Folk Art: Canada's Cultural Heritage*. His work is found in the collections of the Art Gallery of Nova Scotia and the Canadian Museum of History, among others. In 2000 the AGNS mounted a retrospective exhibition curated by Bernard Riordon: *Joe Norris: Painted Visions of Nova Scotia*, which toured the country.

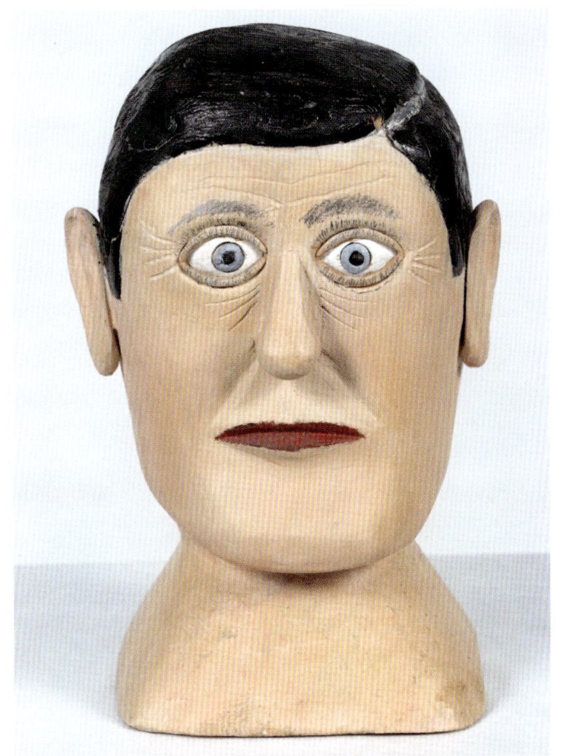

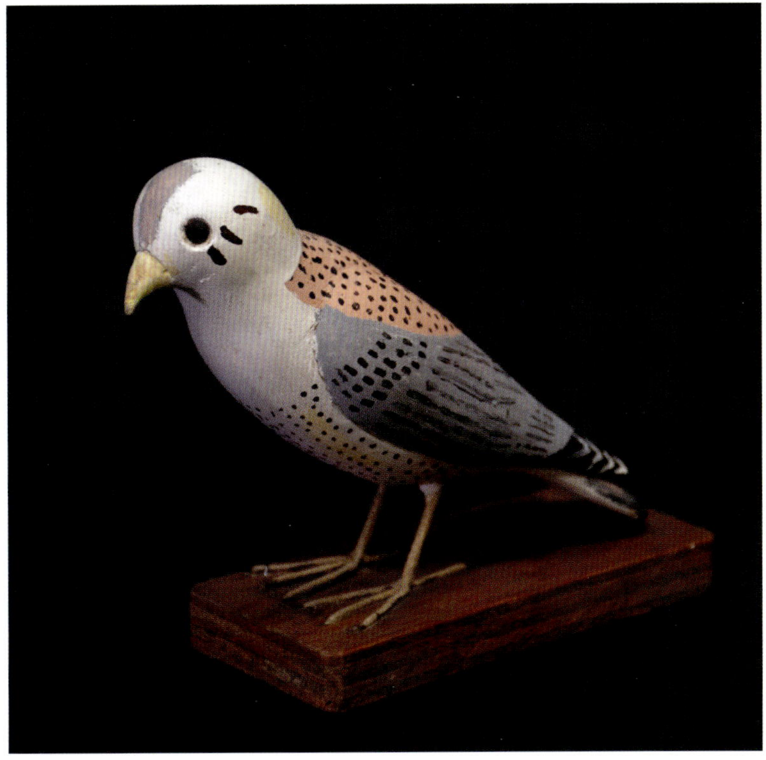

EMERY NOWLAN

(BLACK RIVER, KINGS COUNTY)

1887–1982

LEFT: *Man's Head*, Emery Nowlan

(AGNS)

RIGHT: *Sparrow Hawk*, Emery Nowlan

(AGNS))

EMERY NOWLAN SPENT MOST OF HIS LIFE IN BLACK RIVER, KINGS County, where he was a carpenter and a farmer. He took up carving in his retirement and was active for about ten years. His primary subject was birds, which he carved singly but often displayed in groups, clustered on "trees" made from painted branches.

In the catalogue for *Folk Art of Nova Scotia* an anecdote is told about a carving Nowlan did: "Some time ago he made a head of a man which his wife made him take to the woodshed where it was neglected for four years."[43] It was taken from the woodshed and acquired by Ellen Huntington and then subsequently by the Art Gallery of Nova Scotia in 1977. It was also included in *Folk Art of Nova Scotia* along with *Five Birds in a Tree*.

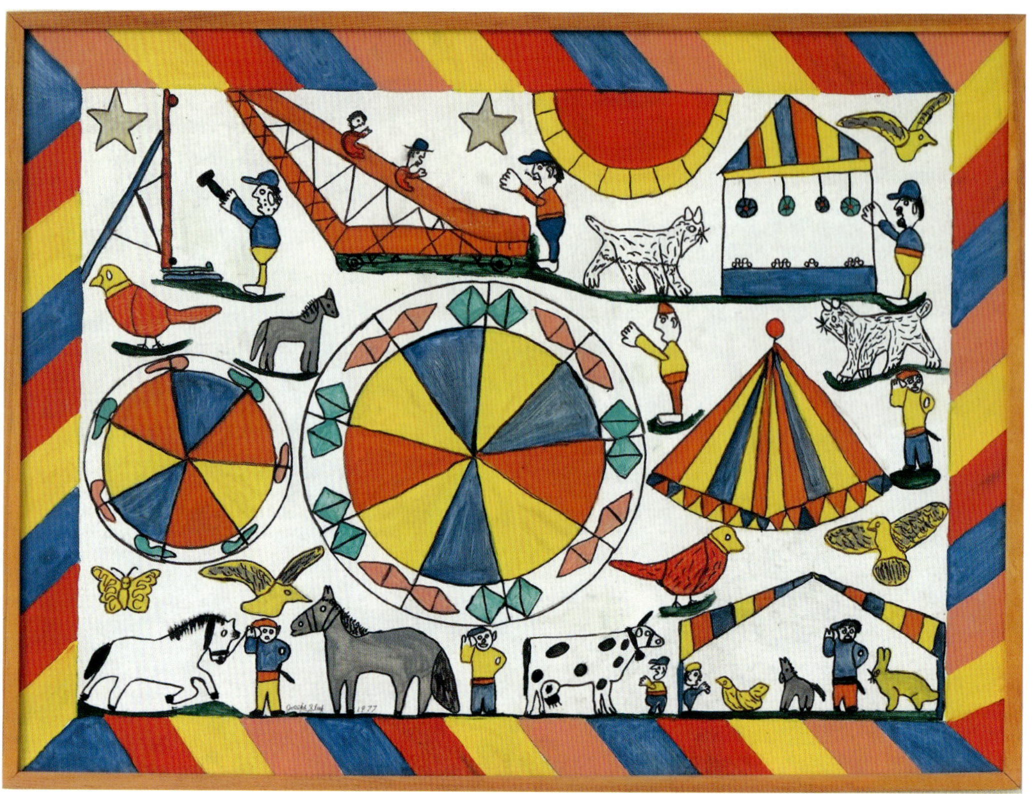

Carnival with Animals, Joseph Sleep

(AGNS)

JOSEPH SLEEP

(HALIFAX, HALIFAX COUNTY)

1914–1978

IN 1981, THREE YEARS AFTER HIS DEATH, THE ART GALLERY OF NOVA Scotia mounted a retrospective exhibition of Joseph "Joe" Sleep's work. Sleep, a former carney (he spent most of his adult life working for the Bill Lynch shows, a travelling Maritime carnival), was hospitalized for high blood pressure in 1973. While in hospital he was introduced to painting. "They gave me posters to colour, and I started drawing my own and I ain't stopped since."[44] Once released from the hospital, no longer able to work in the carnival, he took up picture-making as a means to make a living.

Sleep worked by making stencils drawn from many sources—colouring books, magazines, and book illustrations among them. He would trace the

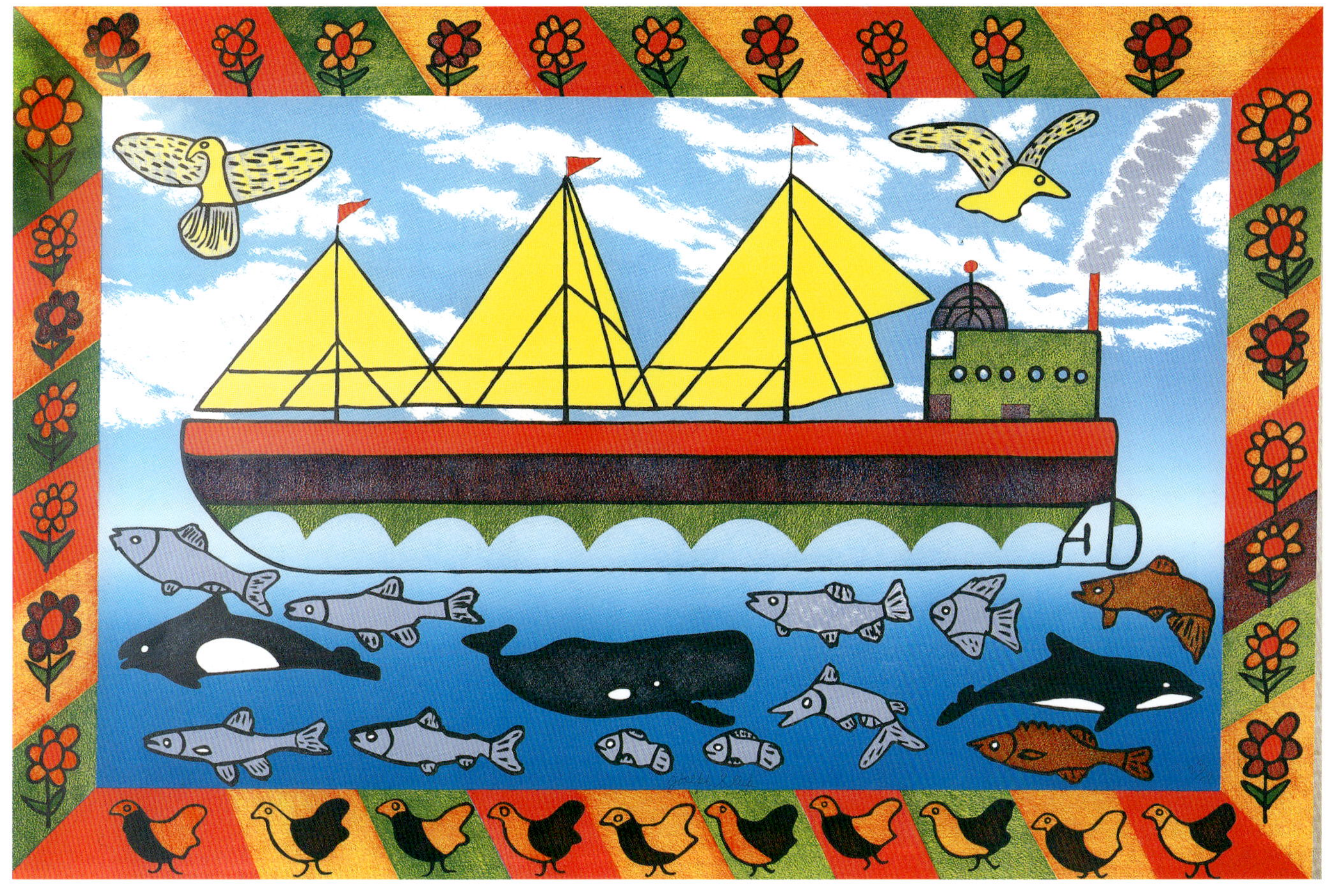

Ship and Creatures, Joseph Sleep

(AGNS)

images onto stiff cardboard and then cut them out to use over and over as stencils for his drawings. He began to display his works on the railings of the fence around the Halifax Public Gardens and deliberately sized them so that they would easily fit into the suitcases of the tourists who were his main customers.

Sleep's work depicts what curator Bruce Ferguson called "a good-natured world in which the elements co-exist in a perpetual tranquility."[45] As with so much Nova Scotia Folk Art—one thinks of Maud Lewis in particular—Sleep's idylls bore little resemblance to the real world, or even to the world of his memories. The seas he depicts are teeming with fish, for instance, with whales, eels, narwhals, sharks, and manta rays all swimming together. It is a world without violence. "All the natural creatures, including humans, portray a desire for pacifism, a content imposed by the artist," noted Ferguson. "This wishfulness was neither reflective of the true circumstances of Joe Sleep's social existence, nor, presumably, of the existence of most of his clientele."[46]

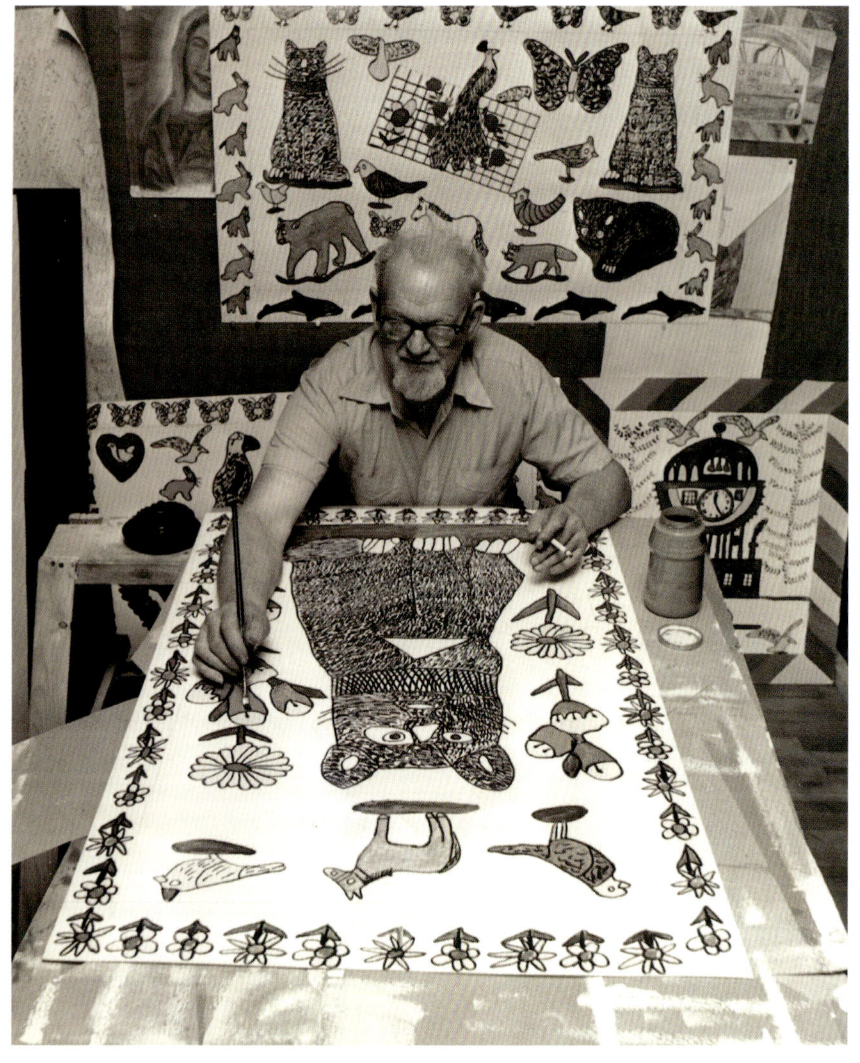

Joseph Sleep
(AGNS)

Of course, as Chris Huntington said repeatedly in talking about the appeal of Nova Scotia Folk Art, the art creates a world of its own—a world simpler, and perhaps better, than the one lived in by the artist. Sleep depicted fantasy, certainly, but he did so with an honest desire that the fantasy would prove to be reality. Who wouldn't rather live in a peaceable kingdom reminiscent of the Garden of Eden?

In 1976 Sleep was invited by Gerald Ferguson, a professor at the Nova Scotia College of Art and Design and a fervent collector of folk art, to make a print as part of NSCAD's renowned Lithography Workshop. In doing so, Sleep joined a select group that included famous contemporary artists such as John Baldessari, Eric Fischl, Sol LeWitt, and Joyce Wieland.

Sleep never framed his works, choosing instead to design decorative borders that are part of the overall design. Frames, he maintained, "interfere with the composition."[47] Sleep's work was included in *Folk Art of Nova Scotia*, *From the Heart: Folk Art in Canada*, and *Nova Scotia Folk Art: Canada's Cultural Heritage*.

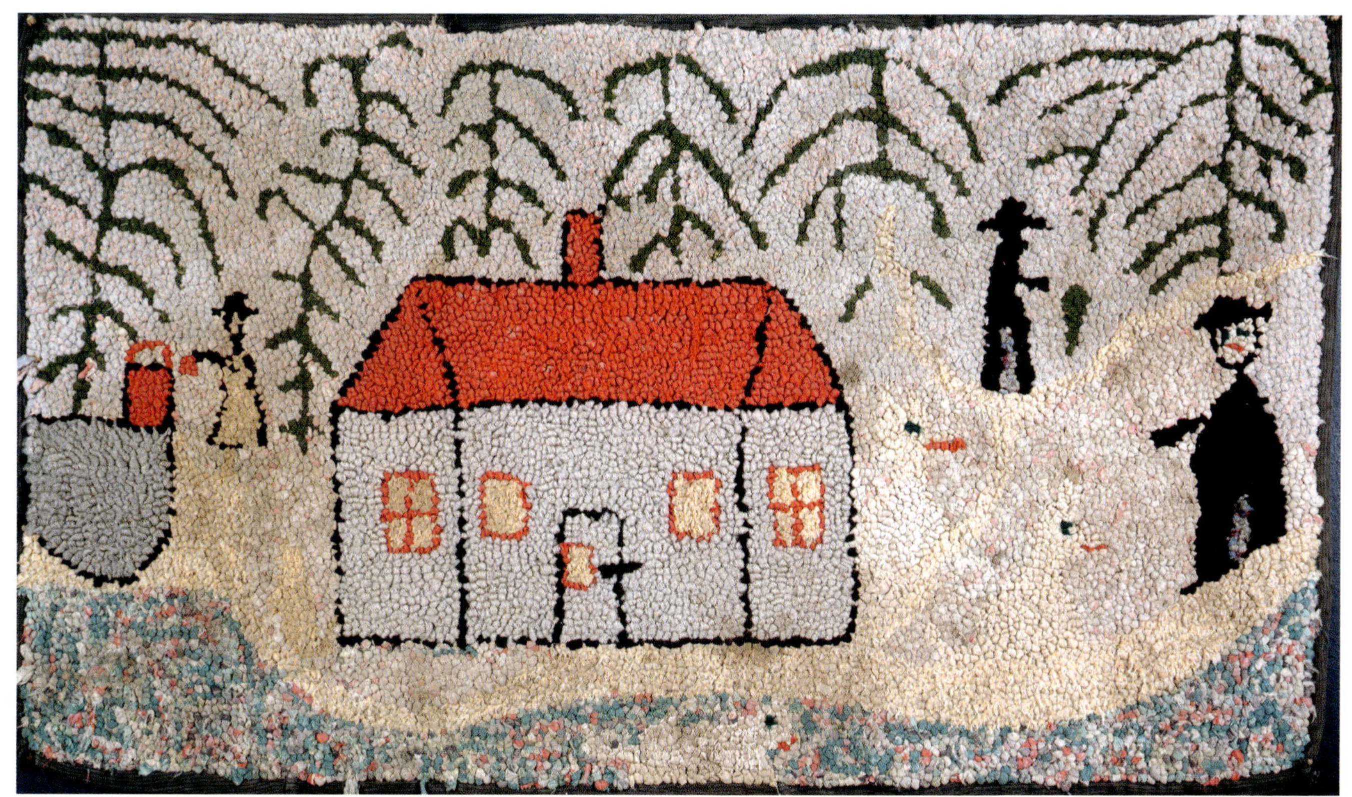

ELLEN GOULD SULLIVAN

(HALLS HARBOUR, KINGS COUNTY)

1907–2004

Woman at the Well with Two Men, Ellen Gould Sullivan

(AGNS)

ELLEN GOULD SULLIVAN WAS BORN AT BLACK ROCK IN KINGS COUNTY. With her husband she moved to the North Mountain, near Halls Harbour, and lived there for the rest of her life. Sullivan leaned to hook rugs from her mother, and for her whole career she used a rug hook that had been made for her by father: the hook was fashioned from a table fork and the handle was carved to fit her hand. Hooked rugs have long been features of homes in Nova Scotia and the rest of Atlantic Canada, and they often feature geometric or floral patterns based on popular patterns. The Grenfell Mission hooked rugs,

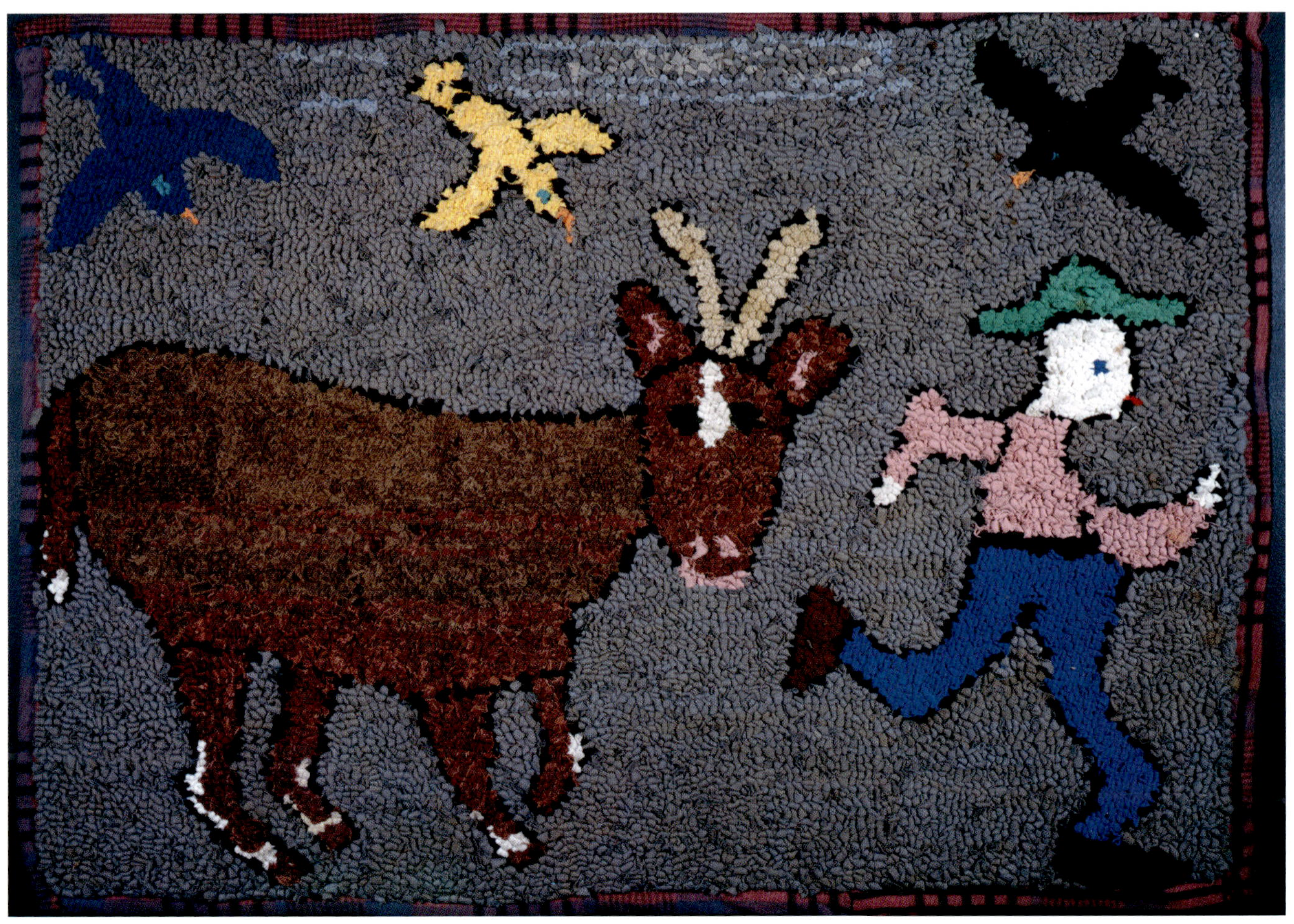

Bull Chasing Man, Ellen Gould Sullivan (AGNS)

from rural Newfoundland and Labrador, are among the best-known examples of this genre, and they include many pictorial scenes, again made from patterns supplied to the "hookers."

What sets the rugs of Ellen Gould Sullivan apart are the designs that she made herself—domestic and biblical scenes, scenes from memories of her childhood, and humorous set pieces made to amuse family members. One of her earliest known works, *Woman at the Well with Two Men* (1956), refers to the old family homestead in Black Rock. In 1979 Ellen Gould Sullivan was the subject of a solo exhibition at the Art Gallery of Nova Scotia; it subsequently toured to three other venues in the province. Her work was also included in the exhibition *Nova Scotia Folk Art: Canada's Cultural Heritage*, which toured through England and Scotland in 1989–90.

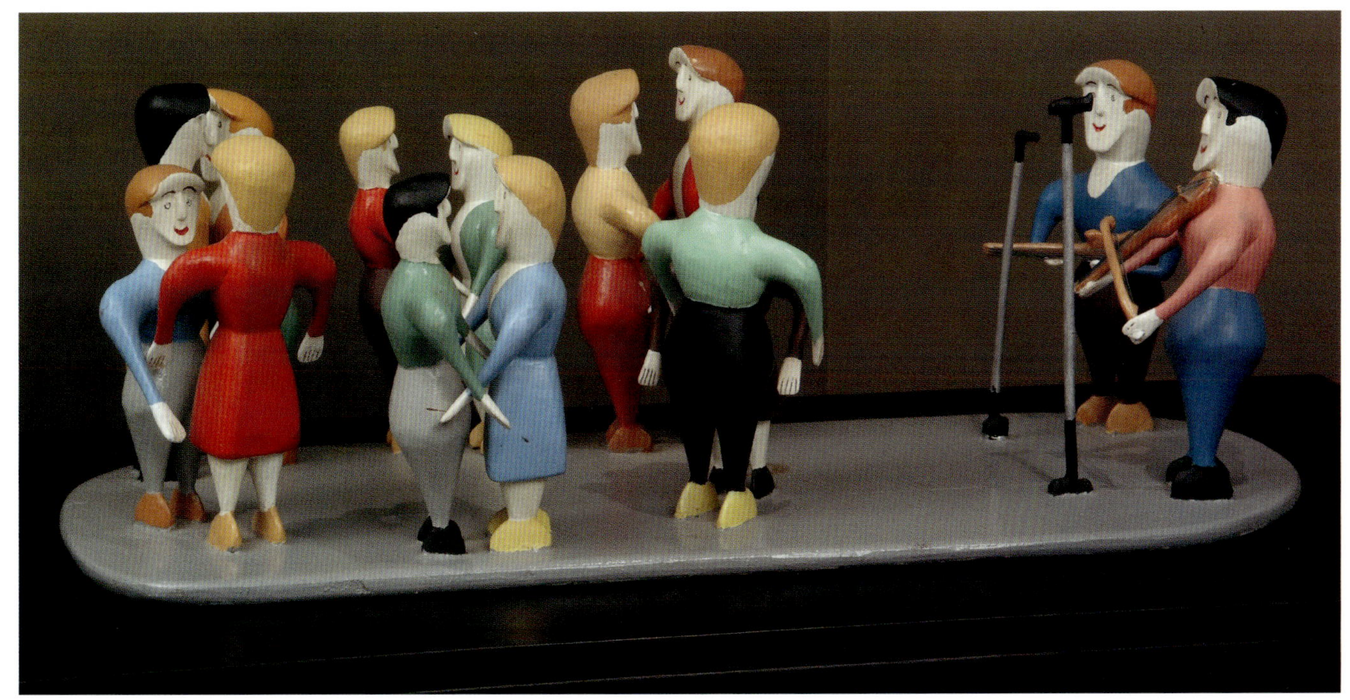

Square Dance, Charles Tanner

(AGNS)

CHARLES TANNER

(EAGLE HEAD, QUEENS COUNTY)

1904–1982

CHARLES "CHARLIE" TANNER WAS BORN IN STONEHURST, LUNENBURG County, and first went to work in his teens as a Grand Banks dory fisher. After a few years as a rum-runner, he eventually moved to Eagle Head in Queens County, and in 1929 he bought his own boat and started fishing. He fished until he had to retire for health reasons in 1973.

He took up carving as a hobby and in 1974 a new neighbour—collector and curator Chris Huntington—saw a small figure of a man in Tanner's yard. He knocked on the door, introduced himself, and asked Tanner if he had any more work like the yard sculpture. He had a sculpture on his mantel and promised Huntington that he could make many more. For the next eight years Tanner worked on making small figurative sculptures. After his death, his wife, Helen, estimated that he had made three thousand sculptures in his career.

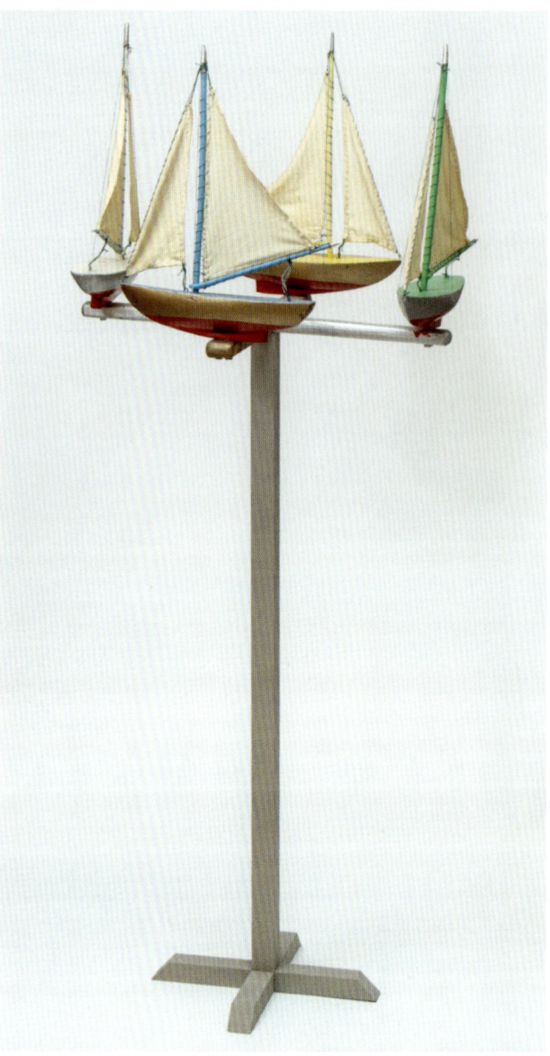

Sailboat Whirligig, Charles Tanner

(RAW PHOTOGRAPHY FOR AGNS)

Tanner's figures are quite unique with their rounded shoulders, flat faces, and colourful painted clothing. His works were all small (the largest known work by Tanner is ironically named *Dwarf*—it is thirty inches high and in the AGNS collection), and he often maintained that he never knew what a carving would be when he started it. "I don't really think much about it," he said. "I just keep settin' and whitllin,' carvin' them out the best way you can."[48] While most of his figures are singular, Tanner also made many group subjects—most notably his *Square Dance* from 1981. In addition to his figures, Tanner also made animals, cats in particular, and decoys, and, like Collins Eisenhauer, he also made the occasional erotic piece, such as *Face to Face* (a nude male and a nude female figure depicted making love), which was included in his 1984 retrospective exhibition. Tanner's work was featured in the touring exhibitions *Folk Art of Nova Scotia* in 1976 and *Nova Scotia Folk Art* (1989–90).

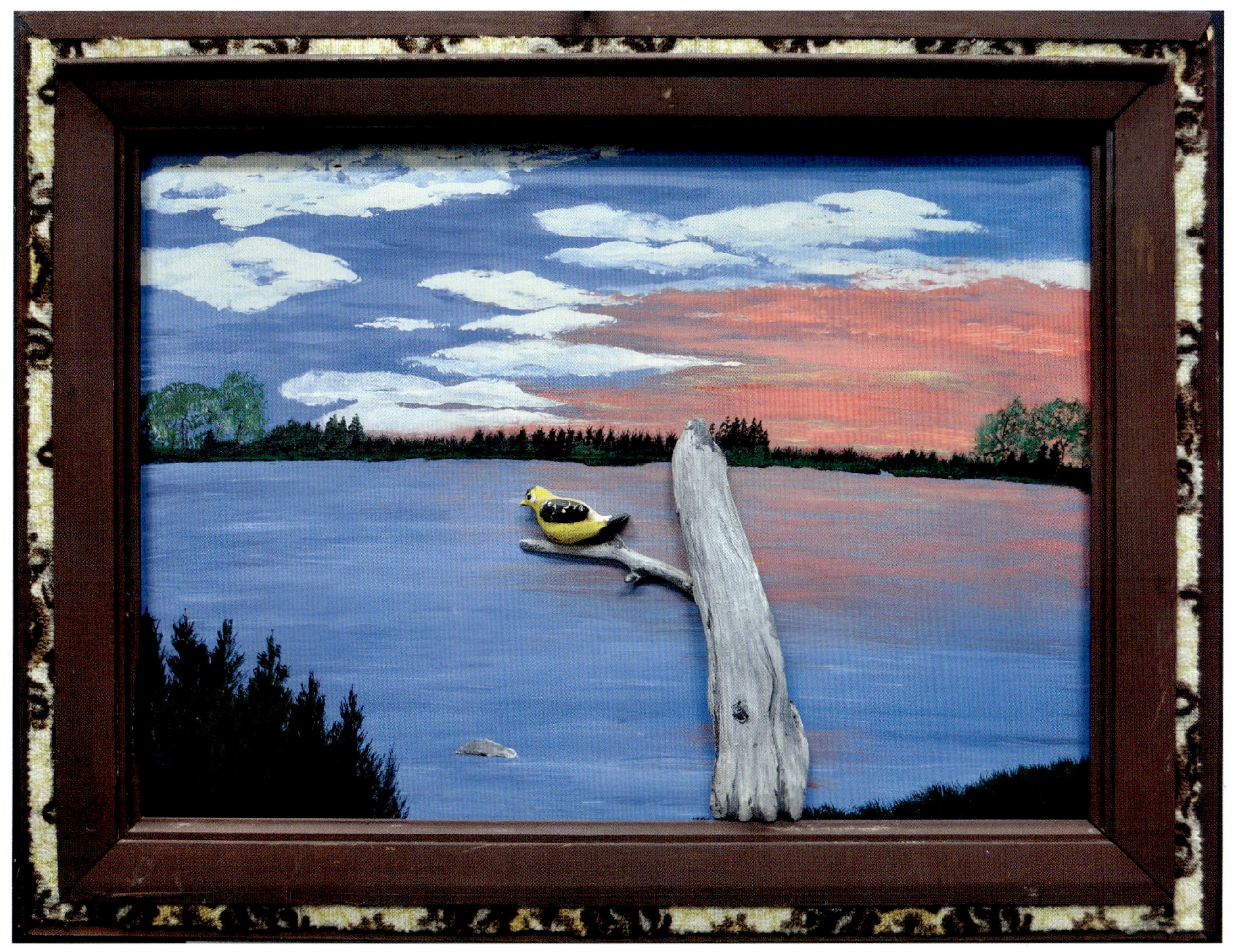

Untitled (Sunset on Lake), Eli Whiteway

(AGNS)

ELI WHITEWAY

(SHELBURNE, SHELBURNE COUNTY)

1914–1987

ELI WHITEWAY WAS A SHOEMAKER AND MERCHANT IN SHELBURNE, NOVA Scotia. He took over his father's shoe repair business before opening "Eli's Store," which sold "general merchandise"—a precursor to our familiar convenience stores. Whiteway had whittled as a boy, and he returned to that in his later years,

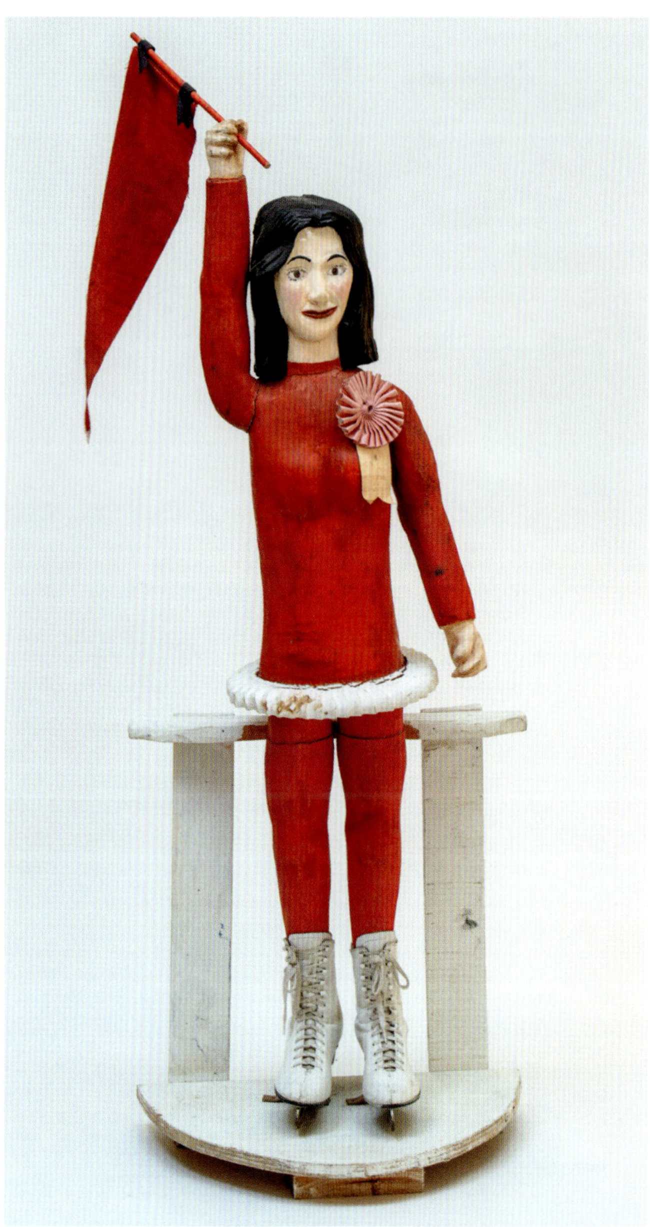

Teenage Skater, Eli Whiteway

(RAW PHOTOGRAPHY FOR AGNS)

making souvenirs to sell in his store. Along with items such as salt and pepper shakers in the forms of various animals, Whiteway did stand-alone carvings of animals, birds, and fish. He also made a few portraits, two of which are in the collection of the Art Gallery of Nova Scotia. *Roxanne*, from 1976, is a portrait of his daughter. His *Teenage Skater* from 1977 is a full figure of a young girl standing at a podium. In a typical folk art touch, she is wearing real skates.

Whiteway made several sculptures of animals with their babies, a good example of which is *Blue Heron with Young*, from around 1980. Whiteway also painted, combining painted sculptures with painted backdrops to make hybrid relief sculptures. One of his odder works is a wooden sculpture of a potted plant—*The Philodendron*, from 1982. Whiteway's sculpture of his daughter was included in *Folk Art of Nova Scotia*.

HARRY WILE

(NORTH RIVER, LUNENBURG COUNTY)

1891–1978

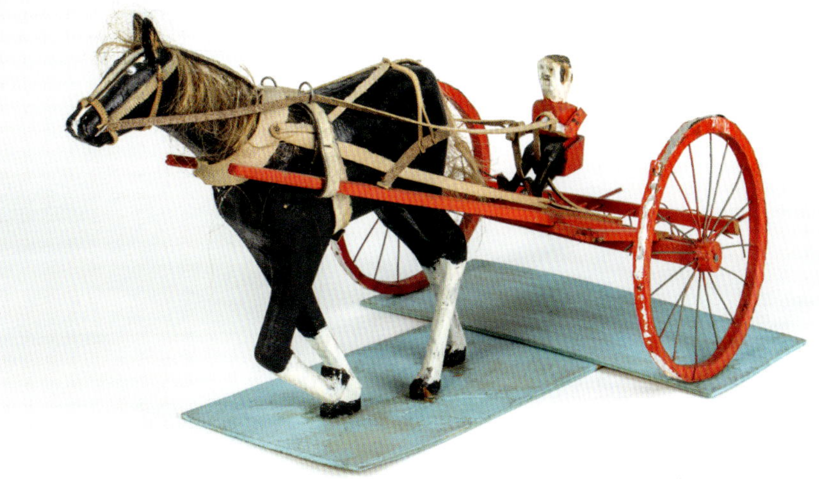

BORN IN SIMPSONS CORNER, Lunenburg County, Harry Wile worked in lumber camps in Ontario as a cook. He whittled as a hobby, making at least one miniature axe a day throughout his working life. On his retirement he returned to Lunenburg County, moving to North River.

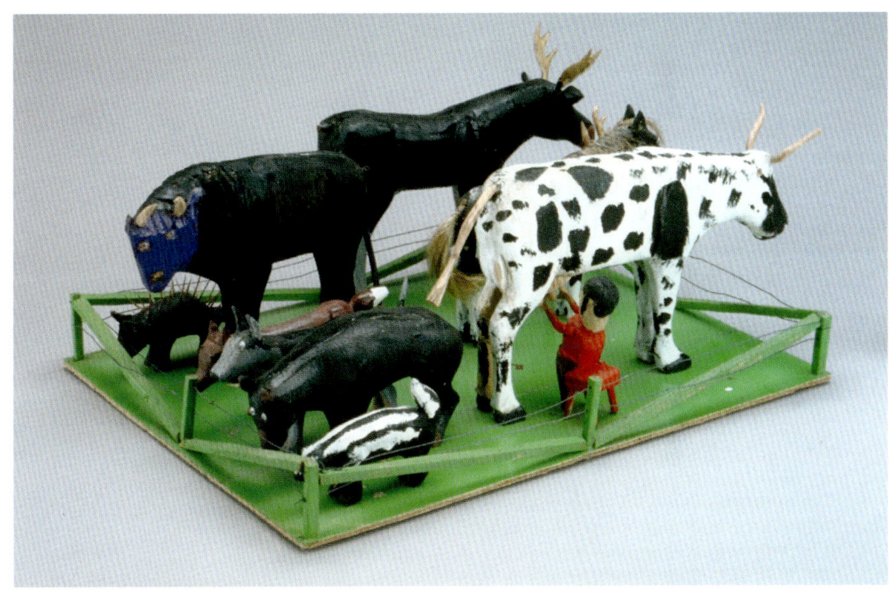

He began carving more seriously in 1965, mostly working on horses with carts and people. In 1975 he created *Collection of Canadian Animals*, which featured, among others, a moose, a bear, a porcupine, an elk, and an ox. Wile's work was included in the 1976 touring exhibition *Folk Art of Nova Scotia*. His carving production dropped in 1976 due to his failing eyesight, and he died in 1978.

TOP: *Hayraker*, Harry Wile

(RAW PHOTOGRAPHY FOR AGNS)

BOTTOM: *Collection of Canadian Animals*, Harry Wile

(CMH)

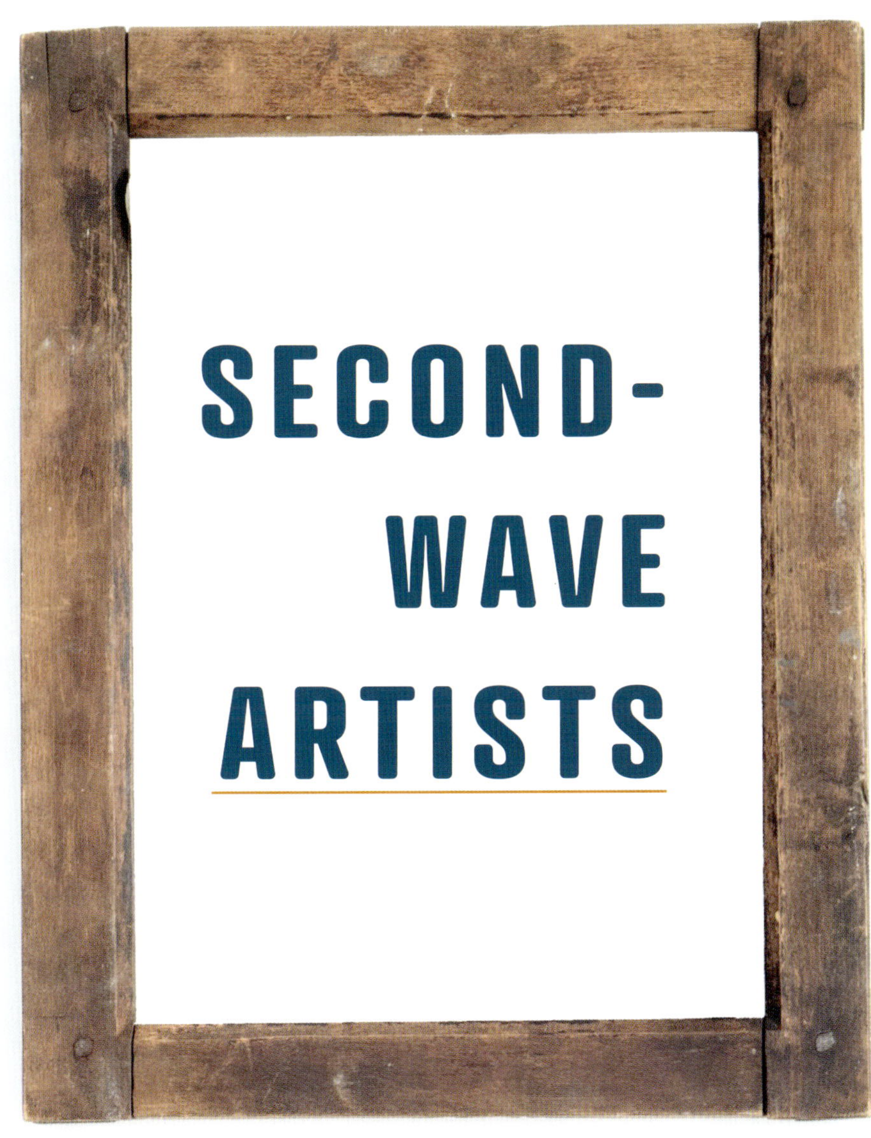

SECOND-WAVE ARTISTS

DONALD BOUDREAU

(ST. BERNARD, DIGBY COUNTY)

1917–2000

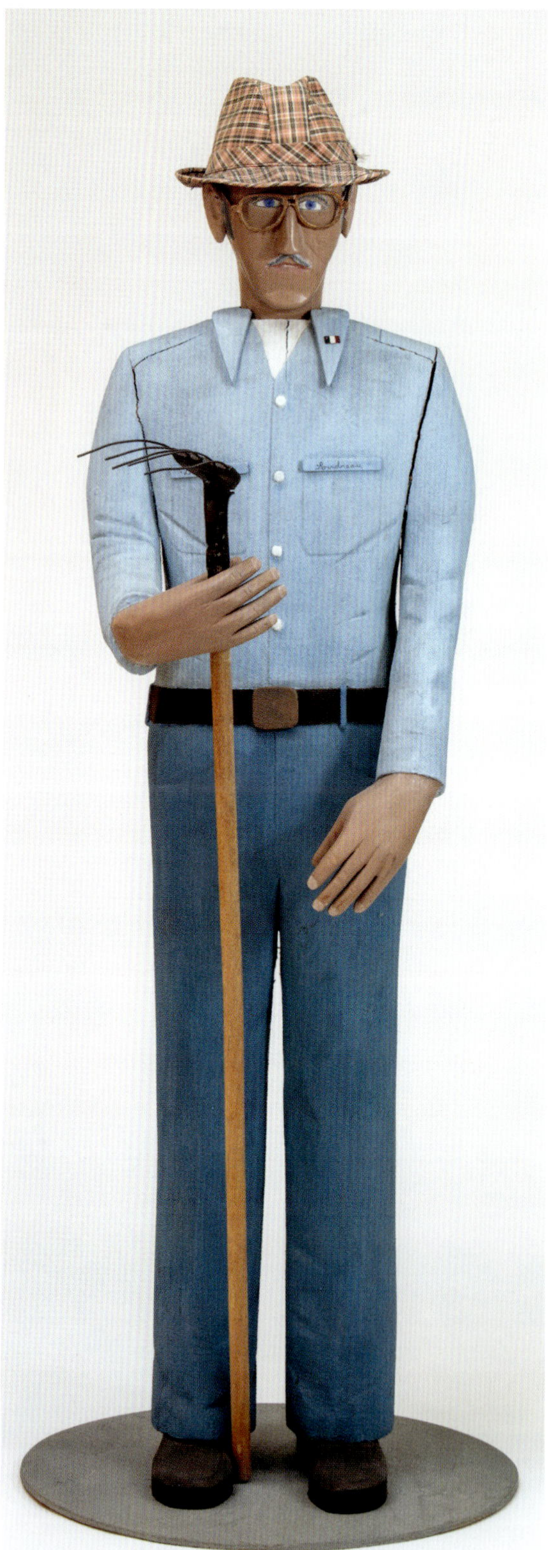

Man Raking, Donald Boudreau

(RAW PHOTOGRAPHY FOR AGNS)

A FORMER FISHER, LUMBERJACK, and woodworker, Donald Boudreau lived all his life in the Acadian community of St. Bernard, Digby County. According to former AGNS curator Patrick Condon Laurette, Boudreau began carving in 1976 after seeing objects in a local novelty store that inspired him.[49] His figures, some nearly life-sized, often carry Acadian flags. The Acadian flag also features prominently in Boudreau's whirligigs, where the wind turns his figures into exuberant flag-wavers. His *Acadian Flagman Windtoy* (1980) was included in the internationally touring exhibition *Nova Scotia Folk Art: Canada's Cultural Heritage*. The same sculpture, though renamed *Acadian Man*, was included in the exhibition *A Life of Its Own: Chris Huntington and the Resurgence of Nova Scotia Folk Art 1975–1995*.

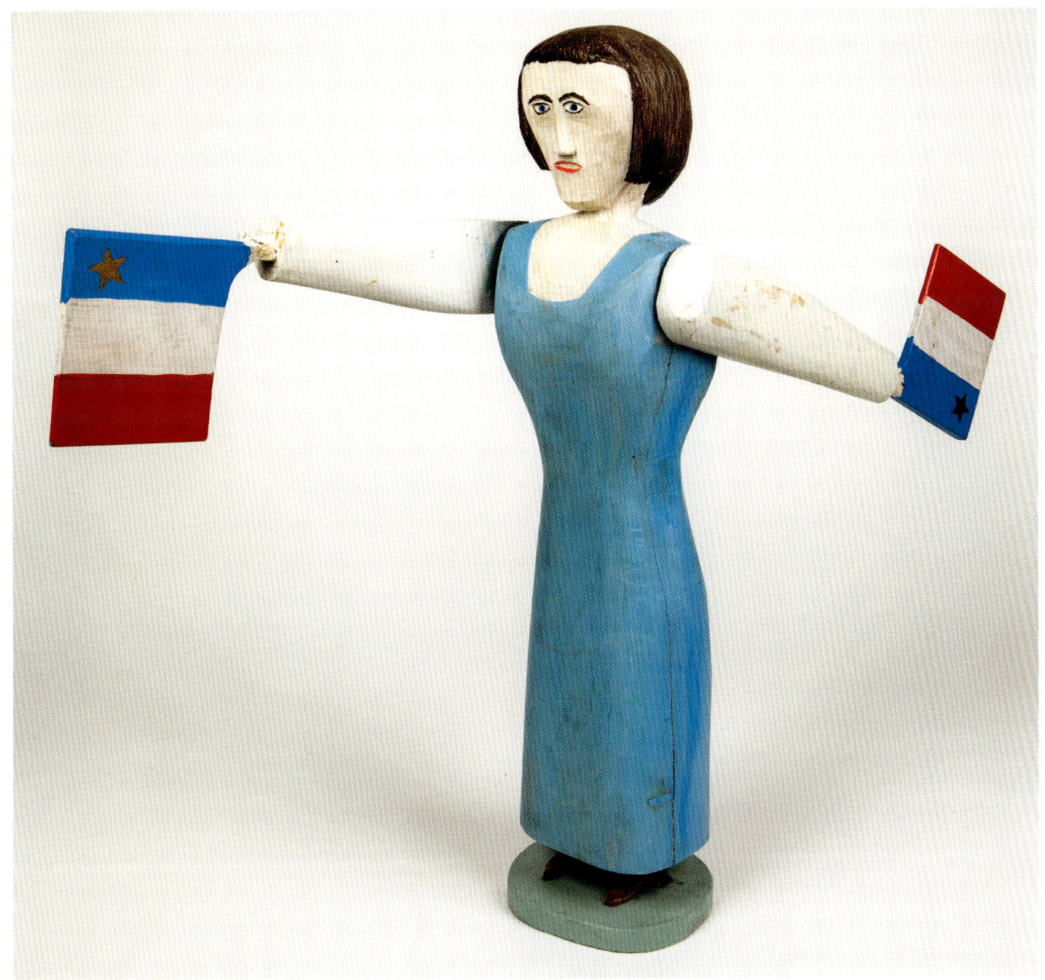

Whirligig: Woman with Acadian Flag, Donald Boudreau

(RAW PHOTOGRAPHY FOR AGNS)

Boudreau also painted and carved animals and birds, but it is his figures, especially his wind toys, that have proven to be most popular. In them, as Condon Laurette noted in 1983, Boudreau was able to "capture a distinctive Acadian psychology and bearing."[50]

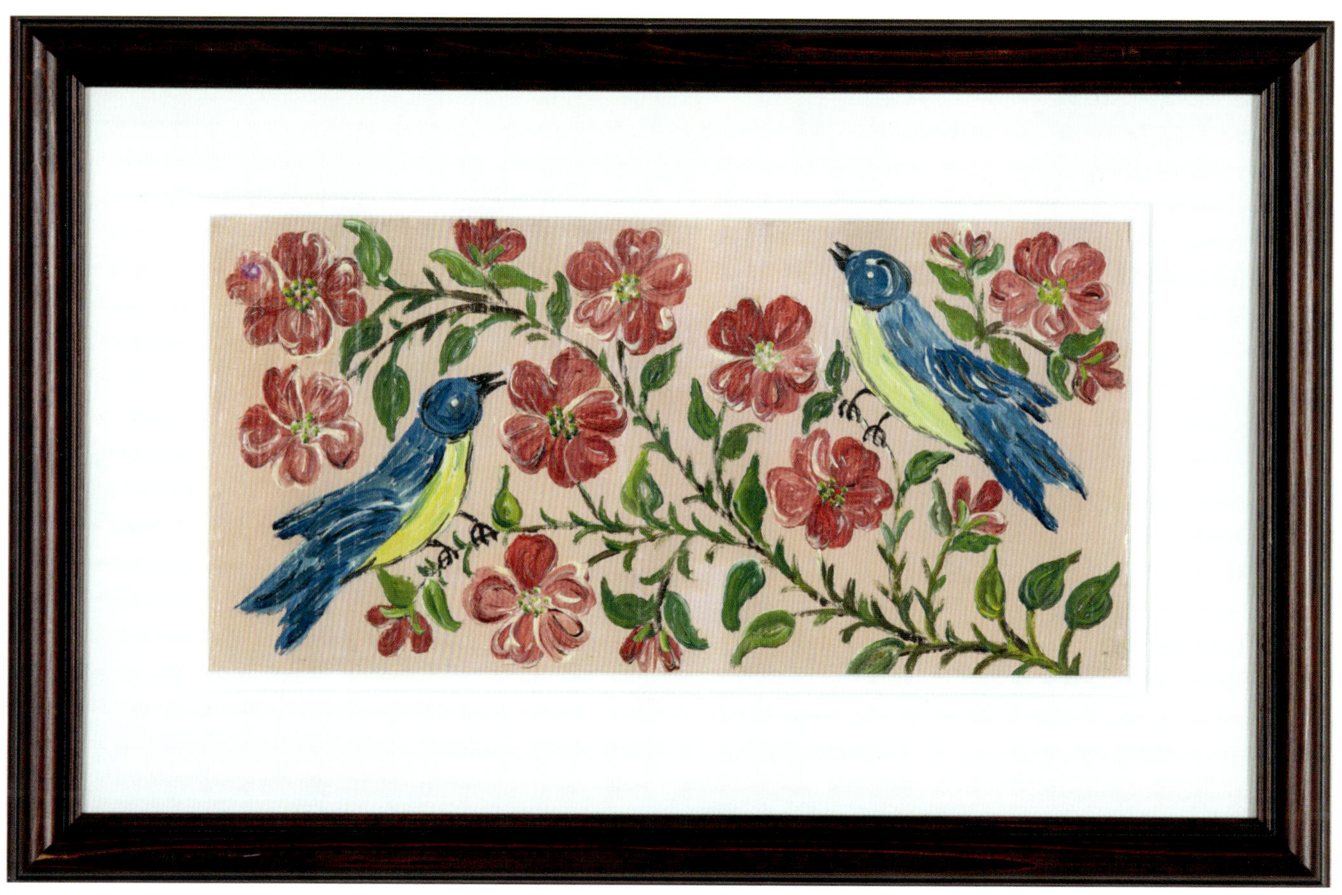

Blue Jays and Wild Rose, Eva Comeau-Hersey

(RAW PHOTOGRAPHY FOR AGNS)

EVA COMEAU-HERSEY

(LITTLE RIVER, DIGBY NECK, DIGBY COUNTY)

1897–1979

EVA COMEAU-HERSEY WAS BORN IN LITTLE BROOK STATION, NEAR Saulnierville in Digby County, the eldest of seventeen children. She left home at seventeen to travel to New England, seeking work as a domestic servant. She eventually came to live and work in New York. She married Ulysse Melanson and the two returned to Nova Scotia, living near Digby. They later separated and Eva returned to the United States, living there until 1949 when she returned to Nova Scotia permanently.

She brought back with her paints and stretched canvases, and painting would remain her hobby for the rest of her life. Through the 1950s she lived in Clare, until she married Bill Hersey in the early 1960s. The two moved to his Digby Neck where they lived for twenty years until his death. She returned to Clare for the final years of her life, dying in 1979. Comeau-Hersey painted hundreds, if not thousands, of paintings over her lifetime—pictures that she gave away to friends and family. Unlike her near-contemporary, Maud Lewis, she never sold her work, not did she ever show her paintings outside the small circle of her community and friends.

Daniel Comeau, who grew up in Clare and remembered Comeau-Hersey from his childhood, decided to do research on her work twenty years after her death, and the Art Gallery of Nova Scotia mounted the exhibition *Eva Comeau-Hersey: A Gift of Art* in 1998.

WALTER COOK

(SHERBROOKE, GUYSBOROUGH COUNTY)

1923–1991

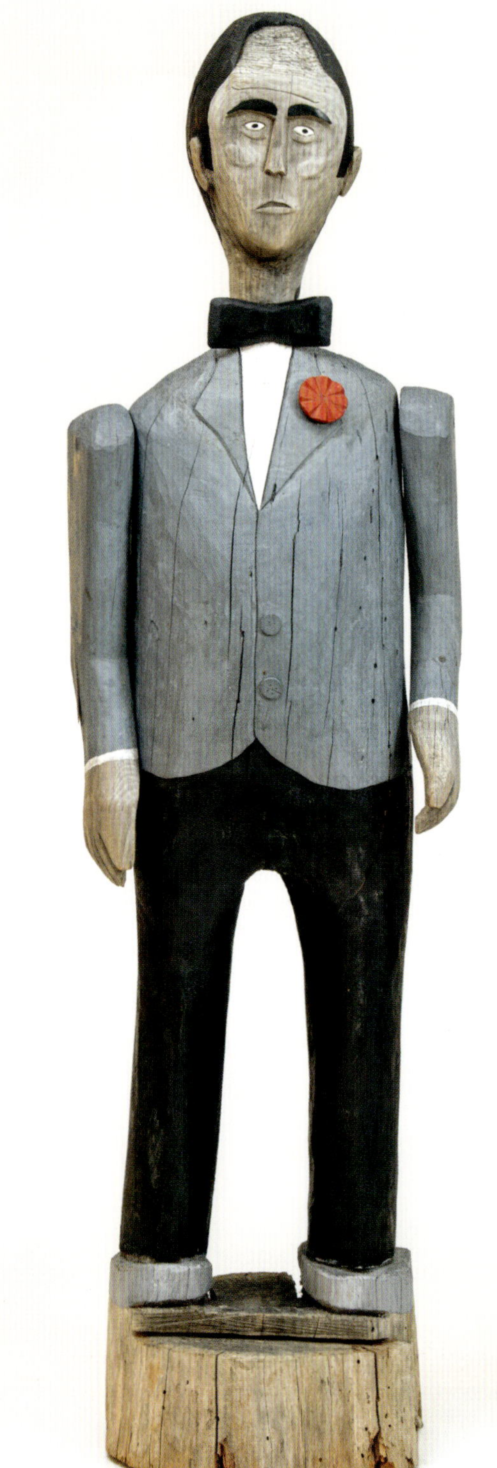

Trudeau,
Walter Cook

(RAW PHOTOGRAPHY FOR AGNS)

WALTER COOK WAS A SOLDIER for most of his working life, serving two tours of duty, from 1943 to 1947 and from 1954 to 1973. During his second (peacetime) stint with the Royal Canadian Horse Artillery, he started woodcarving as a way to fill his idle hours while on manoeuvres. His canes and walking sticks, with fanciful animal heads, were popular with his peers. On his retirement he returned to Sherbrooke with his family.

Sherbrooke Village, a historical "living" museum, was across the road from the Cook home, and Cook began to sell carvings at the village store. He would also make larger-scale carvings that he would exhibit on the front lawn as a means of advertising his work. In the early 1980s collector Chris Huntington met Cook and began to acquire his work, including the now-iconic Cook statue of

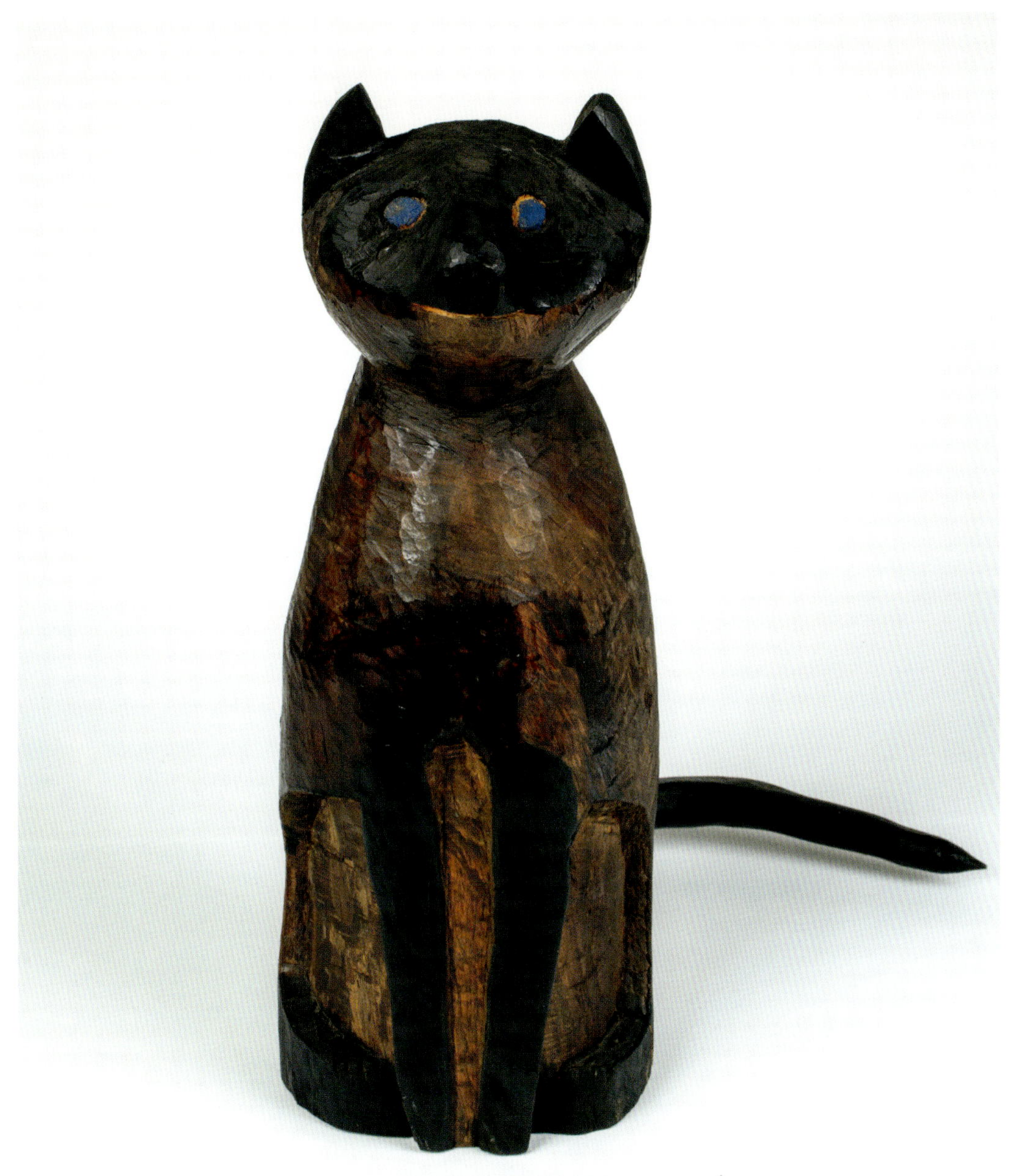

Cat,
Walter Cook

(RAW PHOTOGRAPHY FOR AGNS)

Pierre Elliot Trudeau. He was one of the folk artists in the inaugural Nova Scotia Folk Art Festival in 1989, and his work was included in the AGNS exhibition *A Life of Its Own: Chris Huntington and the Resurgence of Nova Scotia Folk Art 1975–1995*. Walter Cook died of cancer in 1991.

PHYLLIS COSMAN

(AVONPORT, KINGS COUNTY)

1927–2020

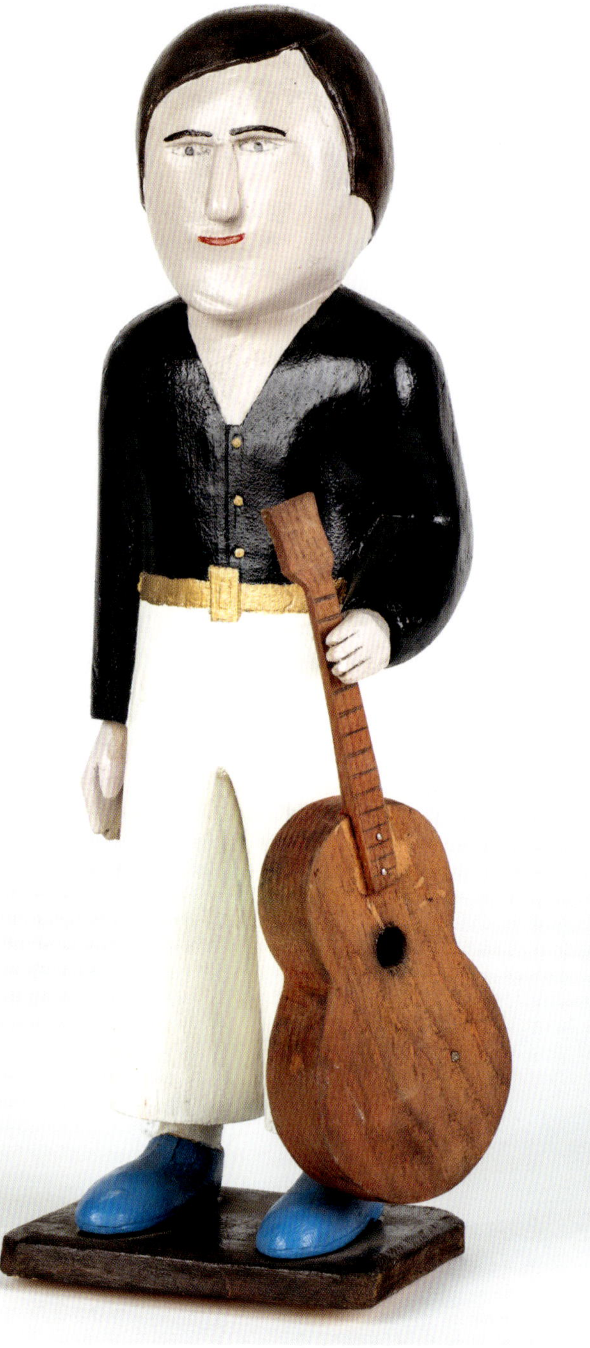

Guitar Player, Phyllis Cosman

(AGNS)

PHYLLIS COSMAN BEGAN carving in 1984, and in 1990 she first exhibited at the Nova Scotia Folk Art Festival in Lunenburg. Unlike the work of many of her male peers, Cosman's sculptures are all modestly sized, and exclusively figurative. Her figures are quite distinctive: doll-sized with large round heads and a lot of character. Cosman is able to convey individual personalities in her works that, while they are not portraits, can be thought of as character studies.

In 1994 the Art Gallery of Nova Scotia bought four sculptures from Cosman. This represented most of her production for that year, as arthritis was making it harder for her to carve. She stopped carving in 1996.

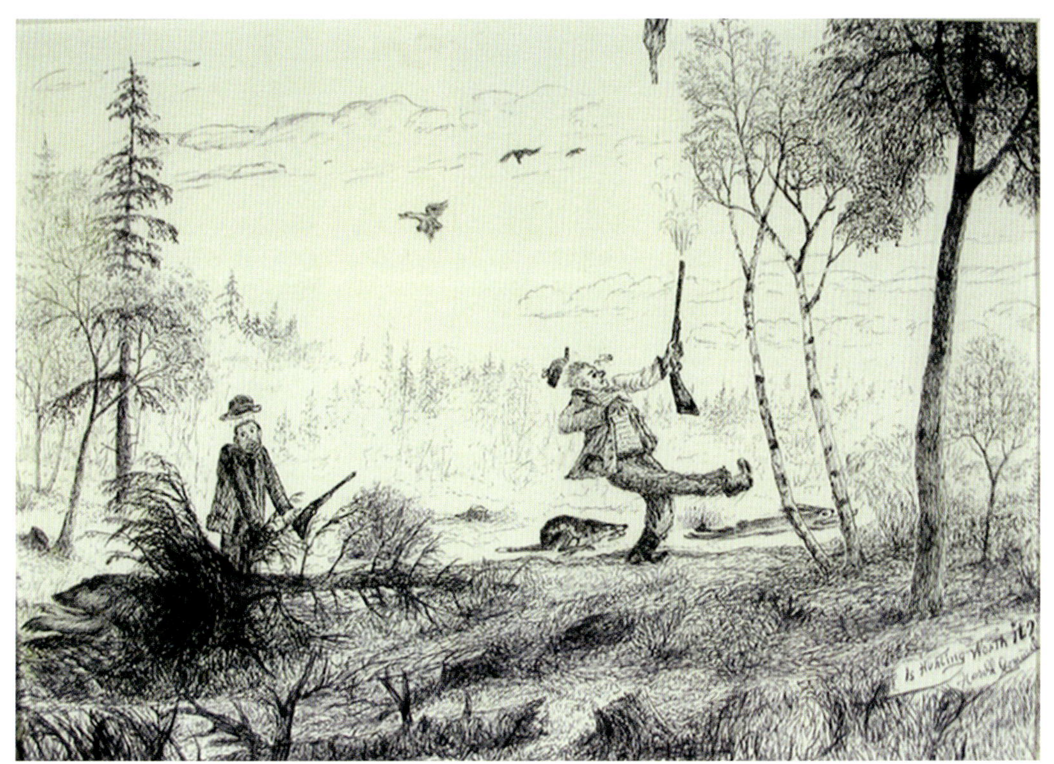

Rural Black Life in Nova Scotia: Is Hunting Worth It?, Harold Cromwell

(AGNS)

HAROLD CROMWELL

(WEYMOUTH, DIGBY COUNTY)

1919–2008

WHILE HAROLD CROMWELL WAS WELL-KNOWN IN HIS OWN COMMUNITY, he never achieved the level of recognition that many thought he deserved. David Woods, then-curator of African Nova Scotia Art at the AGNS, said upon Cromwell's death: "He would have been a Canadian folk art icon had the public seen the scope of his works."[51] Cromwell, who lived in Weymouth for most of his life, was unique among the major Nova Scotia folk artists in two ways—he was African Nova Scotian, and his work consisted almost completely of drawings.

Cromwell was a Second World War veteran, and while he was in the military hospital at Debert recuperating from wounds received overseas he was given drawing materials by the nurses to help him pass the time. Those first drawings tended to be racy, he said in 2007. "Oh, I drew some naughty things there—

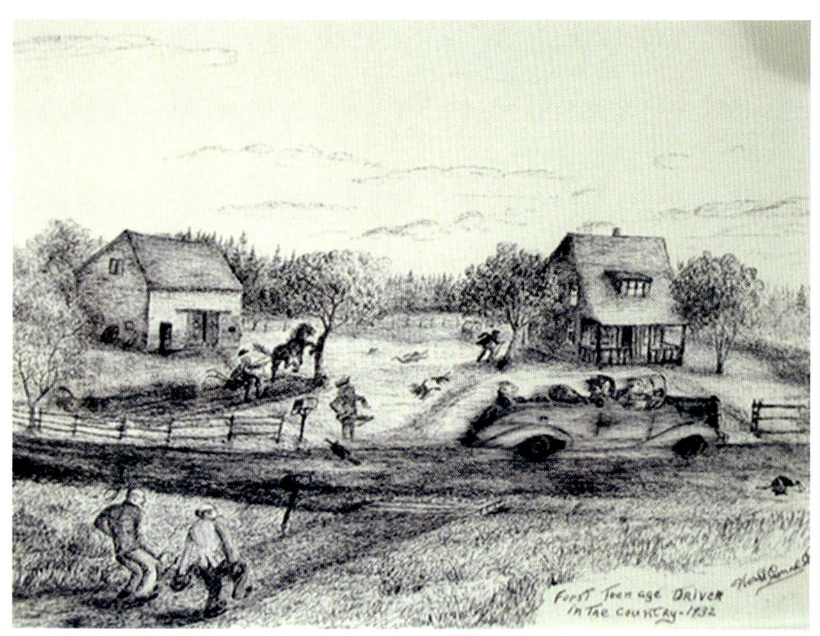

Rural Black Life in Nova Scotia: First Teenage Driver in the Country, 1932, Harold Cromwell

(AGNS)

some of them were a little raw."[52] He soon started drawing the doctors and nurses, as well as the landscape he saw out the window.

After the war he continued to draw, and after a five-year stint as a miner in Sudbury, Ontario, he returned to Weymouth. He worked several jobs there, and when he retired, he took up drawing more intensely, working mostly in pen and ink to create scenes that depicted his memories of the rural life of Weymouth Falls and his community. He also made larger works where he used coloured markers to offset the mostly monochrome ink of his drawings.

Cromwell's work depicts life in an African Nova Scotian community in the early twentieth century. He also made works illustrating stories about the settlement of the area by his ancestors—Black Loyalists who came to Nova Scotia after the American Revolution. Former soldiers, many of the Black Loyalists had been enslaved in the United States and had earned both freedom and land grants by serving in the British Army.

Cromwell's work is included in the collection of the Art Gallery of Nova Scotia, but much of his work is held in private collections; institutions have had difficulty securing the loans to mount exhibitions of this important artist's work. "It is very unfortunate that during his lifetime Cromwell never had the recognition that was his due," David Woods said in 2008. "But that will come."[53]

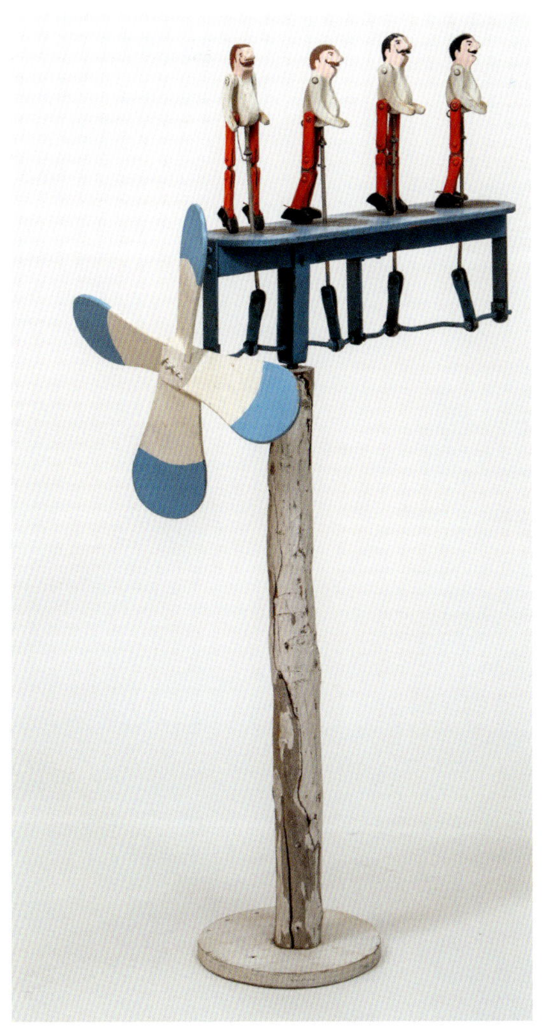

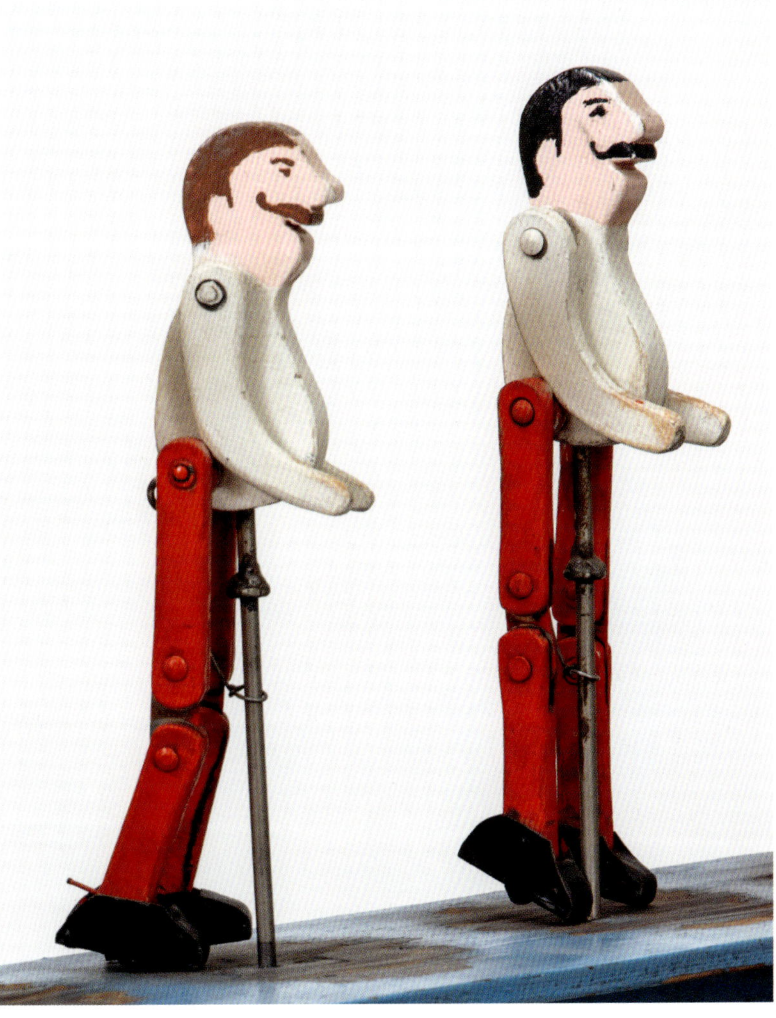

Whirligig Lumberjack Dancers, Joseph Deveau

(RAW PHOTOGRAPHY FOR AGNS)

JOSEPH DEVEAU

(CHÉTICAMP, INVERNESS COUNTY)

1904–1986

A CARPENTER AND LIFELONG RESIDENT OF CHÉTICAMP, JOSEPH DEVEAU had a reputation in his community as one of the best builders around. A general contractor, in his time he built homes, motels, and restaurants. His last job before retiring was as a maintenance worker at the Chéticamp Hospital.

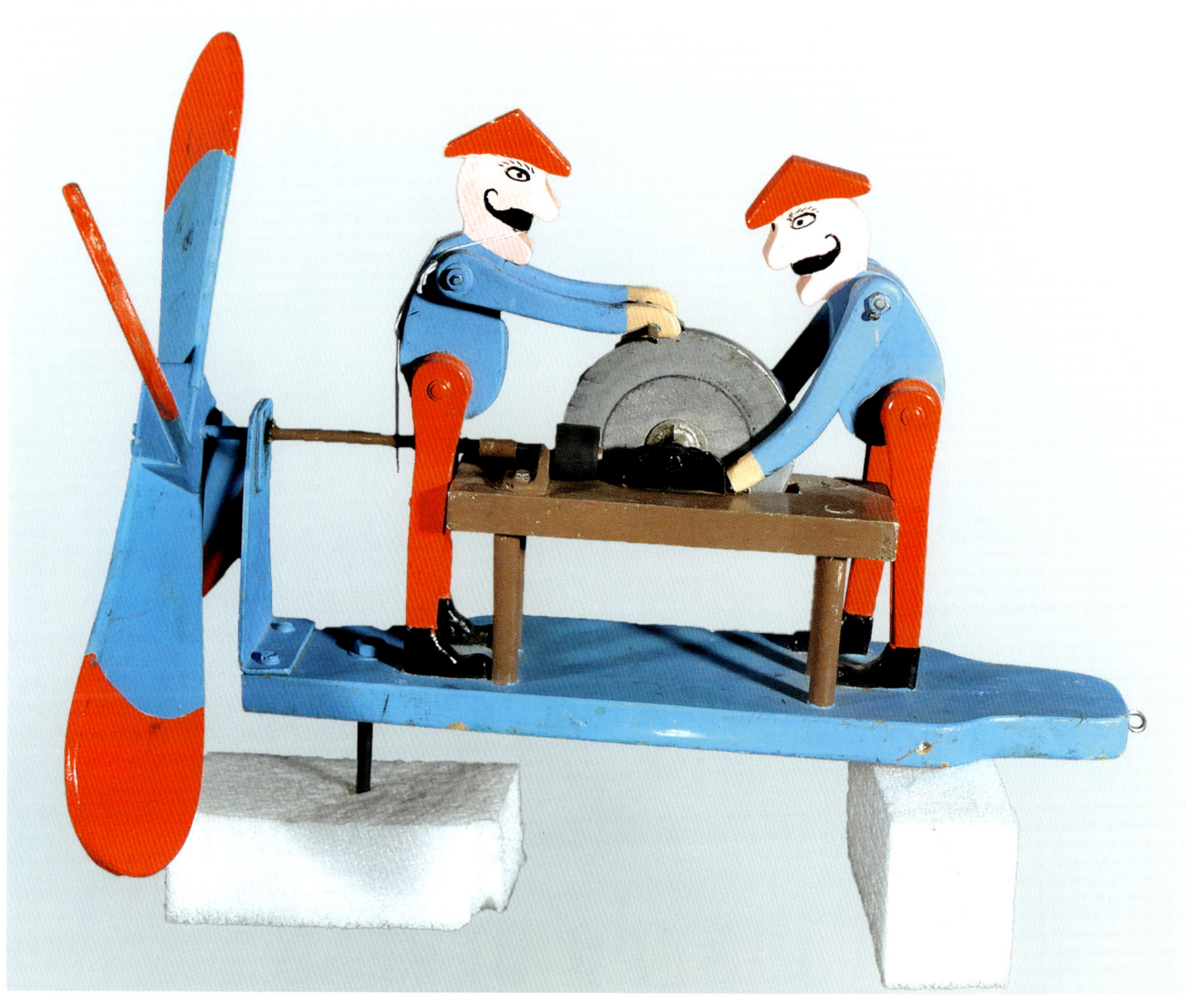

Whirligig Axe Grinders, Joseph Deveau (AGNS)

As a hobby he made whirligigs, birdhouses, and lighthouses. These were gifts for family or friends or were sold to tourists. The AGNS has three particularly fine examples in its collection, including a large wind machine that features a circle of dancing lumberjacks. Deveau's *Whirligig Axe Grinders* was included in the exhibition *Nova Scotia Folk Art: Canada's Cultural Heritage*, and was also included in a tour to seven UK cities including London, Glasgow, Edinburgh, and Birmingham.

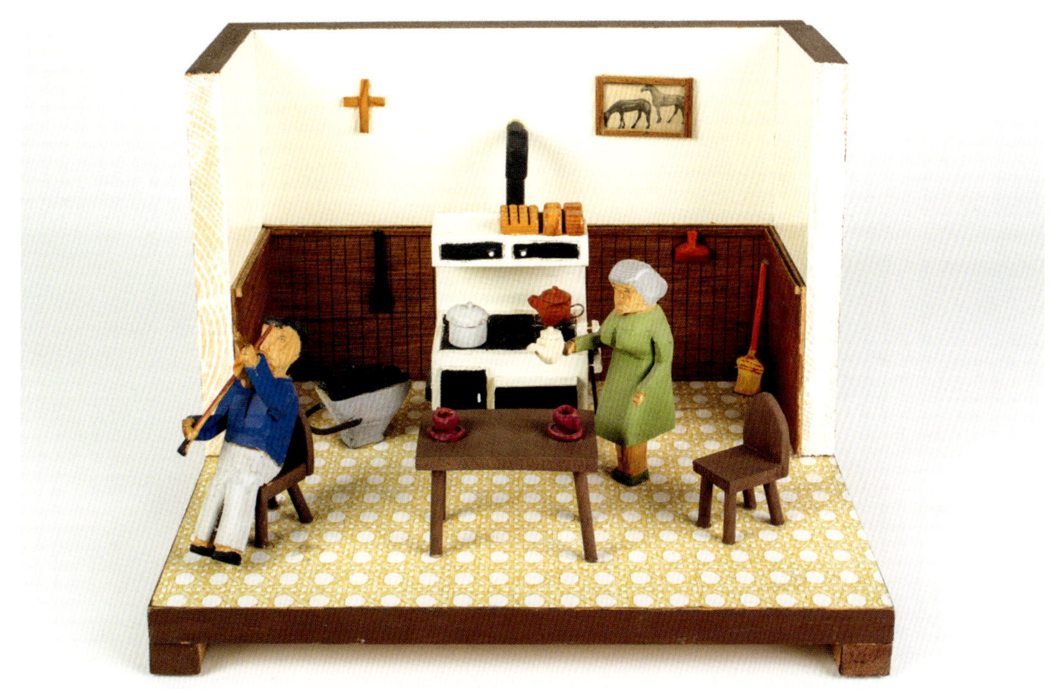

Kitchen Scene,
Murray Gallant

(RAW PHOTOGRAPHY FOR AGNS)

MURRAY GALLANT

(NEW WATERFORD, CAPE BRETON COUNTY)

b. 1938

MURRAY GALLANT WORKED FOR THE TOWN OF NEW WATERFORD UNTIL a back injury forced his retirement. He took up carving in his spare time and was discovered by Cape Breton folk artists Lorne Reid and David Stephens, who exhibited his work in their folk art gallery. They also encouraged him to show his work in the inaugural Nova Scotia Folk Art Festival in 1989, and he has participated ever since. In 2017 the festival chose Gallant as its feature artist. He told the *Cape Breton Post* in 2019 that he will always be grateful to Stephens and Reid. "I didn't even know it was folk art I was doing," he said. "I just love doing it."[54]

The Art Gallery of Nova Scotia has been collecting Gallant's work since 1990 and now has fifteen works by the artist in its folk art collection. The first acquisition, *Cape Breton Coal Miner* (1988), was a gift of Lorne Reid.

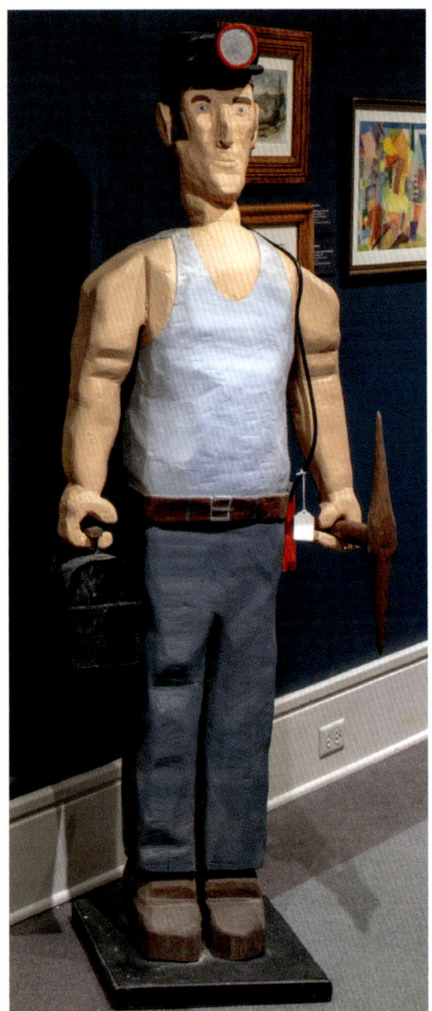

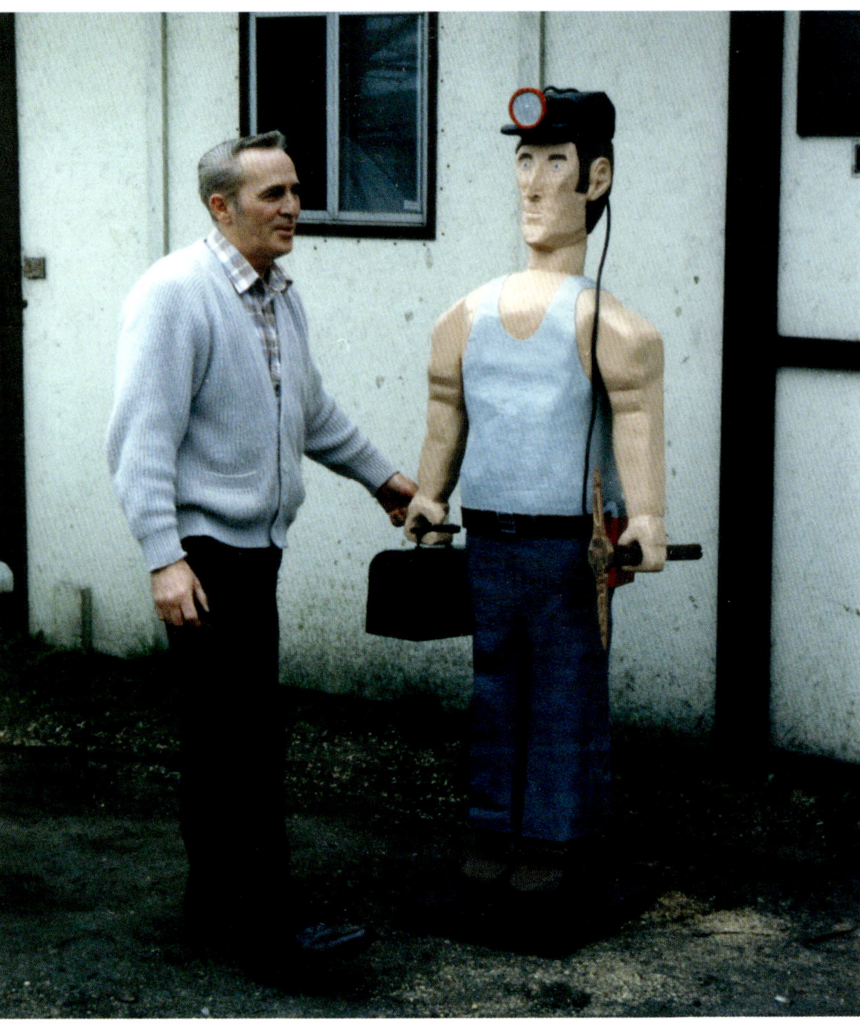

LEFT: *Cape Breton Coal Miner*, Murray Gallant

(AGNS)

RIGHT: Murray Gallant

(AGNS)

Gallant is mostly known for his small figures and whirligigs, though he has also been known to make more erotic sculptures, including a whirligig of a couple making love on a single bed. He told the now-defunct website *Folk Art Maritime*: "I don't want to offend anyone, but I like to do whatever comes into my mind. Often humour seems to come in and if I can make people laugh, I do a good job."[55]

Gallant's work is usually on view at the AGNS, and it has also been included in the permanent collections of the Canadian Museum of History, the Beaverbrook Art Gallery, and the Cape Breton University Art Gallery. In 1989–90, his *Grinning Boy* (1989) was included in the UK touring exhibition *Nova Scotia Folk Art: Canada's Cultural Heritage*.

Despite his work's popularity with collectors, Gallant refuses to create work to order. "If I do one for you and I'm trying to please you and it doesn't work, then we're both disappointed," he says. "But if I do what I want and you like it, that's better for everybody."[56]

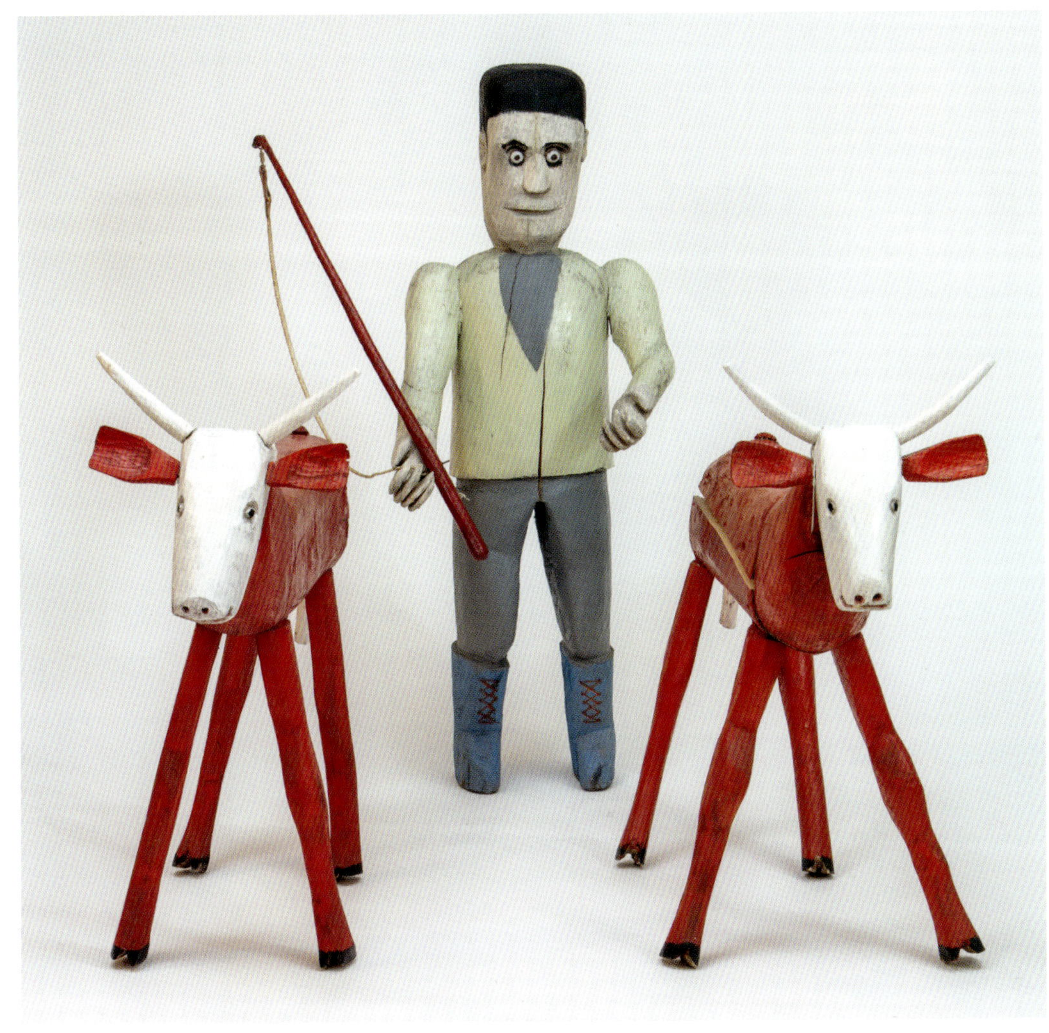

Young Ox Trainer, Wesley Hubley

(RAW PHOTOGRAPHY FOR AGNS)

WESLEY HUBLEY

(BRIDGEWATER, LUNENBURG COUNTY)

1920–1991

WESLEY HUBLEY WORKED VARIOUS JOBS OVER HIS LIFETIME, FINISHING his working life as a burial supervisor for funeral homes in his home of Bridgewater. A relative of folk artist Eddie Mandaggio, Hubley started making folk art in the mid-1980s. He was one of the nineteen artists in the inaugural Nova Scotia Folk Art Festival in 1989 and was represented by

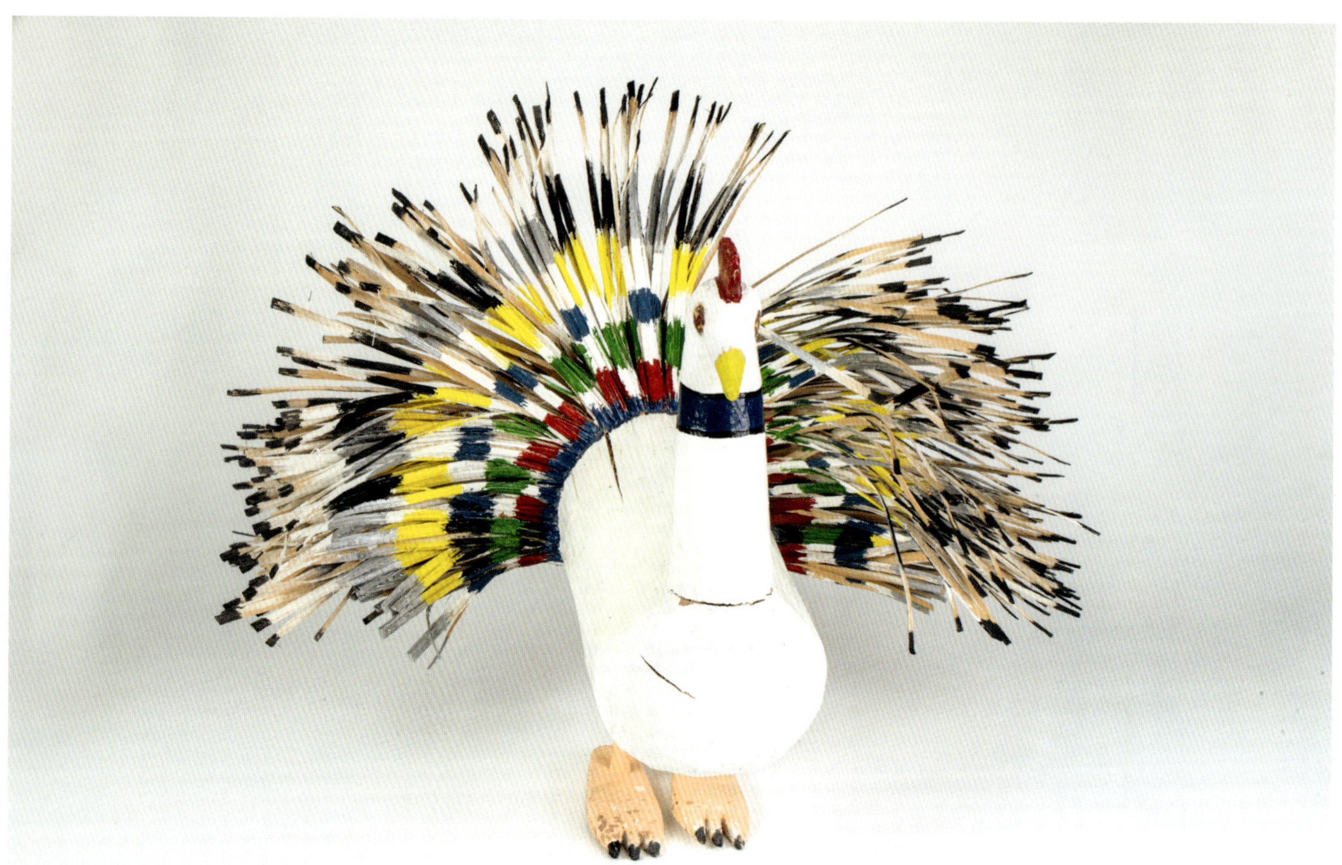

Peacock, Wesley Hubley
(RAW PHOTOGRAPHY FOR AGNS)

Chris Huntington's Wild Goose Chase Gallery, which Huntington opened that same year in Blockhouse, Lunenburg County. One of the first "second-wave" folk artists, Hubley died just as his work was becoming better known.

His largest known piece, and his best, is *Young Ox Trainer*, currently in the collection of the Art Gallery of Nova Scotia. It was included in the internationally touring exhibition *Nova Scotia Folk Art: Canada's Cultural Heritage*, and in *A Life of Its Own: Chris Huntington and the Resurgence of Nova Scotia Folk Art 1975–1995*.

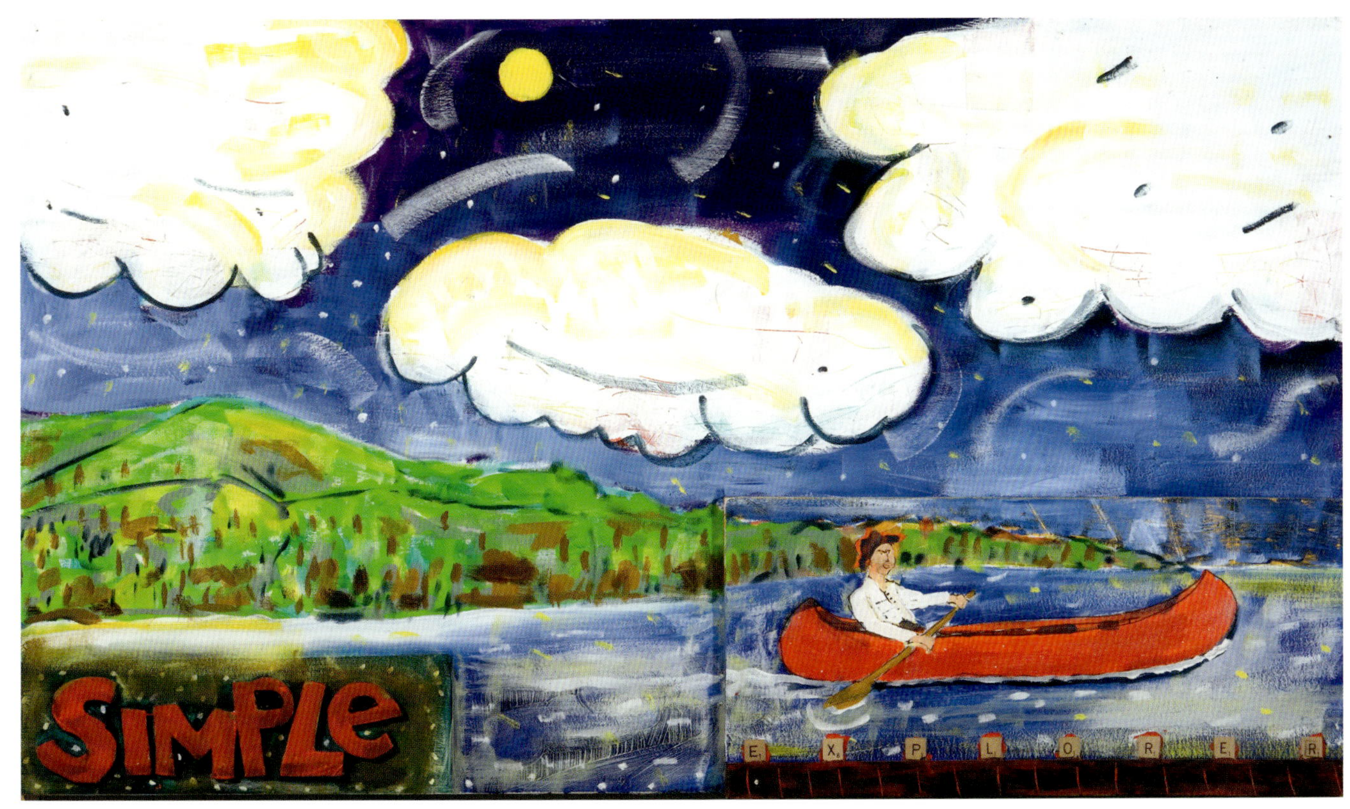

Simple Explorer, Kyle Jackson

(KYLE JACKSON)

KYLE JACKSON

(HALIFAX, HALIFAX COUNTY)

b. 1960

BY THE LATE 1980S NOVA SCOTIA FOLK ART WAS BECOMING BIG BUSINESS, and more and more artists were aligning themselves with what had been an art created by mostly rural, mostly untrained (and often uneducated) retirees. One such artist, Kyle Jackson, put his formidable energy into promoting folk art and artists at the popular restaurant he co-owned in Halifax—the SoHo Kitchen. He started showing work by folk artists at the restaurant, and the SoHo Kitchen was one of the hosts of the first annual Nova Scotia Folk Art Festival and Picnic held in Blockhouse. The guiding force behind the festival

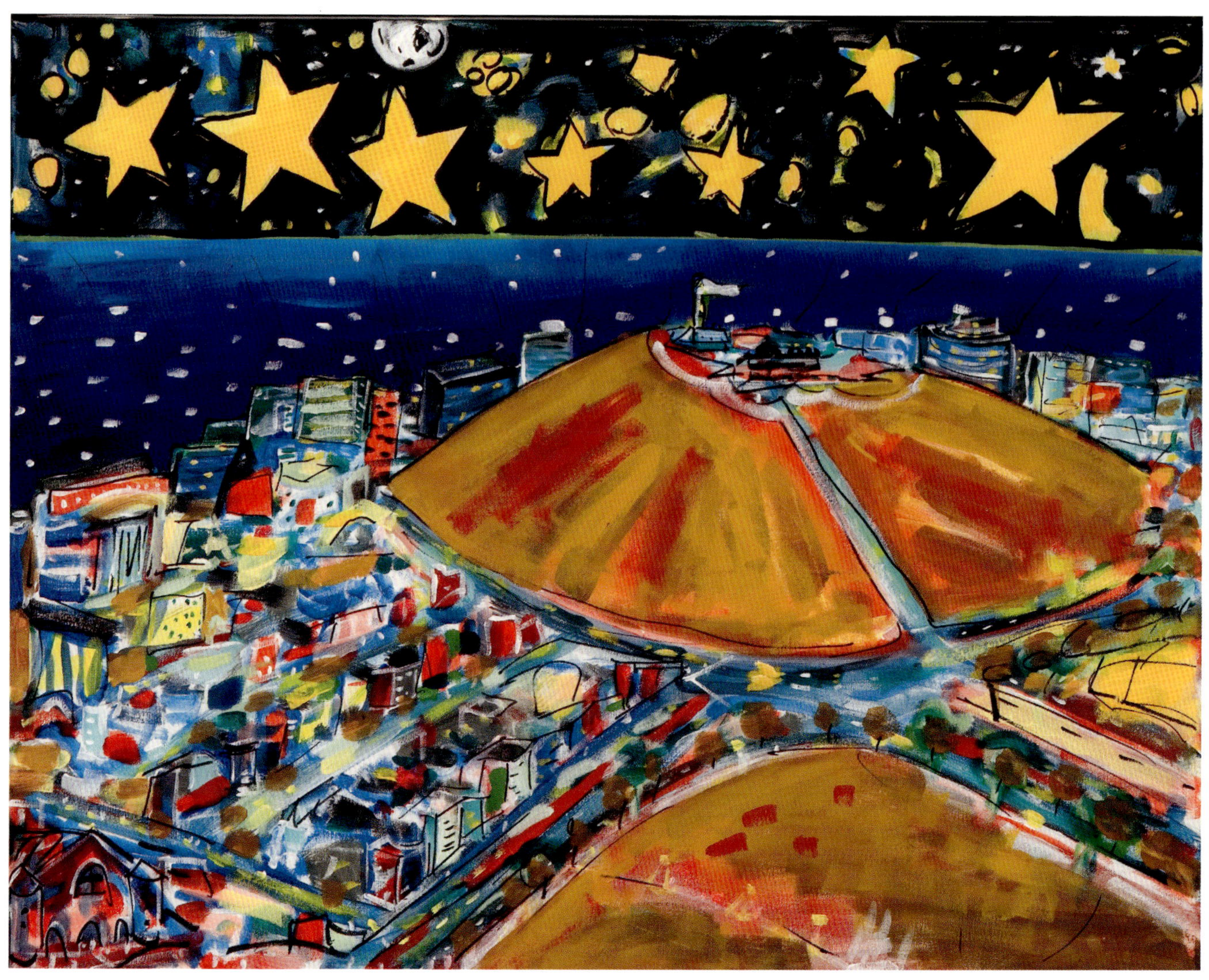

Halifax at Night, Kyle Jackson

(KYLE JACKSON)

was Chris Huntington, but Jackson was one of the founders and also one of nineteen exhibiting artists.

Jackson's paintings, often built up with added pieces to give 3-D effects, featured folk art themes such as boats and seascapes, and for many years he was considered part of the folk art scene. "I imagine this is why my work has been associated with folk art, with my sculptural paintings full of bright colors and protected whimsy," he said.[57]

Jackson came to Halifax from Ontario in 1984 to study at the Nova Scotia College of Art and Design (NSCAD). He dropped out and eventually opened the SoHo Kitchen, which he co-owned for eighteen years. He returned to

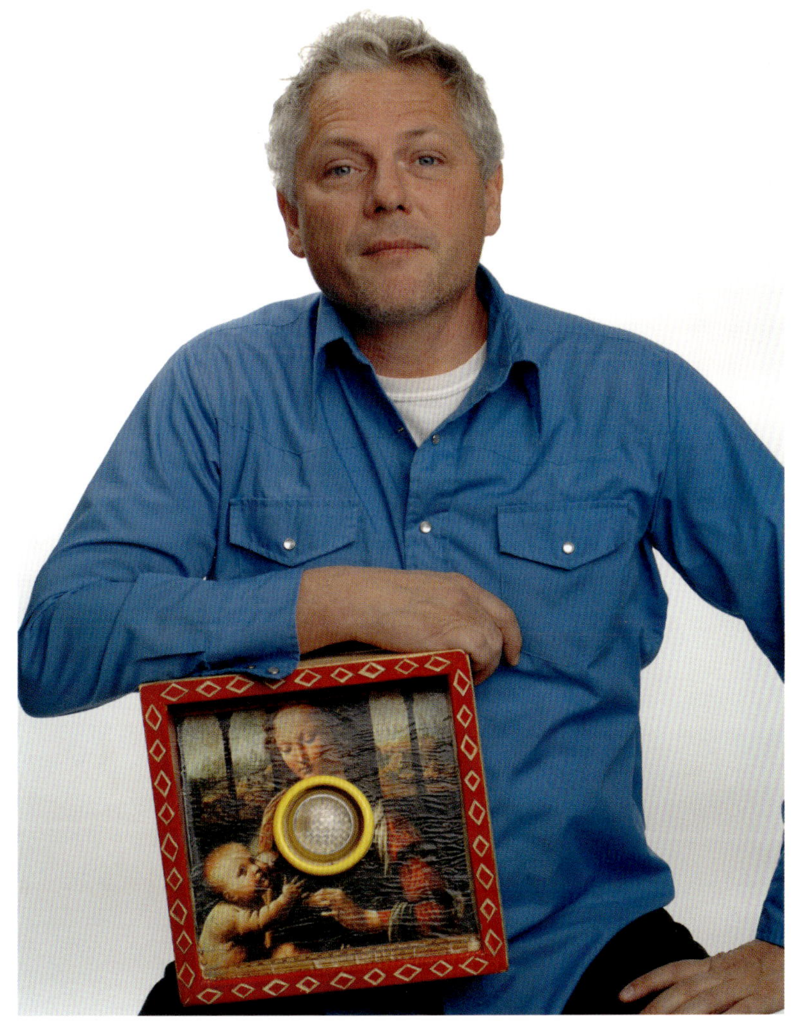

Kyle Jackson

(CHRIS REARDON)

NSCAD several years ago and completed his degree. Jackson does not identify as a folk artist any longer, preferring to simply be known as an artist. Nonetheless, in 2013 he was a featured artist at the twenty-fifth iteration of the Nova Scotia Folk Art Festival.

For the past several years Jackson has been active as a community-based artist, working with schools through Visual Arts Nova Scotia's PAINTS program. He was artist-in-residence at the Pier 21 Museum of Immigration in 2016. In 2013 the Cape Breton University Art Gallery mounted a full-career survey exhibition called *True Grit: The Urban Folk Creations of David P. Stephens and Kyle B. Jackson*.

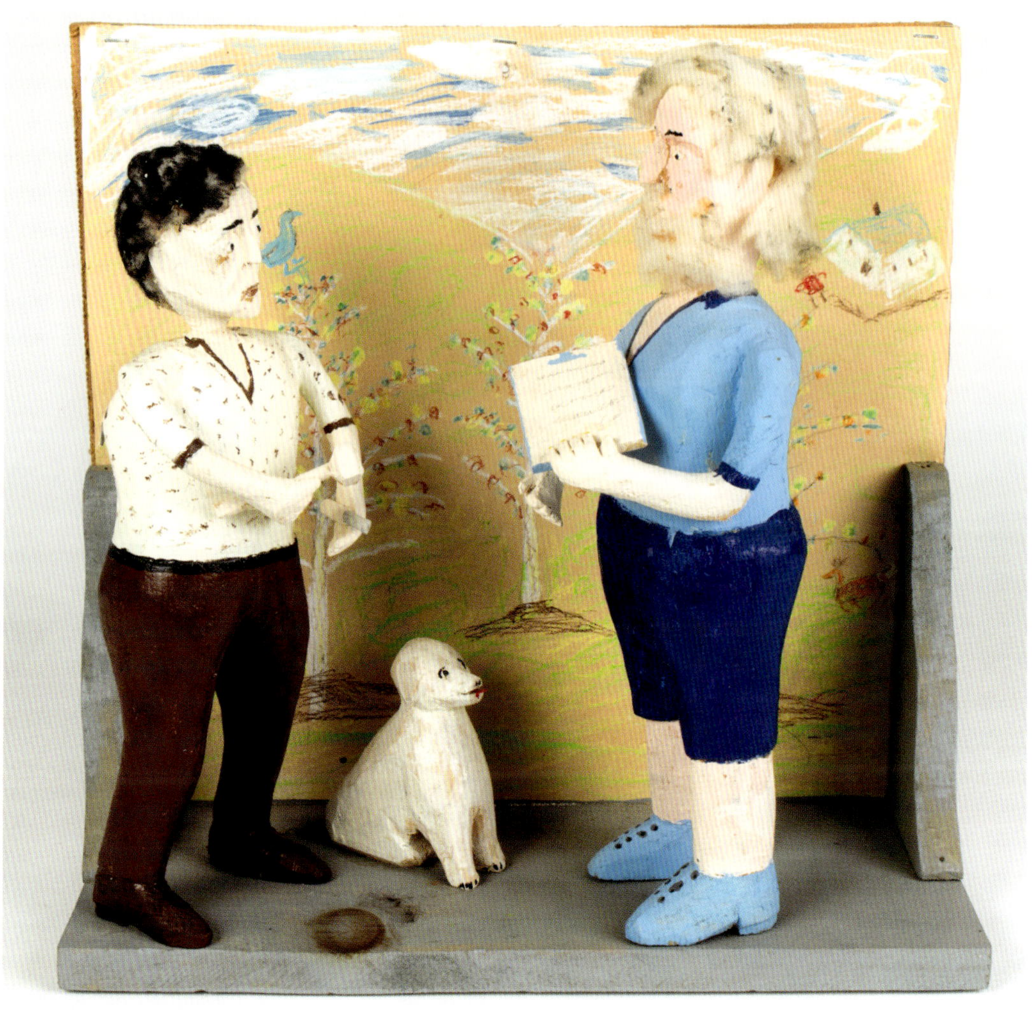

Elmer and Chris (Self-Portrait with Chris Huntington), Elmer Killen

(RAW PHOTOGRAPHY FOR AGNS)

ELMER KILLEN

(COOKS BROOK, HALIFAX COUNTY)

1908–2000

THE SON OF IRISH IMMIGRANTS, ELMER KILLEN WORKED AS A DROVER (responsible for moving herds of cattle to market, drovers came to be called "cowboys" in Western North America) until he took over the family dairy farm in the 1930s. He was a dairy farmer for over forty years, until he retired and took up carving as a hobby. Killen was one of many artists discovered by Chris Huntington.

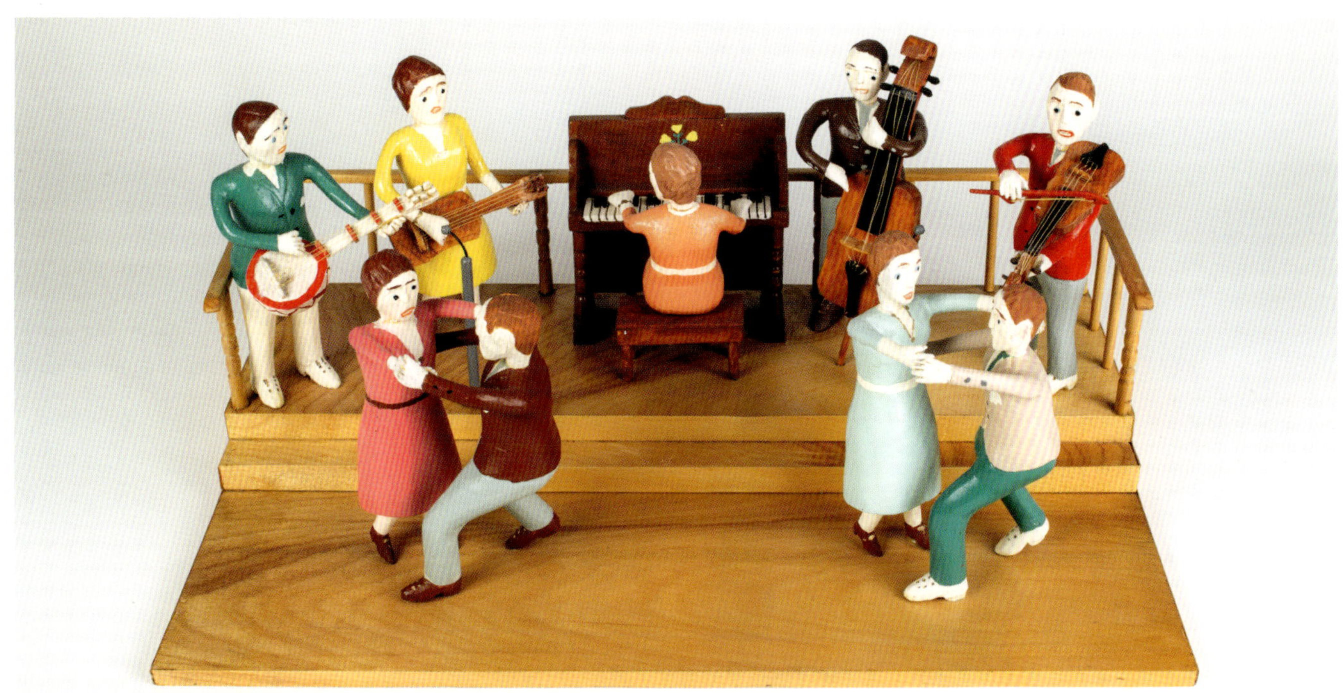

Band and Dancers, Elmer Killen

(RAW PHOTOGRAPHY FOR AGNS)

In fact, in an interview with Killen conducted by Patrick Condon Laurette of the AGNS, Killen told the curator that he made his carvings with a jackknife and with a traditional crooked knife that he had been given by Huntington.[58]

One of the artists in the inaugural Nova Scotia Folk Art Festival, Killen made small figures and figure groupings depicting his memories of his community's past. Square dances and bands were a popular subject for Killen, as were depictions of everyday chores such as churning butter, sharpening tools, and doing laundry.

While it is relatively common for Nova Scotia folk artists to do self-portraits, or portraits of popular figures such as entertainers and politicians, Killen's self-portrait is unique, as he depicts himself with his first, and most important, supporter—Chris Huntington.

Killen participated in several iterations of the Nova Scotia Folk Art Festival, and his work was included in the exhibitions *Nova Scotia Folk Art: Canada's Cultural Heritage* and *A Life of Its Own: Chris Huntington and the Resurgence of Nova Scotia Folk Art 1975–1995*.

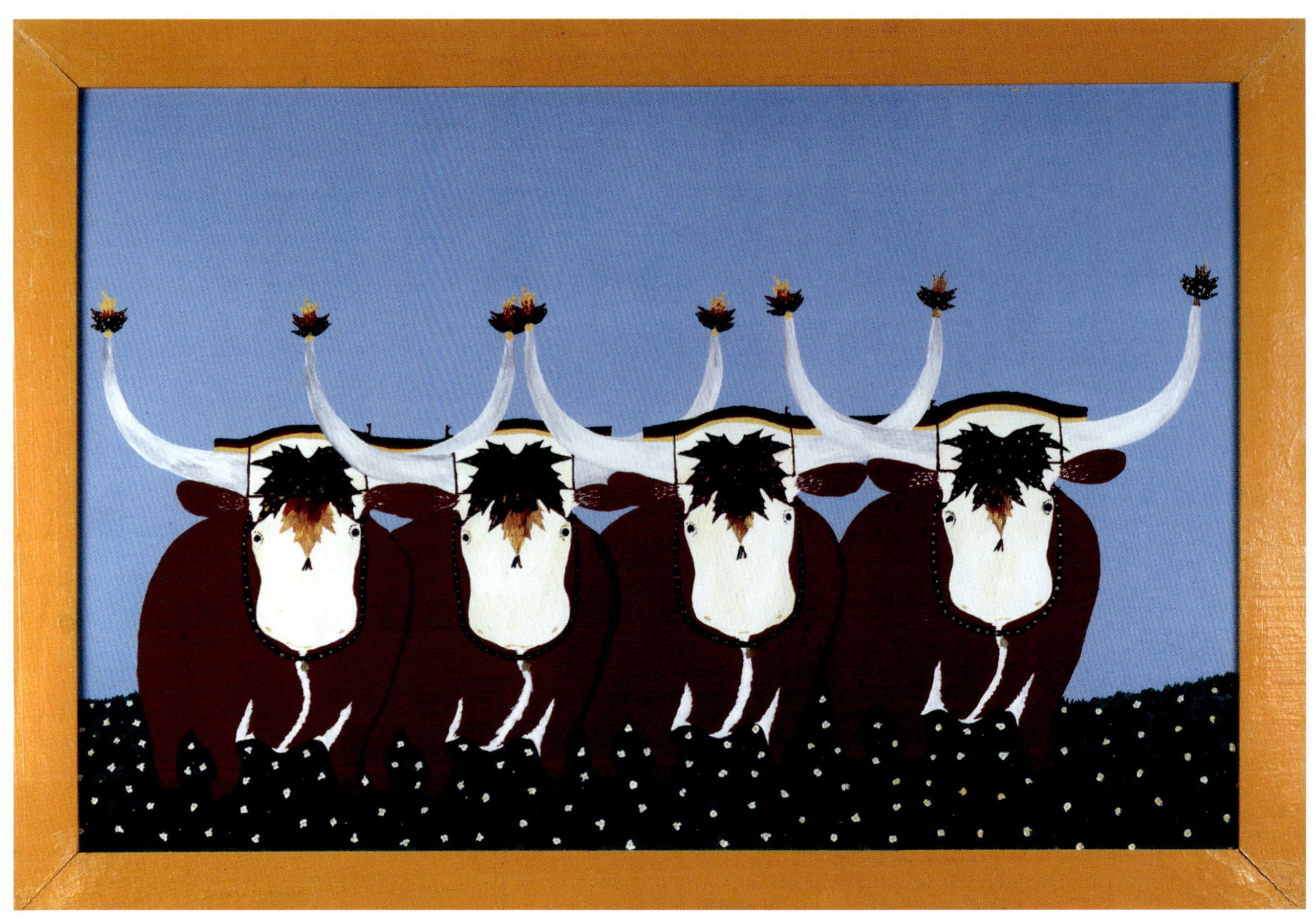

Oxen with Olympic Torches, Eddie Mandaggio

(AGNS)

EDDIE MANDAGGIO

(CAMPERDOWN, LUNENBURG COUNTY)

1928–2020

EDDIE MANDAGGIO WAS BORN IN ONTARIO, WHERE HE WORKED AS A trapper and a hunting and fishing guide. He moved to Nova Scotia in 1951, to Camperdown in Lunenburg County, where he lived until his death in 2020. He initially made carvings to decorate his cabin. His work was first brought to public attention in the early 1980s by John Houston of the Houston North Gallery in Lunenburg.

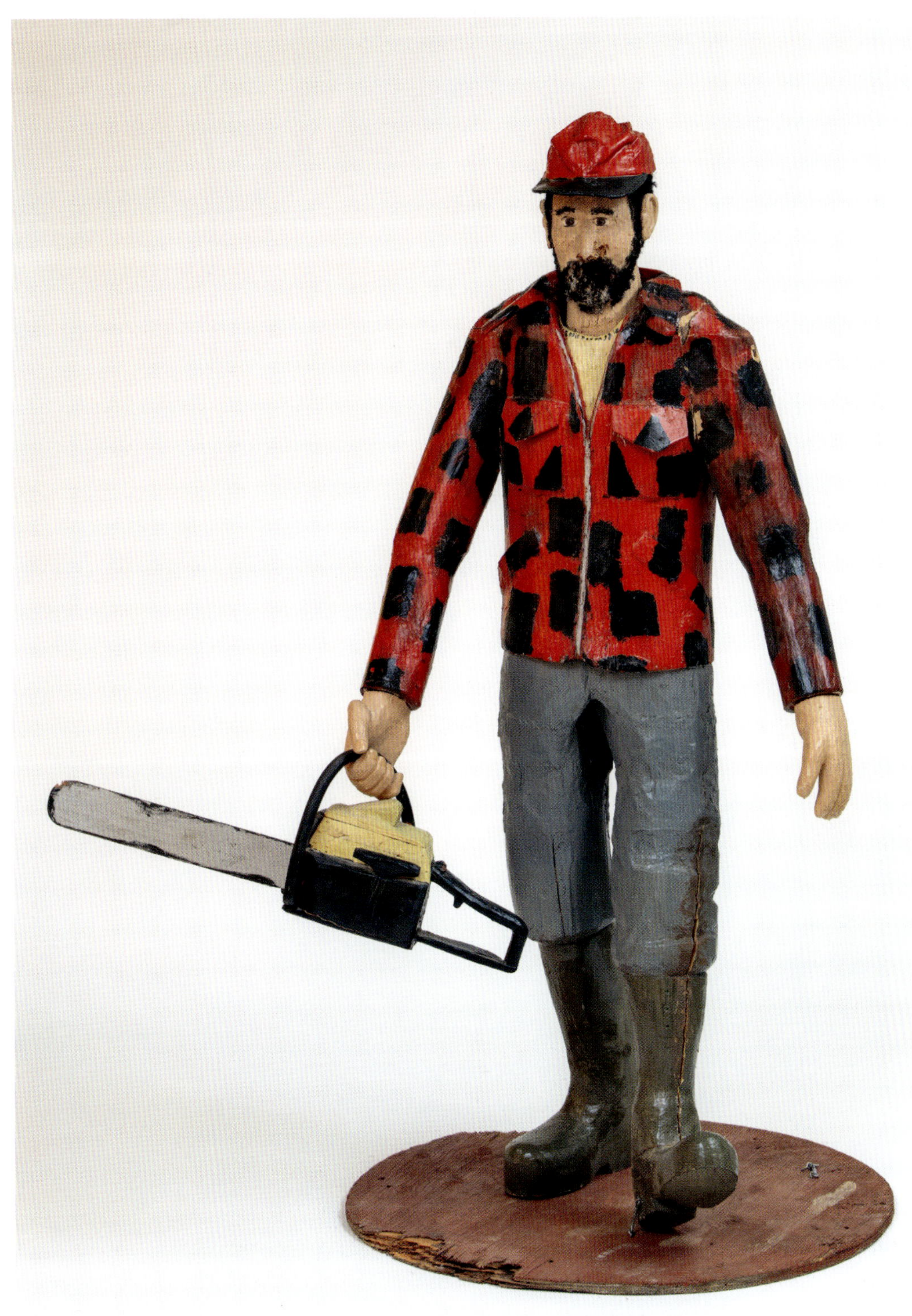

Self-Portrait,
Eddie Mandaggio

(RAW PHOTOGRAPHY FOR AGNS)

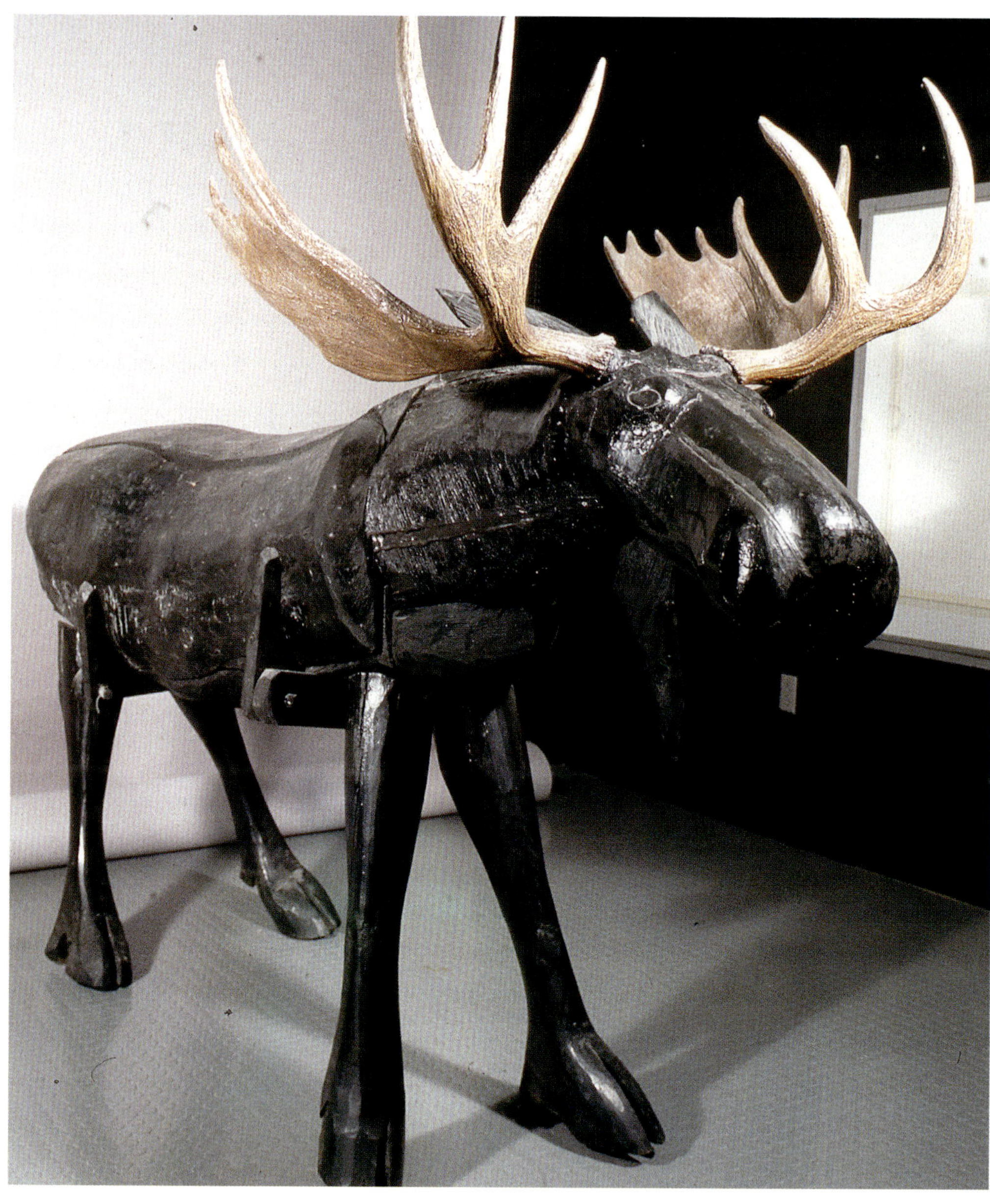

Bull Moose, Eddie Mandaggio (AGNS)

In 1988 Mandaggio was one of the artists included in the inaugural Nova Scotia Folk Art Festival, and he was prominently featured in the 1994 National Film Board documentary *Folk Art Found Me*. "You got to study a piece of folk art," he said in the film. "The more you look at it, the more it grows onto ya."[59]

Mandaggio made large and small carvings, as well as painted panels and furniture. For twenty years he was one of the most prolific folk artists in Nova Scotia. His younger friends and neighbours, Bradford, Leo, and Ransford Naugler, began making folk art under his influence.

Animals were a favourite subject. "I seen a lot of different animals. I watched them; it's amazing," he said in 1988. "Some people never know what nature is. They'll never realize how it works."[60] His work was included in the internationally touring exhibition *Nova Scotia Folk Art: Canada's Cultural Heritage* in 1989–90, and the Art Gallery of Nova Scotia has several of his works in its permanent collection.

DONALD MANZER

(ASHMORE, DIGBY COUNTY)

1912–1990

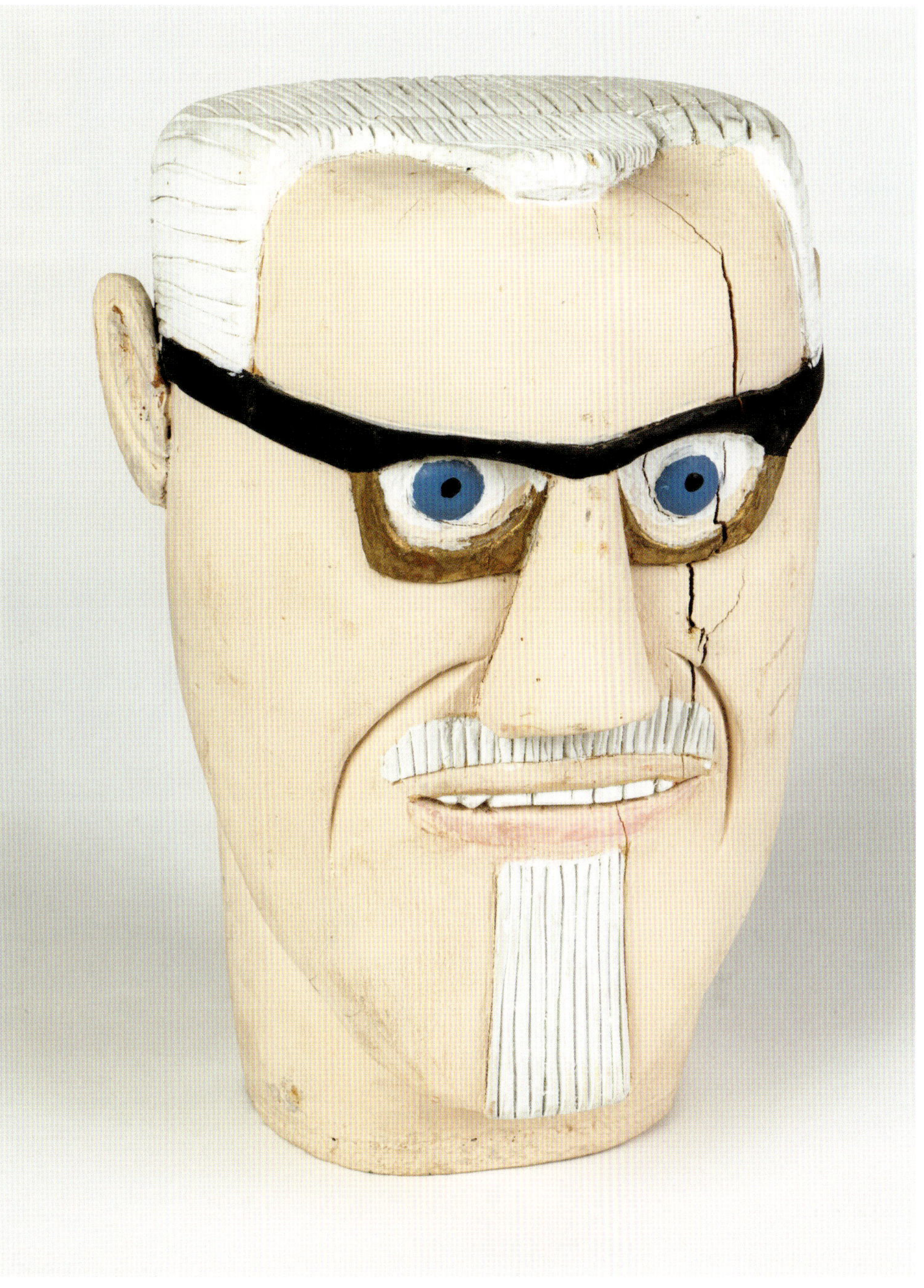

DONALD MANZER BEGAN carving in 1975, first making small animals and figures, but soon expanding to near–life-sized figures. His objects are often fanciful, such as his best-known work, *Cat and the Fiddle*, which illustrates a phrase from a children's nursery rhyme. His *Colonel Sanders* reflects an interest in popular culture often seen in Nova Scotia Folk Art. This portrait head of Harland Sanders, founder of the fast-food chain Kentucky Fried Chicken, may be a direct response to Collins Eisenhauer's treatment of the same topic, which was included in the Folk Art of Nova Scotia exhibition. Both sculptures were originally owned by Chris Huntington (in the case of the Eisenhauer, co-owned with Murray Stewart), until they entered the collections of the AGNS and the Canadian Museum of History, respectively.

Colonel Sanders, Donald Manzer

(RAW PHOTOGRAPHY FOR AGNS)

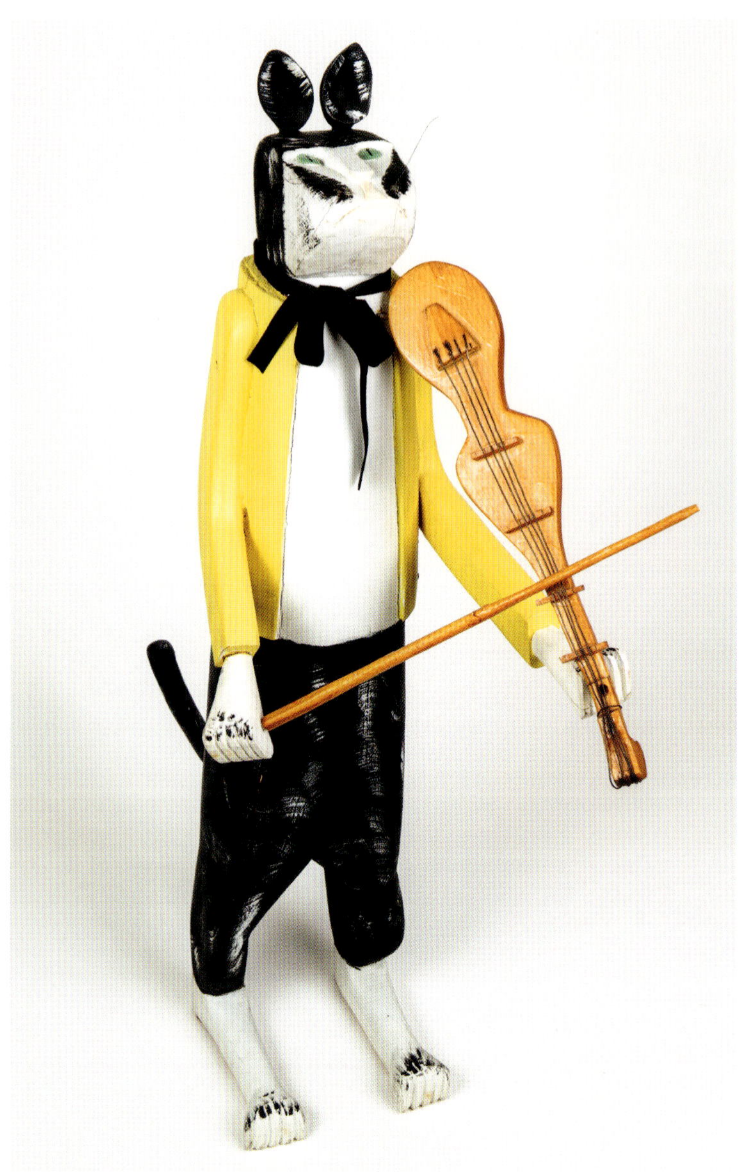

Cat and the Fiddle, Donald Manzer

(RAW PHOTOGRAPHY FOR AGNS)

Manzer's work was included in the internationally touring exhibition *Nova Scotia Folk Art: Canada's Cultural Heritage*; *Cat and the Fiddle* was used as the cover image for the catalogue.

Manzer worked on road crews and as a farmer, retiring as a school bus driver. He took up carving in earnest after his retirement, eventually being represented by the Houston North Gallery in Lunenburg. Manzer's work is included in the collections of the AGNS, the Nova Scotia Art Bank, and the Canadian Museum of History.

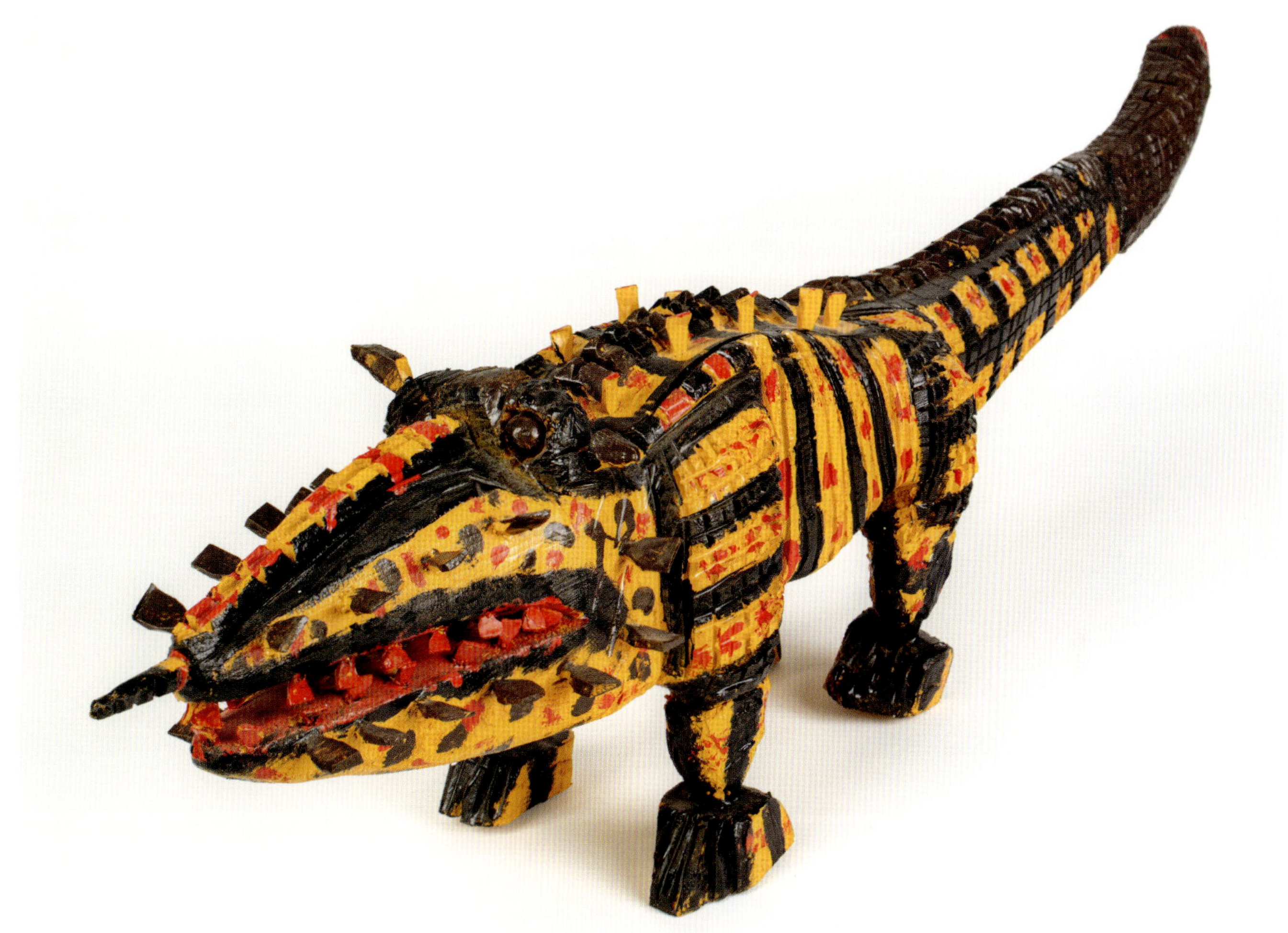

GARNET MCPHAIL

Lizard,
Garnet McPhail

(RAW PHOTOGRAPHY FOR AGNS)

(MELANSON, KINGS COUNTY)

1926–2008

FEATURED PROMINENTLY IN THE NATIONAL FILM BOARD OF CANADA documentary *Folk Art Found Me*, Garnet McPhail was an extremely popular artist from the late 1980s until his death. McPhail had worked many types of jobs during his life, including as a cook, a mason's helper, a woodsman, and a farmer. He eventually took a job as a custodian at Acadia University and he retired from there in 1987.

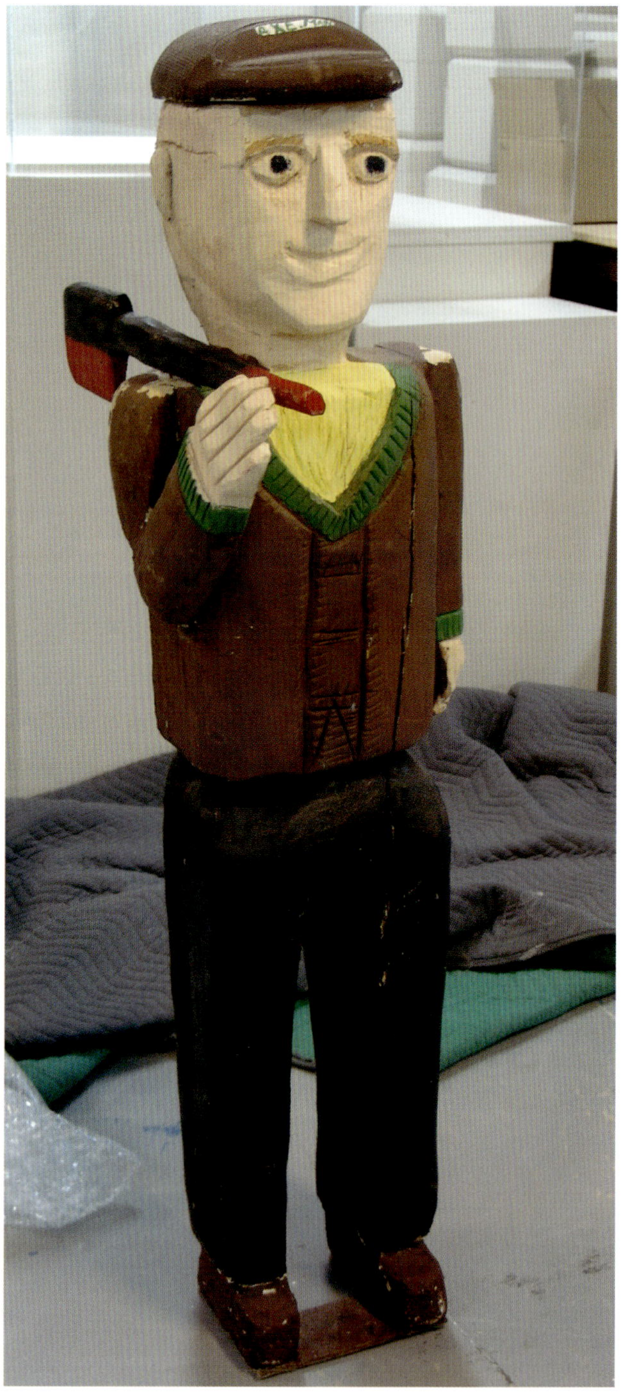

Axeman (Self-portrait), Garnet McPhail

(BEAVERBROOK ART GALLERY)

In 1978, after a knee operation, McPhail took up carving small animals and birds as part of his recovery. On his retirement he began carving larger sculptures, roughing out figures with a chainsaw and then finishing and painting them. In *Folk Art Found Me* he talked about cleaning in a department at Acadia University where they kept stuffed animal specimens. He was fascinated by the exotic animals and remembered them when he started carving. Among his favourite animals to carve were lizards and alligators—animals he only knew from the stuffed versions at the university. He also made life-sized and near–life-sized figures, as well as another popular subject: spotted dogs.

McPhail was one of the nineteen artists included in the inaugural iteration of the Nova Scotia Folk Art Festival and he returned to the festival for many subsequent years. McPhail's work is included in the collections of the Art Gallery of Nova Scotia and the Beaverbrook Art Gallery in Fredericton.

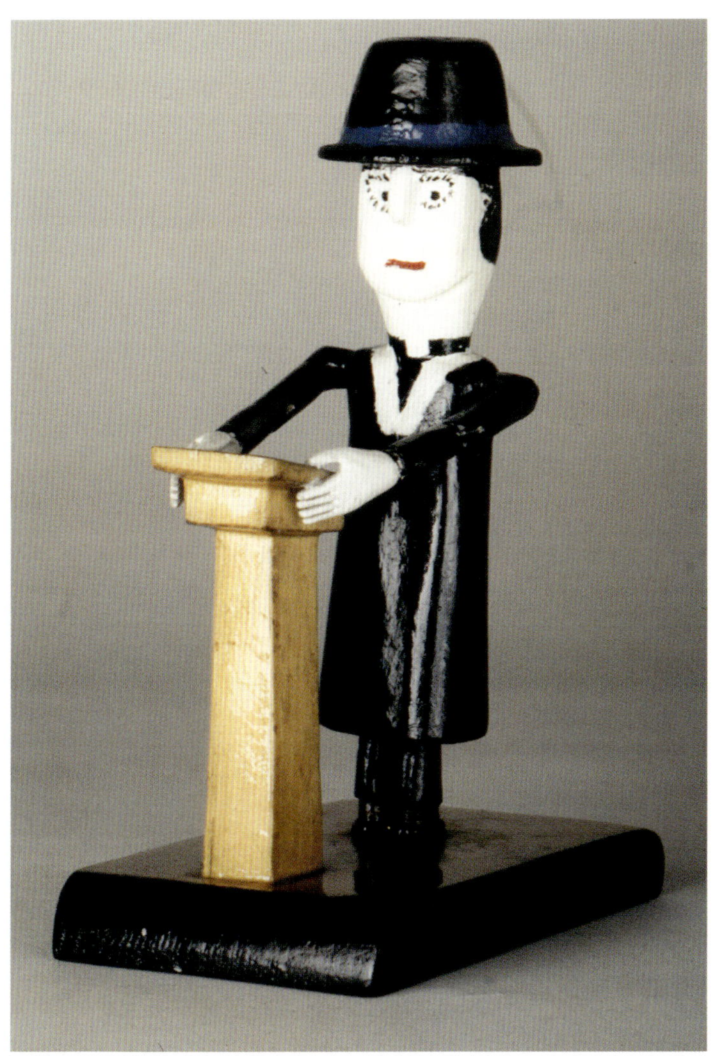

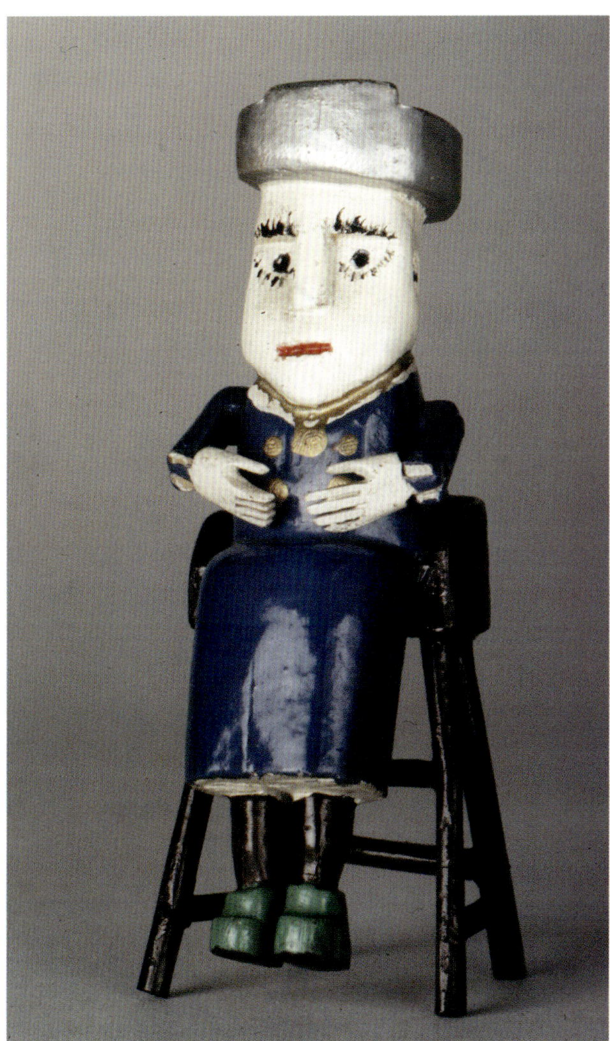

GEORGE MUNROE

(SYDNEY, CAPE BRETON COUNTY)

1902–1983

LEFT:
Congregational Group "In God We Trust": Preacher, George Munroe

(AGNS)

RIGHT:
Congregational Group "In God We Trust": Seated Child, George Munroe

(AGNS)

GEORGE MUNROE WAS BORN IN ENGLAND AND IMMIGRATED TO CAPE Breton where he worked as a rigger in the steel plant in Sydney. He carved as a hobby, giving his carvings away as gifts to family and friends. Munroe died in 1983, and in 1984 and 1985 four of his works were donated to the AGNS.

In 1988, folk artist Lorne Reid convinced Munroe's family members to sell him several pieces, which were the first of Munroe's works to enter the marketplace. Reid's fellow folk artist David Stephens donated one of Munroe's figures to the AGNS in 1991.

Munroe's largest work was the multi-piece *Congregational Group*, of which three pieces are in the AGNS collection: a seated child, a seated man and woman, and a preacher. Munroe's blocky style is fully in evidence here, as is his ability to make his figures expressive through subtle painting, particularly of the eyes and mouths. The seated child, with his feet dangling from the chair, has an expression of boredom that seems all too familiar. Other Munroe works can be considered character studies, such as *Miner in Black* and *A Gentleman with Hat and Cane*.

Munroe's *Congregational Group* was included in the exhibition *Nova Scotia Folk Art*, which toured the United Kingdom in 1989 and 1990.

BRADFORD NAUGLER

(MIDDLEWOOD, LUNENBURG COUNTY)

b. 1948

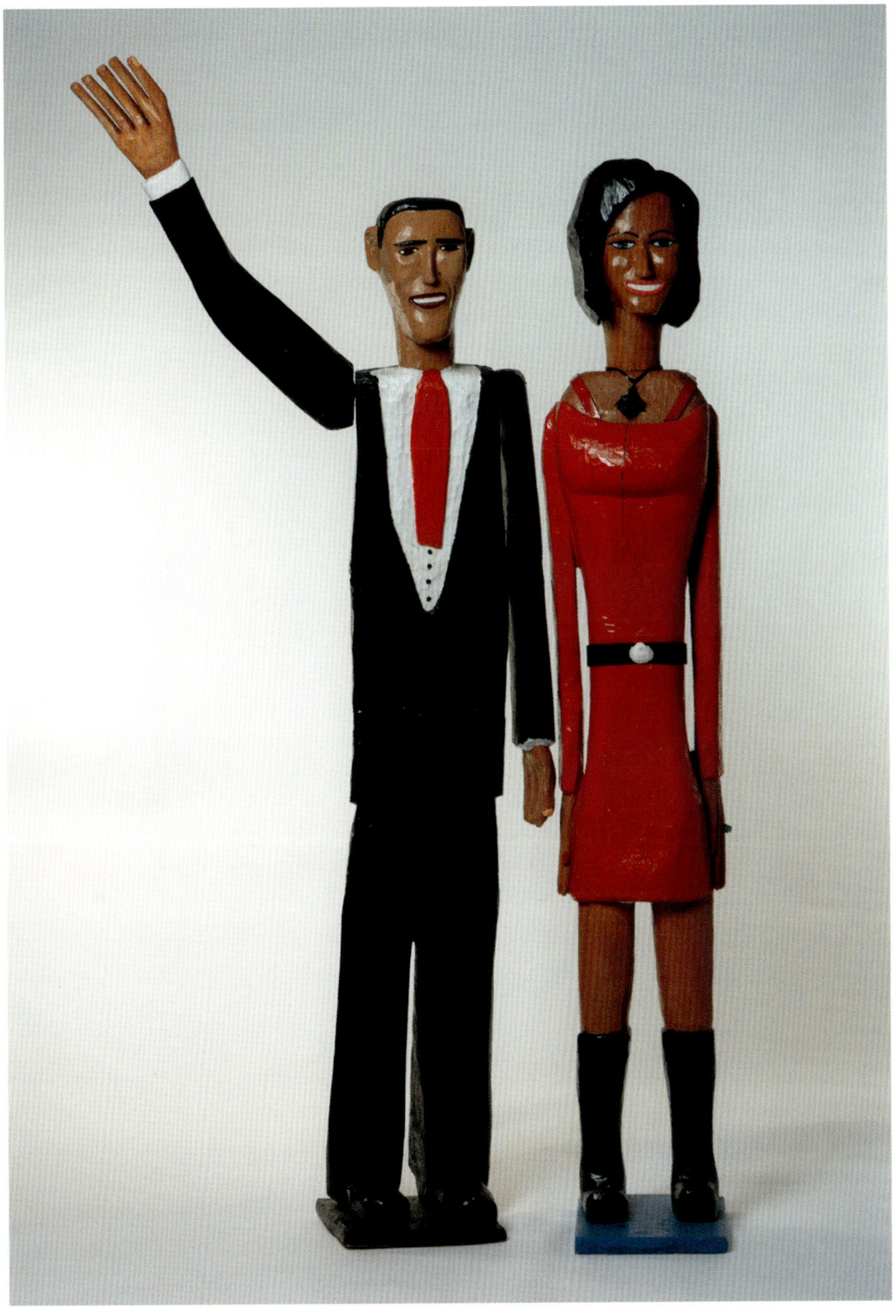

"I STILL DO FOLK ART THE old way, dry your wood outdoors, use a chainsaw to cut it out then use a carving knife to refine, and then paint it." —Bradford Naugler.[61]

Bradford Naugler began making folk art in 1989, inspired by the example of his friend and neighbour, Eddie Mandaggio. That year he was one of the artists featured in the inaugural Nova Scotia Folk Art Festival, and he has participated in every festival since—the only artist to have done so. Along with his brothers Leo and Ransford, Bradford Naugler was prominently featured in the 1994 National Film Board documentary, *Folk Art Found Me*.

Obama Family, Bradford Naugler

(MICHAEL TOMPKINS FOR AGNS)

Bradford Naugler quickly became a favourite of collectors and curators. Initially known for his animals and birds—particularly his brightly coloured roosters—he began, after a few years, to make the life-sized and larger sculptures that have become his signature works. In 1996, the Confederation Centre Art Gallery and Museum commissioned a ten-figure grouping by Naugler of the *Fathers of Confederation*. His *Obama Family* was a standout at the 2009

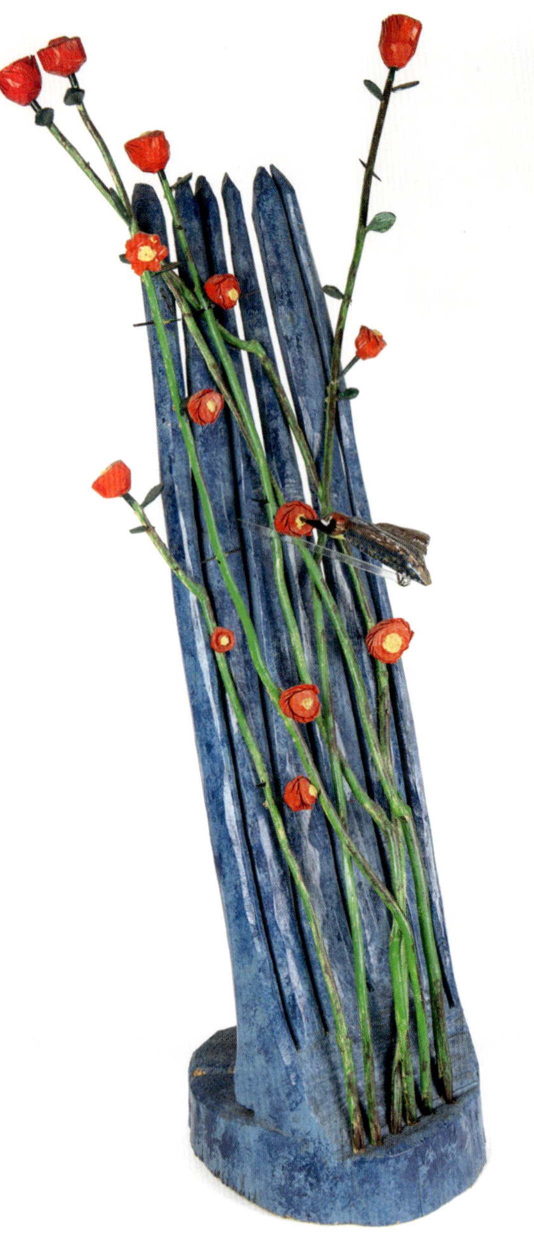

Rosebush with Hummingbirds, Bradford Naugler

(RAW PHOTOGRAPHY FOR AGNS)

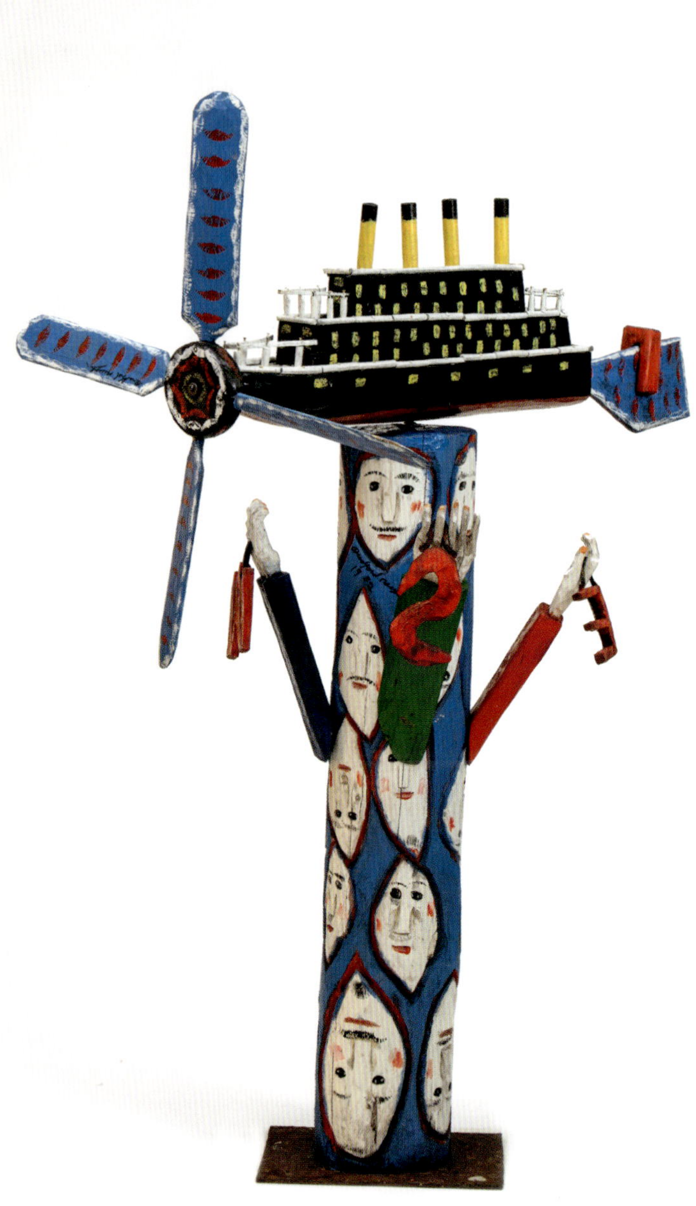

Ship Weathervane, Bradford Naugler

(RAW PHOTOGRAPHY FOR AGNS)

Nova Scotia Folk Art Festival and was acquired by the Art Gallery of Nova Scotia. Politicians, entertainers, sports figures, and such perennial folk art themes as Mounties and fishermen are all part of his repertoire.

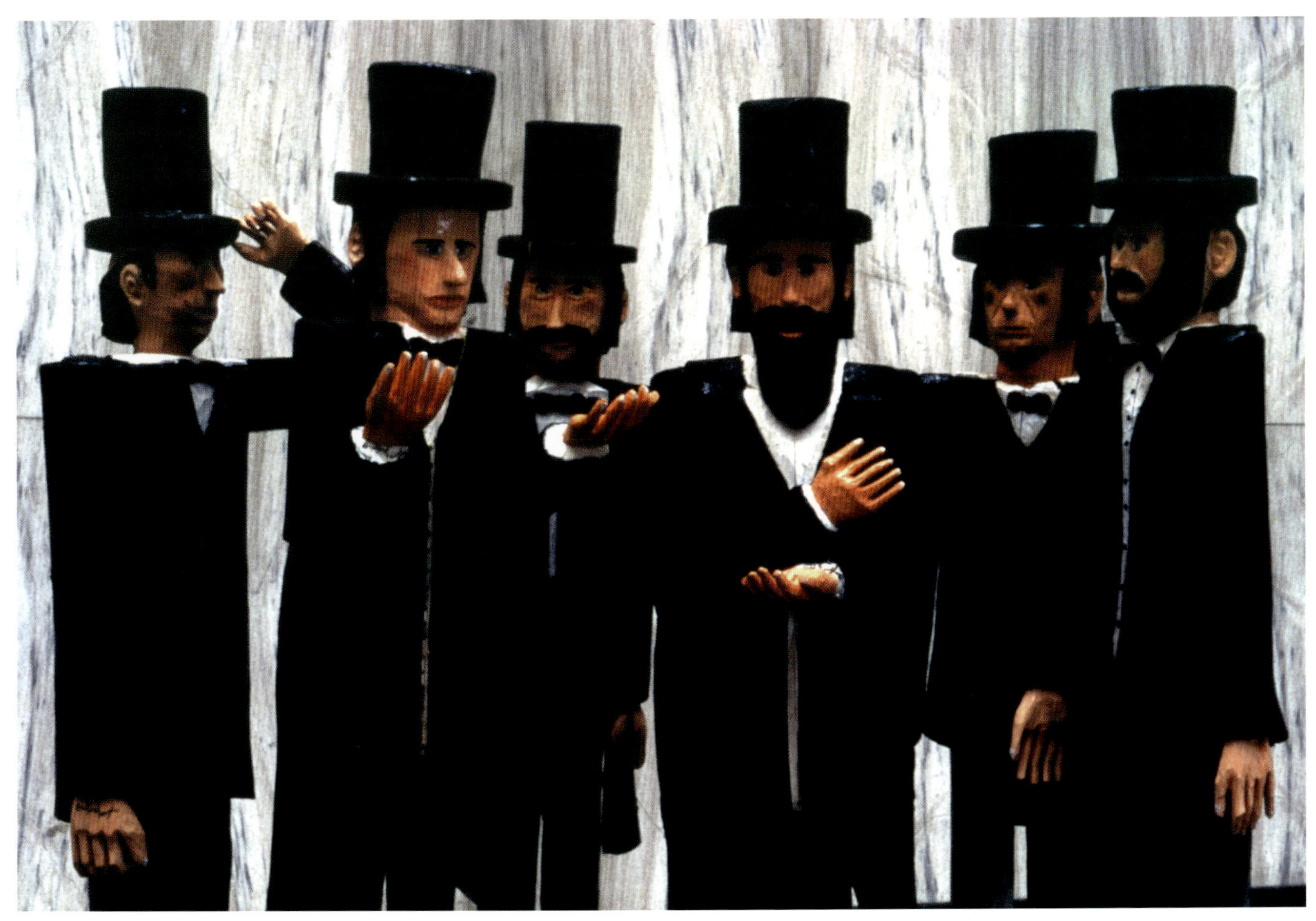

Fathers of Confederation, Bradford Naugler

(CONFEDERATION CENTRE OF THE ARTS)

In 1989–90 his work was included in the internationally touring exhibition *Nova Scotia Folk Art: Canada's Cultural Heritage*, and in 1997 his work was also included in *A Life of Its Own: Chris Huntington and the Resurgence of Nova Scotia Folk Art 1975–1995*. Bradford Naugler's artwork can be found in the permanent collections of the DesBrisay Museum in Bridgewater, the Confederation Centre Art Gallery and Museum, and the Art Gallery of Nova Scotia.

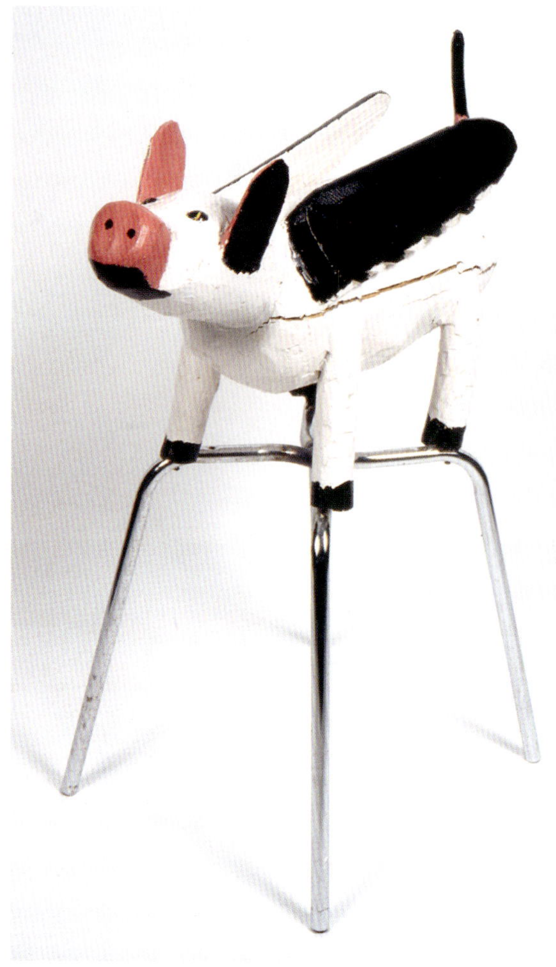

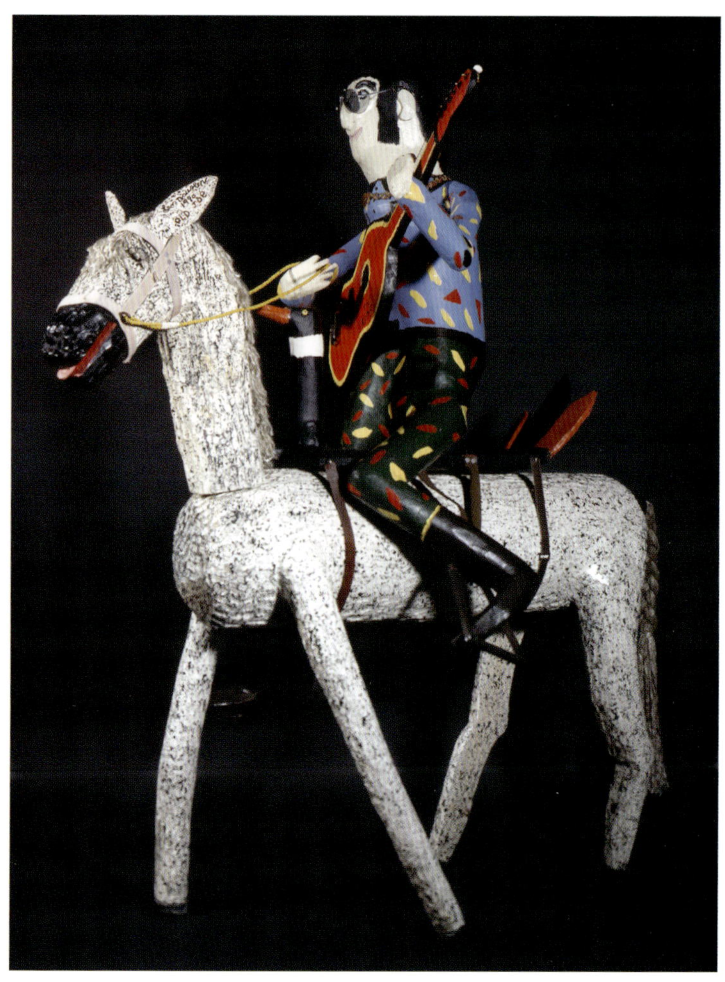

LEFT: *Flying Pig*, Leo Naugler

(AGNS)

RIGHT: *The King and Old Joe*, Leo Naugler

(AGNS)

LEO NAUGLER

(MIDDLEWOOD, LUNENBURG COUNTY)

b. 1956

AFTER WORKING AT VARIOUS ODD JOBS, INCLUDING AS A HIGHWAY labourer, and then running his own auto body shop, Leo Naugler began making folk art in 1989. He and his brothers were encouraged to take up folk art by their friend and neighbour Eddie Mandaggio, who remained an inspiration to all three artists.

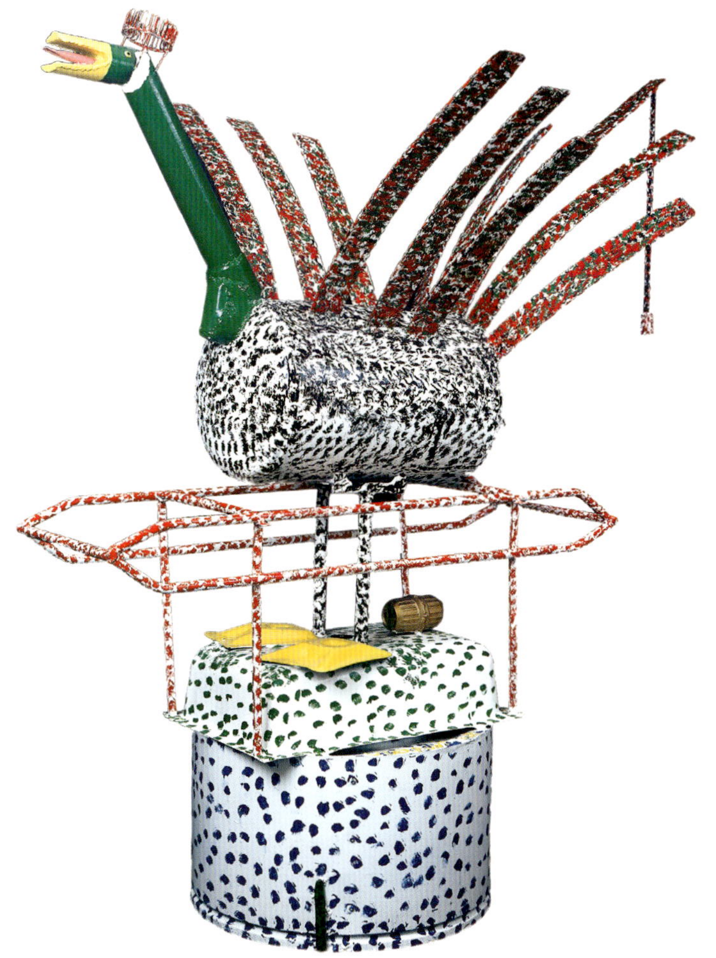

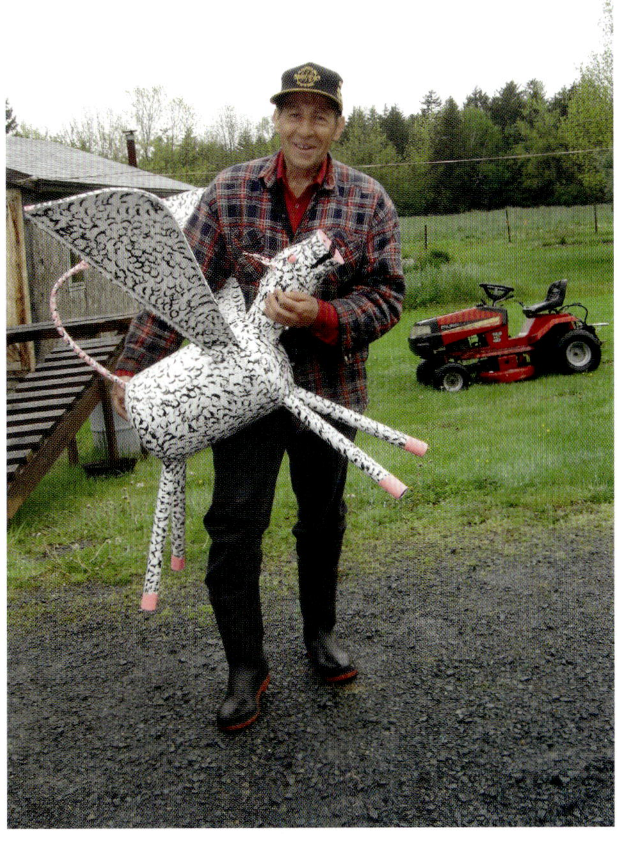

LEFT: *Royal Goose Fountain*, Leo Naugler

(AGNS)

RIGHT: Leo Naugler

(BLACK SHEEP GALLERY)

Leo Naugler made paintings, carvings, and welded sculptures, all featuring bright colours and whimsical subject matter. He was one of the artists included in the first Nova Scotia Folk Art Festival in 1989, and he continued to exhibit at the festival until health issues limited his art-making in 2002. His sculpture *Flying Pig* (1989) was included in the internationally touring exhibition *Nova Scotia Folk Art: Canada's Cultural Heritage* and in *A Life of Its Own: Chris Huntington and the Resurgence of Nova Scotia Folk Art 1975–1995*. Leo was featured prominently in the National Film Board of Canada documentary *Folk Art Found Me* in 1994.

A favourite among collectors, Leo Naugler resisted demands to work "to order," or to replicate popular subjects. "It's hard to paint something when people tell you what colour to put where and stuff," he said. "It'd be no fun doing it, really. I couldn't do it that way."[62]

The largest work he ever made was *Flying Fish Helicopter*, which was featured on the television program *Weird Wheels* in 2002. Leo Naugler's work is included in the permanent collections of the Canadian Museum of History and the Art Gallery of Nova Scotia, among other museums and galleries.

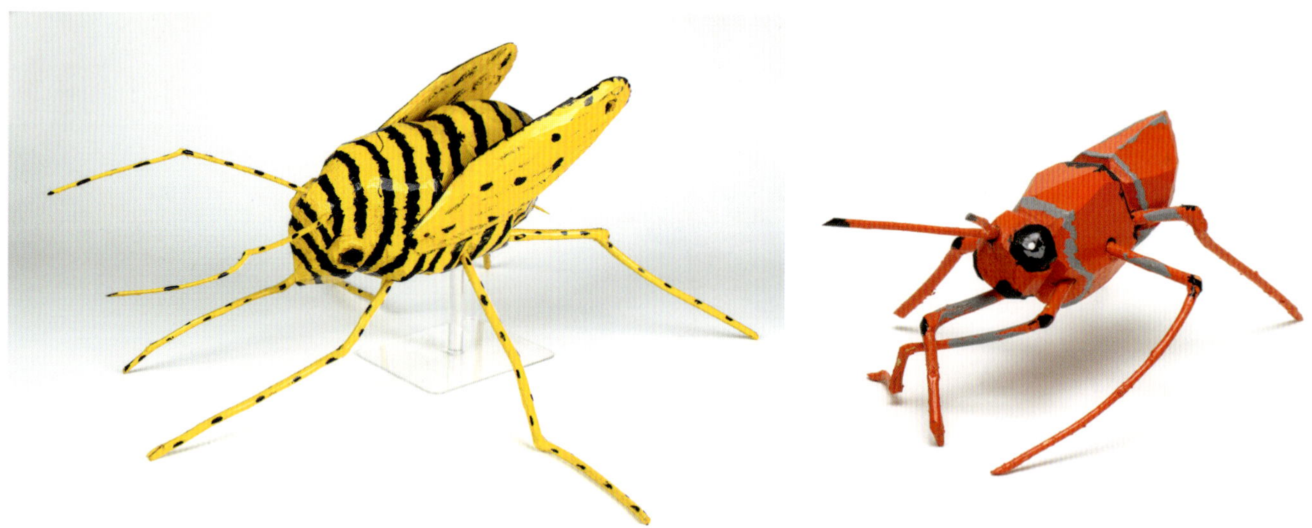

Bumblebee and *Orange Bug*, Ransford Naugler

(RAW PHOTOGRAPHY FOR AGNS)

RANSFORD NAUGLER

(MIDDLEWOOD, LUNENBURG COUNTY)

b. 1953

RANSFORD NAUGLER HAS BEEN MAKING FOLK ART SINCE 1988. IN 1990 he became an exhibitor at the Nova Scotia Folk Art Festival, and has returned most years since. Ransford Naugler has worked many jobs over his lifetime, including as a fisher, a carpenter, and a maintenance worker. Along with his brothers Bradford and Leo, he is a member of the most famous family in Nova Scotia Folk Art. Neighbour and friend Eddie Mandaggio was an inspiration to all three of them, and like Mandaggio, Ransford Naugler makes large figures of animals and people, roughed out with a chainsaw, and then finished and painted.

Unique to Ransford Naugler are his smaller sculptures of insects, three of which are included in the permanent collection of the Art Gallery of Nova Scotia. Ransford Naugler is included in many private and corporate collections, including that of former Governor General Adrienne Clarkson. Ransford was featured prominently in the National Film Board of Canada documentary *Folk Art Found Me* in 1994.

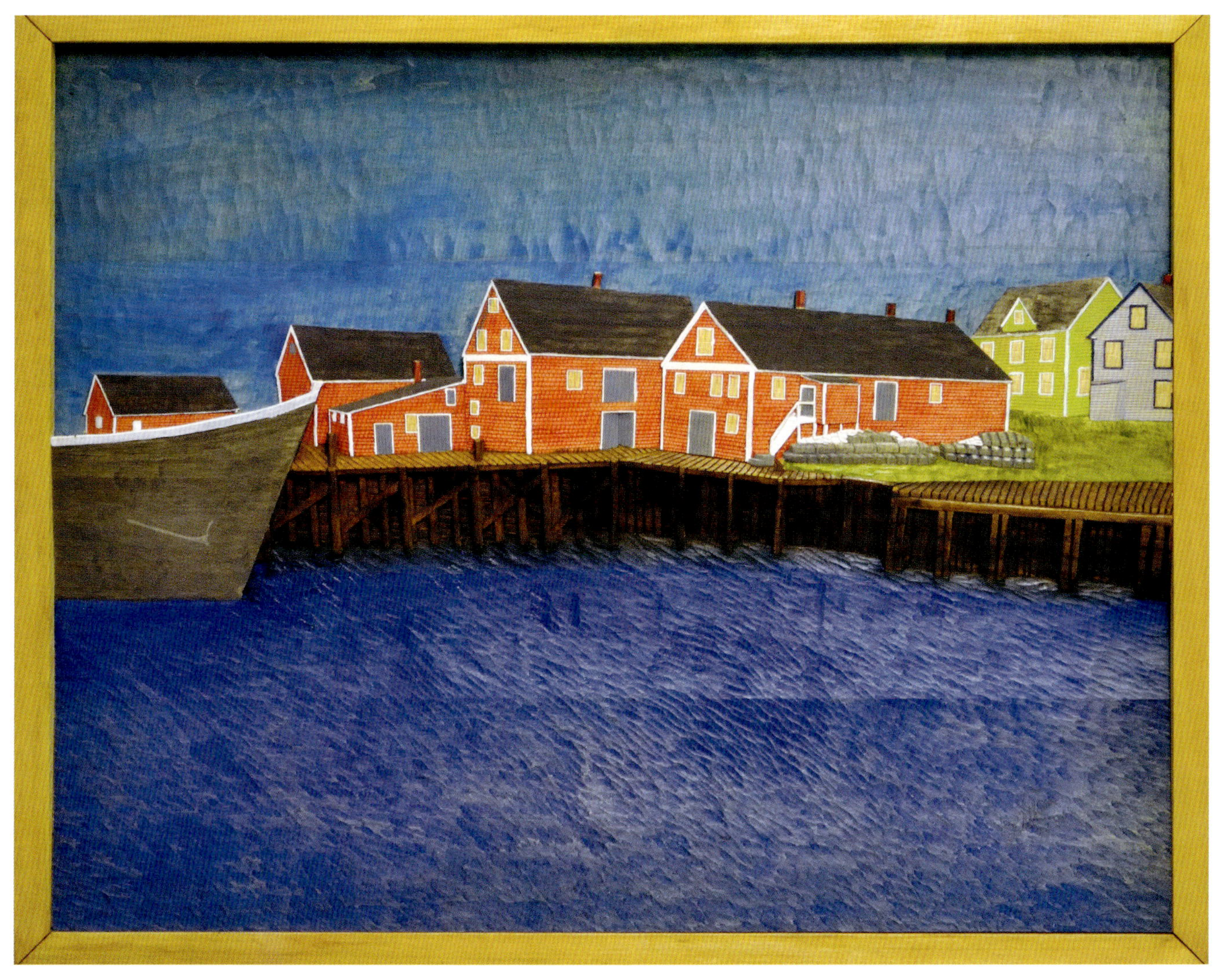

Fish Houses,
Stephen Outhouse

(AGNS)

STEPHEN OUTHOUSE

(DIGBY, DIGBY COUNTY)

1943–2018

STEPHEN OUTHOUSE WAS BORN IN ST. JOHN'S, NEWFOUNDLAND AND Labrador, in 1943 and first began carving while he was stationed in Germany with the Canadian Armed Forces in the early 1960s. He used scraps of wood

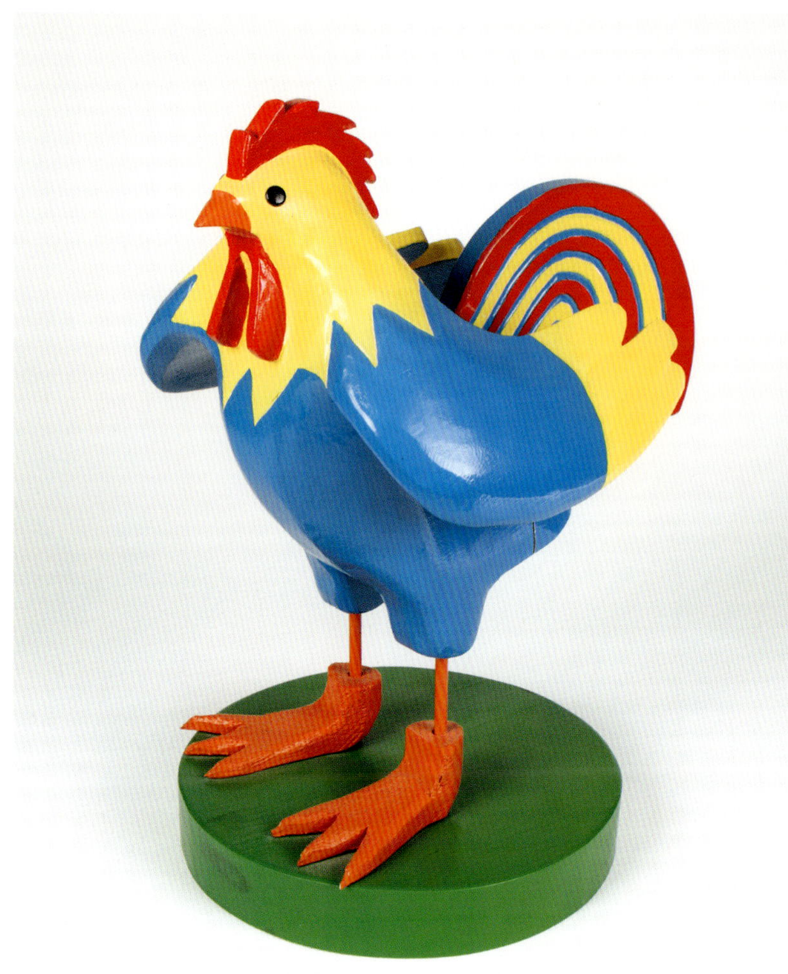

Rooster,
Stephen Outhouse
(RAW PHOTOGRAPHY FOR AGNS)

and scalpels to create female nudes that were very popular with his fellow soldiers. After leaving the army he worked as a carpenter, a labourer, and a mall superintendent, eventually settling in Digby. He was an early member of the Maud Lewis Painted House Society, founded in Digby to preserve the iconic house where Maud and Everett Lewis had lived in Marshalltown, Nova Scotia.

Outhouse was a popular artist at the Nova Scotia Folk Art Festival, first showing in the third iteration of the Lunenburg institution in 1991. His early work consisted mostly of painted relief carvings of local subjects and life-sized people. Outhouse did not come from the sort of isolated background his predecessors had. In fact, while untrained in art, he was aware of art history and trends, even making that awareness part of his work. He said in 1993: "When I first started carving reliefs, I always kept famous artists in mind. I even copied pictures by famous artists, changing them here and there to make them my own. But eventually I found my own thing."[63]

His work is included in the permanent collection of the Art Gallery of Nova Scotia, the McCord Museum in Montreal, and the Admiral Digby Museum.

STANLEY RECTOR

(SOUTHAMPTON, CUMBERLAND COUNTY)

1943–2020

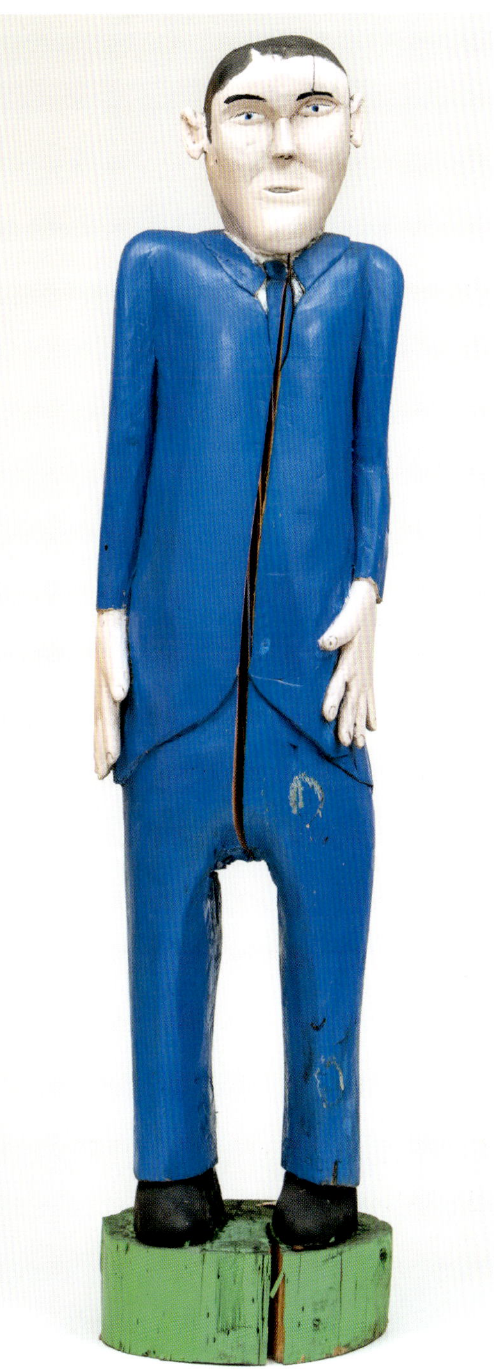

Brian Mulroney,
Stanley Rector

(RAW PHOTOGRAPHY FOR AGNS)

STANLEY RECTOR HAD A NUMBER of jobs, including as a woodsman, a coal miner, a fisher, and a truck driver. He started making carvings in the late 1980s and was included in the second Nova Scotia Folk Art Festival in 1990. His father, Tom Rector, was also a folk artist.

Rector mostly carved figures, from tabletop to life-sized. His best-known work is a full-sized portrait of then-prime minister Brian Mulroney, which is in the collection of the Art Gallery of Nova Scotia. Rector joined a long line of carvers who have depicted politicians, going back to Collins Eisenhauer's four-figure grouping, *Political Figures (Pierre Trudeau, Robert Stanfield, David Lewis, and Gerald Regan)*, which is in the collection of the Canadian Museum of History. The AGNS also has a portrait of John Diefenbaker by Sidney Howard, and a Pierre Trudeau portrait by Walter Cook.

Rector's *Brian Mulroney* (1990) was included in *A Life of Its Own: Chris Huntington and the Resurgence of Nova Scotia Folk Art 1975–1995*.

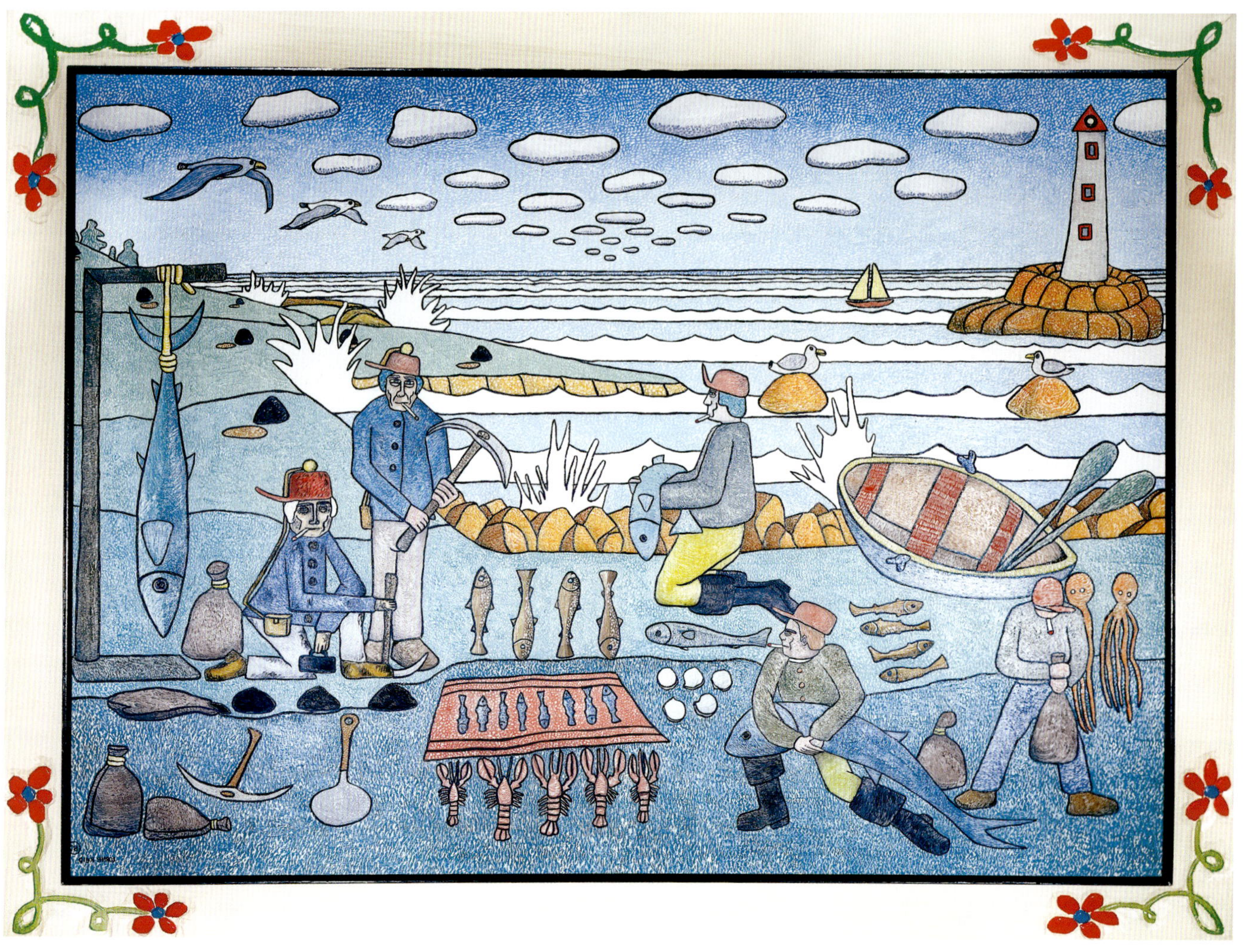

Fishermen Bartering with Coalminers, Lorne Reid

(AGNS)

LORNE REID

(DOMINION, CAPE BRETON COUNTY)

1954–1991

"FOLK ART IS IN DEMAND BECAUSE IT SEEMS TO FREE OUR SOULS FROM the dreadful conflicts that go on around us. It enables us to live life the way it should be lived—in total peace and simplicity."—Lorne Reid.[64]

Lorne Reid was never able to find much in the way of peace and simplicity in his life. The son of a coal miner, he was born in Glace Bay and raised in Dominion. When he was sixteen, he quit school and left home, travelling across North America. He had only one ambition—to paint. He eventually landed in California, but after years of hard living and abusing drugs and alcohol, he returned to Nova Scotia. "California was like living in a circus," he told the *Globe and Mail* in 1990.[65]

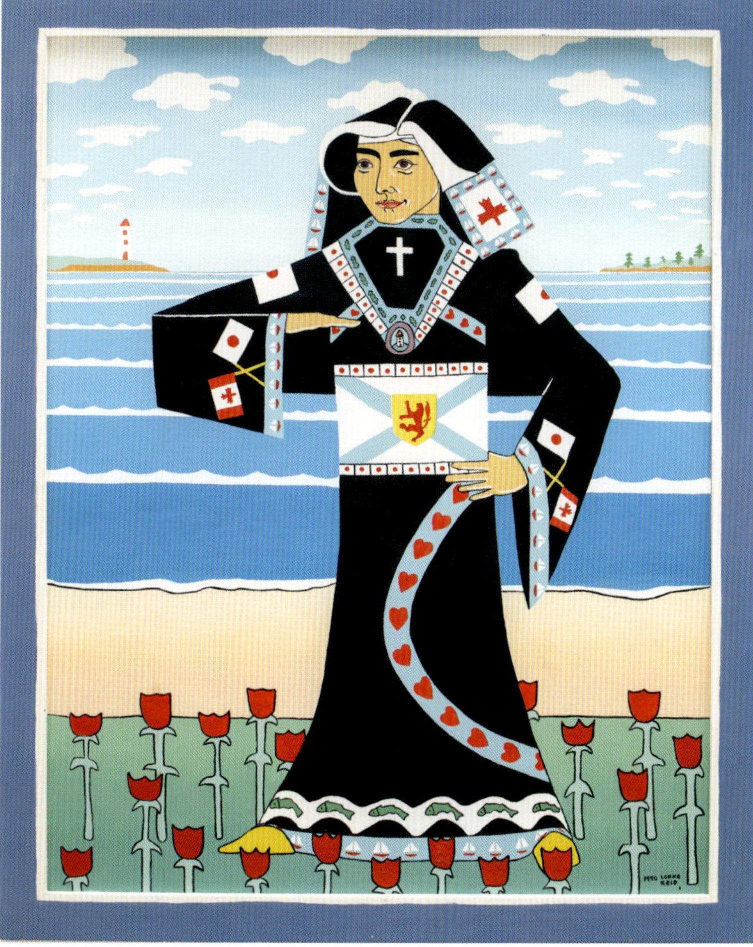

Shino Shimpo from Japan, The Shino Visits Nova Scotia,
Lorne Reid

(RAW PHOTOGRAPHY FOR AGNS)

He tried art school, spending three years at the Nova Scotia College of Art and Design before leaving without graduating. "I just couldn't do the things they were asking me to do. I had to leave."[66] He returned to Cape Breton, moving to Chéticamp and setting up a pizza restaurant with his brother. In a small upstairs room he had a studio for his painting. He began to paint in a folk art style, saying, "I had been painting stuff that was too intense—lots of people staring and hurting—and I just wanted to paint the Bluenose."[67] He began to show his paintings in the pizza parlour. Eventually he opened Reid's Folk Art Gallery with his friend and fellow artist David Stephens. Never a traditional folk artist—he was too educated and edgy to really fit the mould—Reid started to show other folk artists and is credited with discovering Dick Tutty and Murray Gallant. In 1988 he also was one of the founders of the Nova Scotia Folk Art Festival, and showed his work in the inaugural exhibition, along with David Stephens and Kyle Jackson, two other artists who uneasily fit the folk art designation. The Art Gallery of Nova Scotia bought two of his works in 1988, and in 1990 the Atlantic Film Festival used one of his paintings as its poster. He moved to Halifax in 1990 as his career was taking off; he was making a living selling his work and seemed to be growing out of the folk art category. As AGNS Director Bernard Riordon said, "It is folk art, and beyond folk art. Much of it was subconscious. It is very thoughtful and innovative artwork no matter how you categorize it."[68]

Unfortunately, Reid never got to fully enjoy his success, or to further push his remarkable work. Stricken with cancer, he died at his parents' house in Dominion in 1991. He was thirty-seven years old.

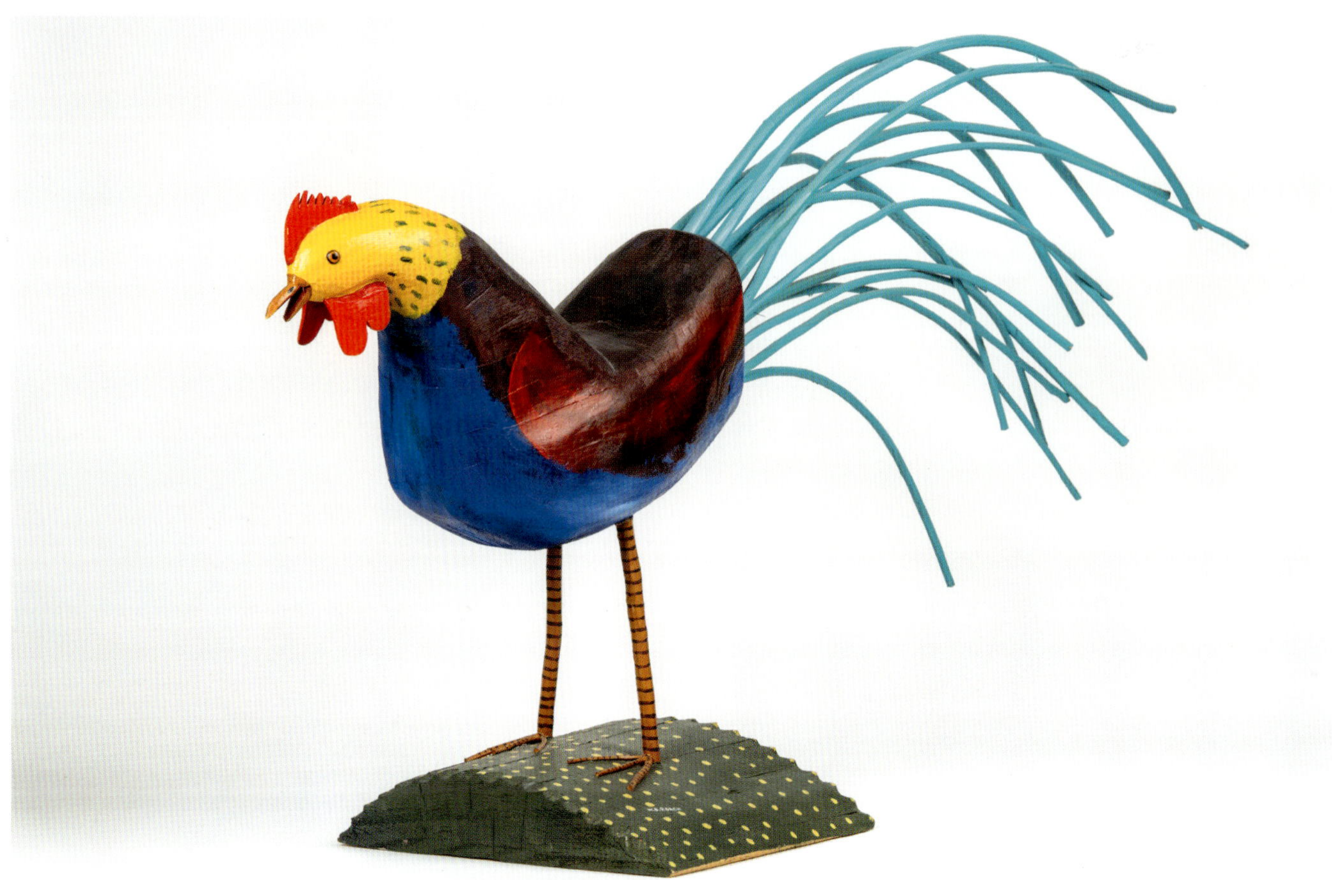

Rooster, William Roach

(RAW PHOTOGRAPHY FOR AGNS)

WILLIAM ROACH

(CHÉTICAMP, INVERNESS COUNTY)

b. 1950

ANYONE TRAVELLING ON THE FAMOUS CABOT TRAIL WILL HAVE PASSED the Sunset Gallery in Chéticamp, just outside the entrance to Cape Breton Highlands National Park. Attached to the modest complex of gallery and coffee shop is a small studio building where visitors can find William "Bill" Roach carving or painting.

Born in Point Cross, Cape Breton, in 1950, Bill Roach was raised in an Acadian community, the son of a bootlegger and occasional woodsman.

His uncle, Auguste Camus, carved as a hobby, and Roach emulated him, taking up whittling birds and animals while still a small boy. To this day Roach keeps a small carving of oxen done by his uncle in his studio.

He had a difficult childhood exacerbated by poverty and his father's alcoholism, a disease that would eventually almost claim Roach's life. He went to work at fourteen and moved to Ontario with an older sister and her husband when he was seventeen. He worked a series of jobs there for twenty years, marrying Linda Needham in 1974. In 1978 the couple moved back to his home of Chéticamp.

Roach shared his father's drinking problem, but with the help of Alcoholics Anonymous he was able to quit drinking in 1980. Being sober also gave him new perspective on his desire to make art, and he took up carving and painting in earnest. In 1989 he quit his job at a fish cannery and became an artist full-time. In 1990 he and Linda opened the Sunset Gallery, and Roach participated in his first Nova Scotia Folk Art Festival. In 1991 his work was included in an exhibition at the Canadian Embassy in Washington. That year also marked the first time his work entered a public collection, when the AGNS bought one of his carved roosters, a subject that is among his most popular.

He became friends with folk artist Sidney Howard who gave him valuable encouragement in the early days. "He'd tell me, 'Bill, get it out of your blood or you'll always be wondering what would have come of it.' That's why when I look at where I am today, I am contented because it went way further than I thought it would."[69] Roach's carving of Sidney Howard is among his works in the collection of the Art Gallery of Nova Scotia.

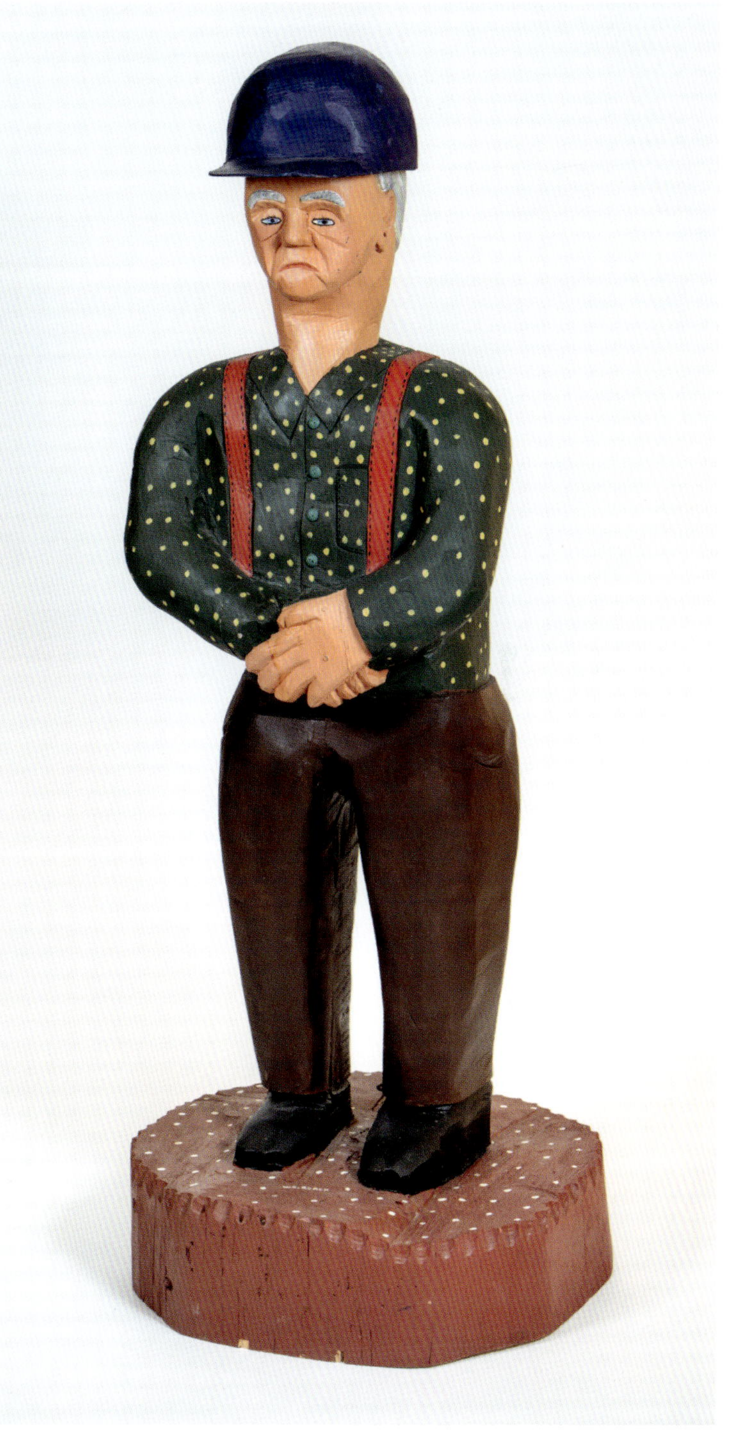

Sidney Howard, William Roach

(RAW PHOTOGRAPHY FOR AGNS)

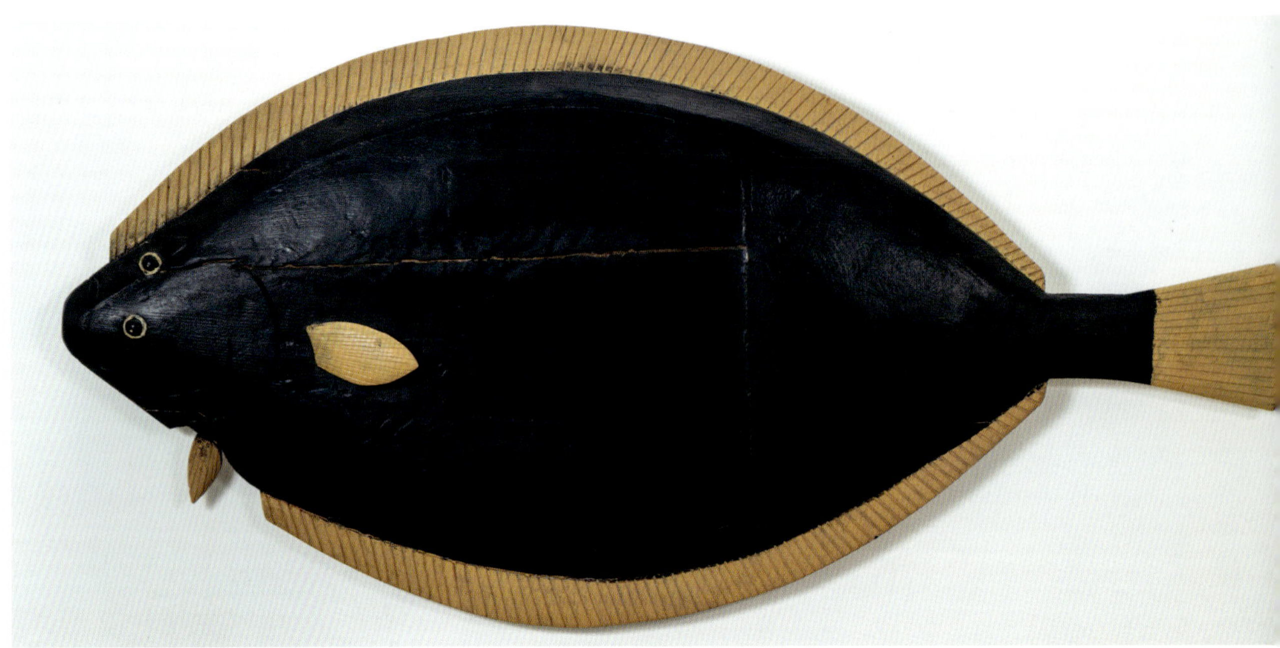

Halibut,
Randall Smith

(RAW PHOTOGRAPHY FOR AGNS)

RANDALL SMITH

(INGOMAR, SHELBURNE COUNTY)

b. 1906

RANDALL SMITH WAS A FISHER, A BOATBUILDER, AND A CARPENTER, and a lifelong resident of Shelburne County in southwest Nova Scotia. In 1970 he began carving to decorate his yard, displaying wooden carvings of fish on poles. He also made a few weathervanes, including a remarkable one featuring a steamship that is in the collection of the Canadian Museum of History.

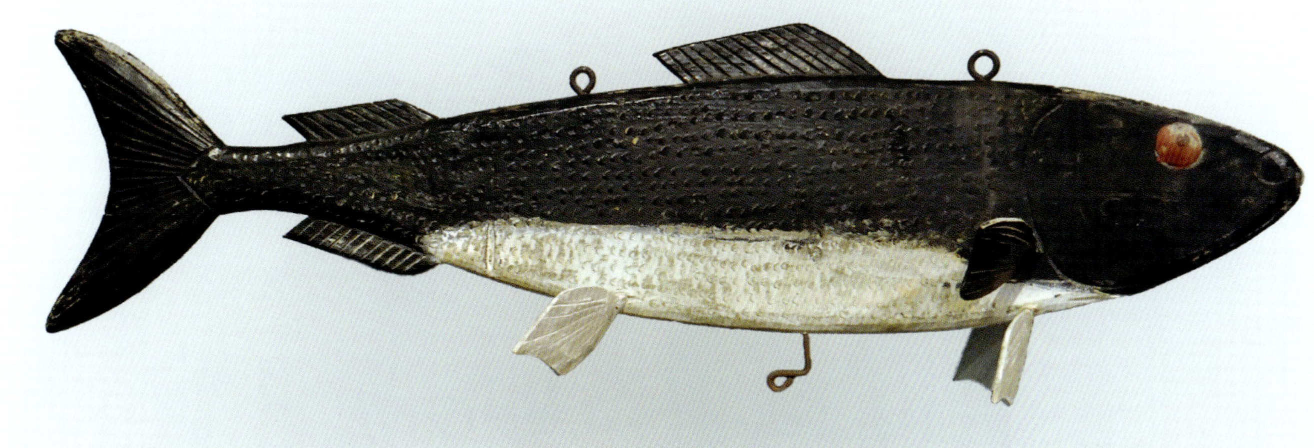

Cod,
Randall Smith
(AGNS)

One of his large wooden cod sculptures was included in the touring exhibition *From the Heart: Folk Art in Canada*, and his *Halibut* is rarely off view at the Art Gallery of Nova Scotia. Fish were his primary subject, because, as he told the Canadian Museum of History, it was "[something] I know all about."[70] Smith's work was also included in *A Life of Its Own: Chris Huntington and the Resurgence of Nova Scotia Folk Art 1975–1995*.

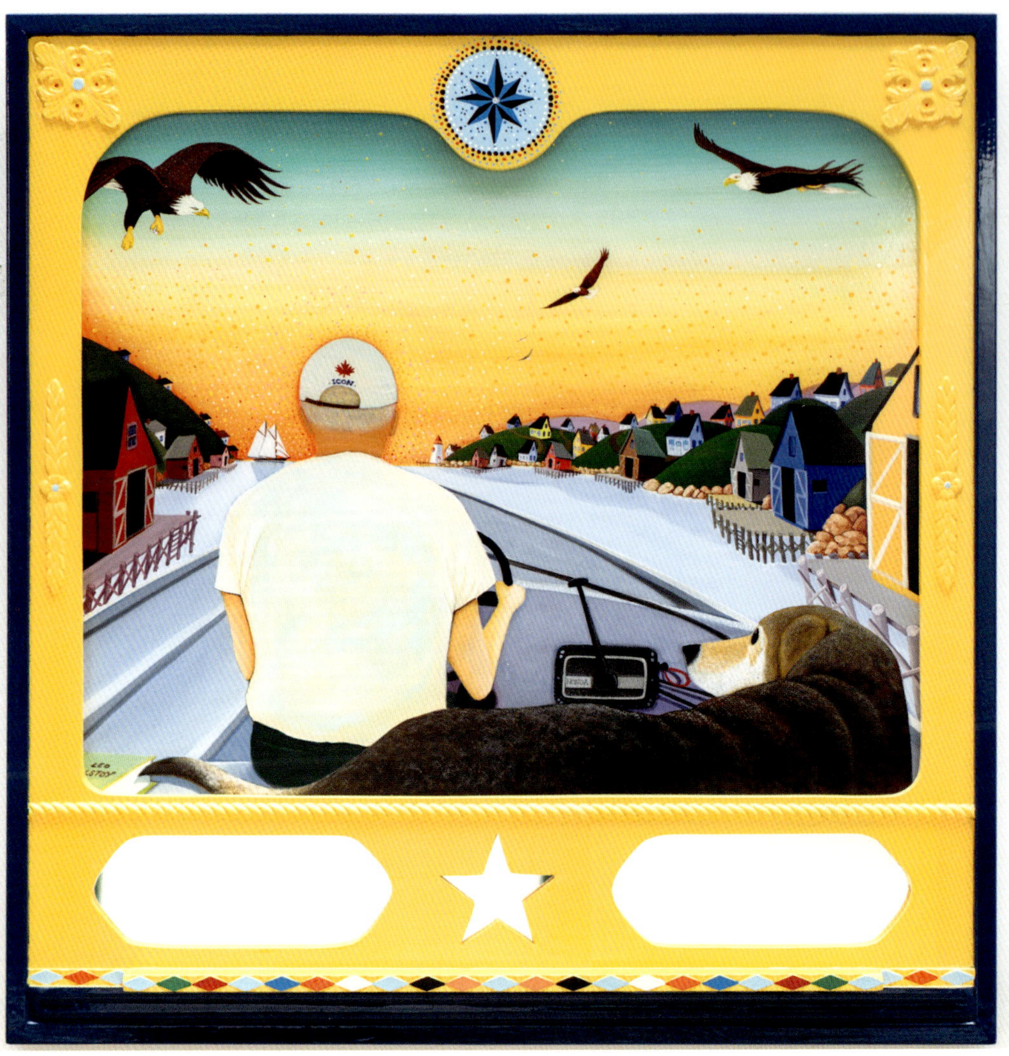

Alex Colville: Won't You Please Come Home, David P. Stephens

(RAW PHOTOGRAPHY FOR AGNS)

DAVID P. STEPHENS

(SYDNEY, CAPE BRETON COUNTY)

b. 1955

DAVID STEPHENS IS AN ATYPICAL FOLK ARTIST. HE WAS BORN AND grew up in Sydney, and after a time off-island he returned to Cape Breton. Stephens worked at a variety of jobs before becoming a folk artist, including in a lumber camp, in the army, and at sea as a marine engineer for

HMCS *Athabaskan*. He also worked as a rigger at the navy dockyard in Halifax. He started painting in 1985, and in 1988 he moved to Chéticamp. There he encountered a childhood friend, Lorne Reid, who was also striving to become an artist. As Stephens remembers, "after previously struggling to seek new directions, we began anew, from a child-centred perspective, with simplified, easy flowing forms, filled with pure unmodulated colours."[71] They also started a gallery to promote folk art.

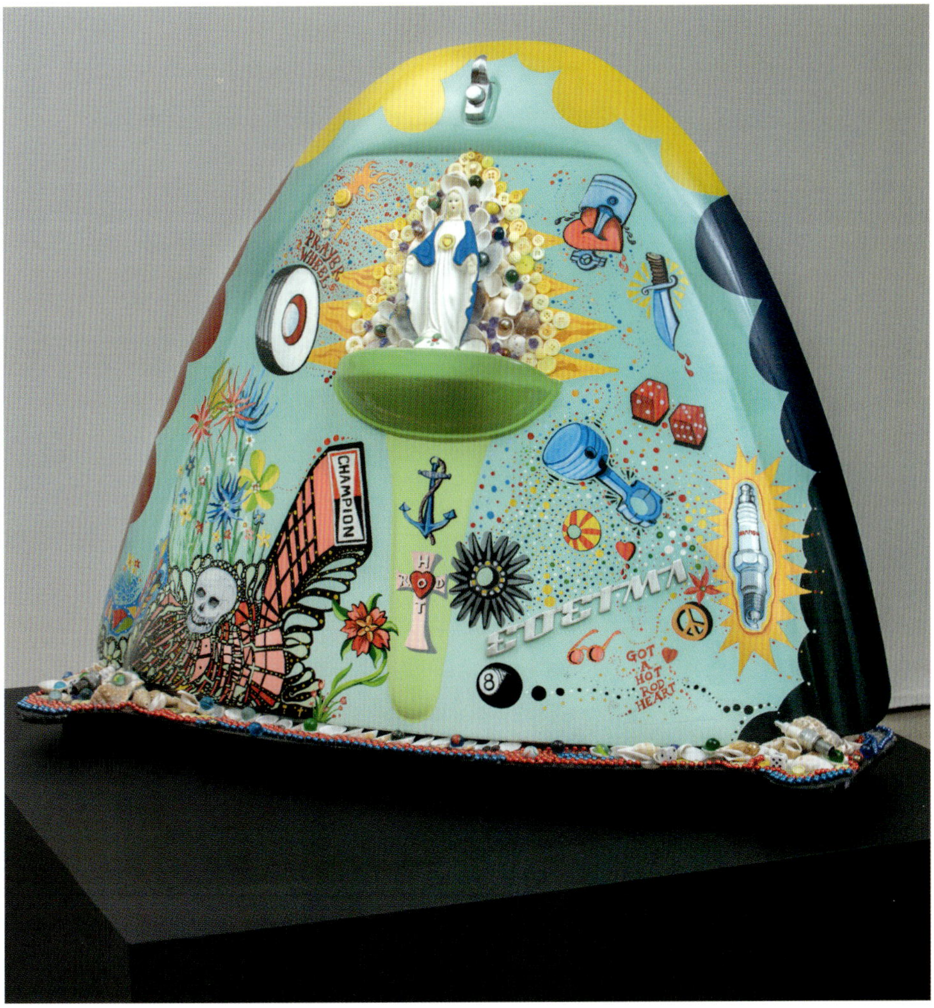

The next year, with Chris Huntington and the SoHo Kitchen's Kyle Jackson, they helped start the Nova Scotia Folk Art Festival. David Stephens was to become the Festival's director as of 1990, and he held down various roles at the festival and exhibited at it for almost twenty years. In 2005 he was the poster artist for the festival.

Saint El Camino: Our Lady of Internal Combustion, David P. Stephens

(AGNS)

In addition to his paintings, Stephens makes decorated art cars—working automobiles that are painted in his unique style. He also makes paintings on car parts, such as his *VW Beetle Art Car Door* (1999) in the collection of the Art Gallery of Nova Scotia. Stephens's work can also be found in the Nova Scotia Art Bank and in the Beaverbrook Art Gallery's collection.

In 2013 the Cape Breton University Art Gallery mounted the full-career survey exhibition *True Grit: The Urban Folk Creations of David P. Stephens and Kyle B. Jackson*. In 2016 Stephens was included in *Terroir*, a survey of contemporary Nova Scotia art at the AGNS.

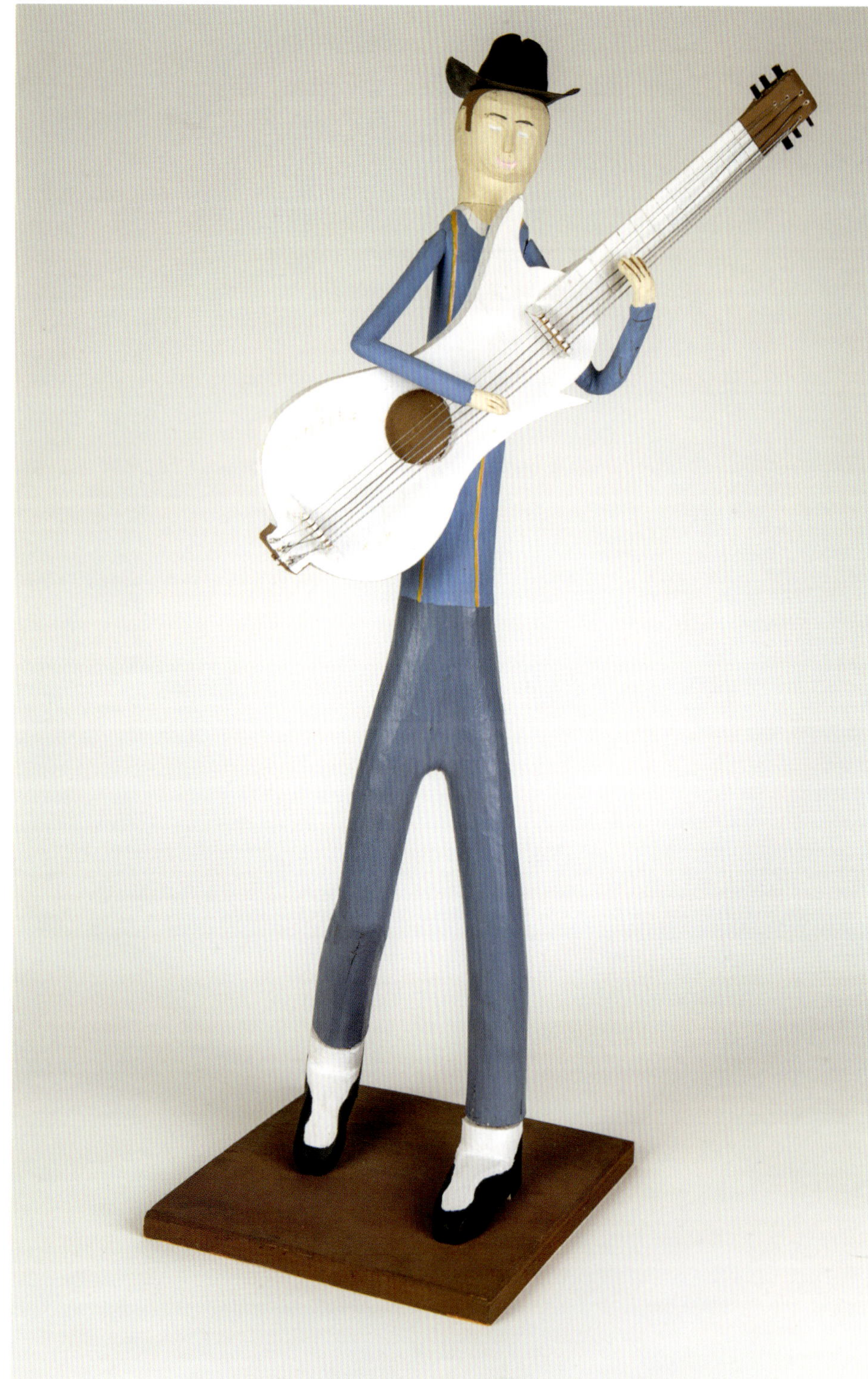

Stompin' Tom, Harold Tutty

(RAW PHOTOGRAPHY FOR AGNS)

HAROLD TUTTY

(GLACE BAY, CAPE BRETON COUNTY)

1919–1995

HAROLD "DICK" TUTTY was a machinist and fisher in Glace Bay who made whirligigs and other ornaments for his property in his spare time. Lorne Reid, who, in addition to being a noted folk artist himself, ran a folk art gallery in Chéticamp, saw Tutty's work while driving by one day, and stopped in and introduced himself. Tutty soon began to show regularly at Reid's Folk Art Gallery, and on his retirement began to make larger sculptures, including full-sized figures, often using the natural fork in a branch to describe the figure, as in *Sheriff* and *Stompin' Tom*, both from 1989 and in the collection of the Art Gallery of Nova Scotia.

He was perhaps best known for his humorous tabletop sculptures, often depicting tableaux of card players and drinkers. Several of his sculptures feature figures who have passed

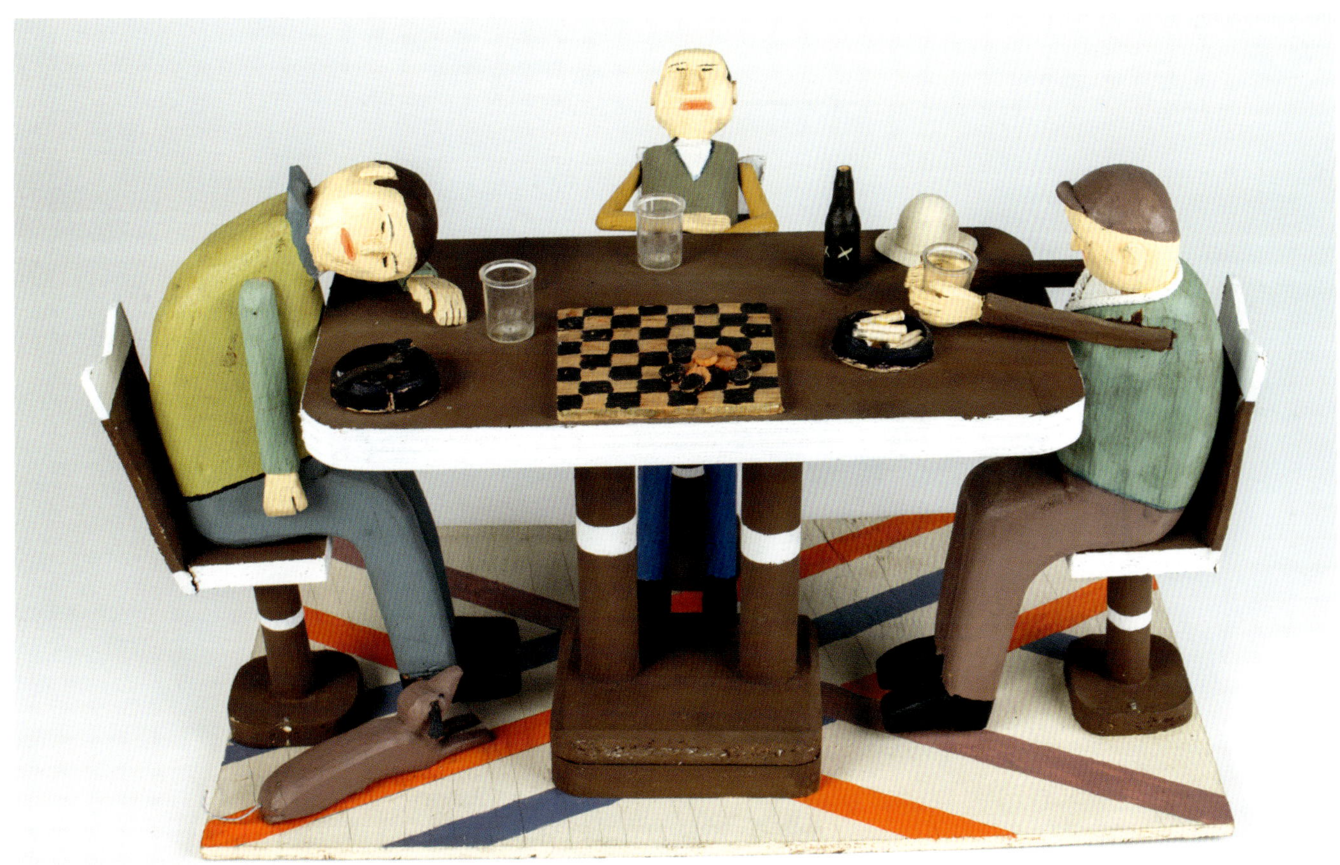

The Night Before the Morning After, Harold Tutty

(RAW PHOTOGRAPHY FOR AGNS)

out on the table from overindulging. *The Night Before the Morning After* (1989) is a good example of this genre of Tutty's work. That work was included in the exhibition *Nova Scotia Folk Art: Canada's Cultural Heritage* that toured the United Kingdom in 1989–90.

While Dick Tutty carved all of his figures, they were painted by his brother, Gerald, who also made a few carvings after Dick's death in 1995.

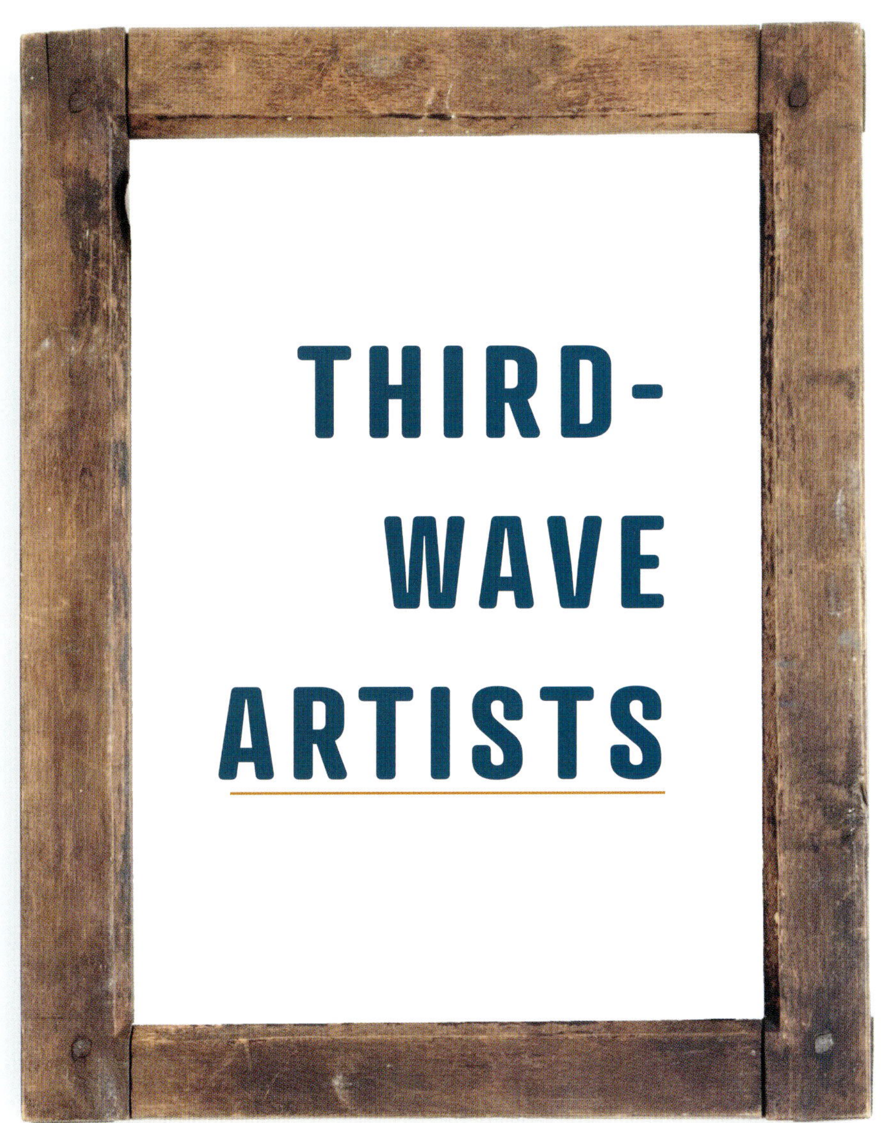

THIRD-WAVE ARTISTS

BARRY COLPITTS

(EAST SHIP HARBOUR, HALIFAX COUNTY)

b. 1960

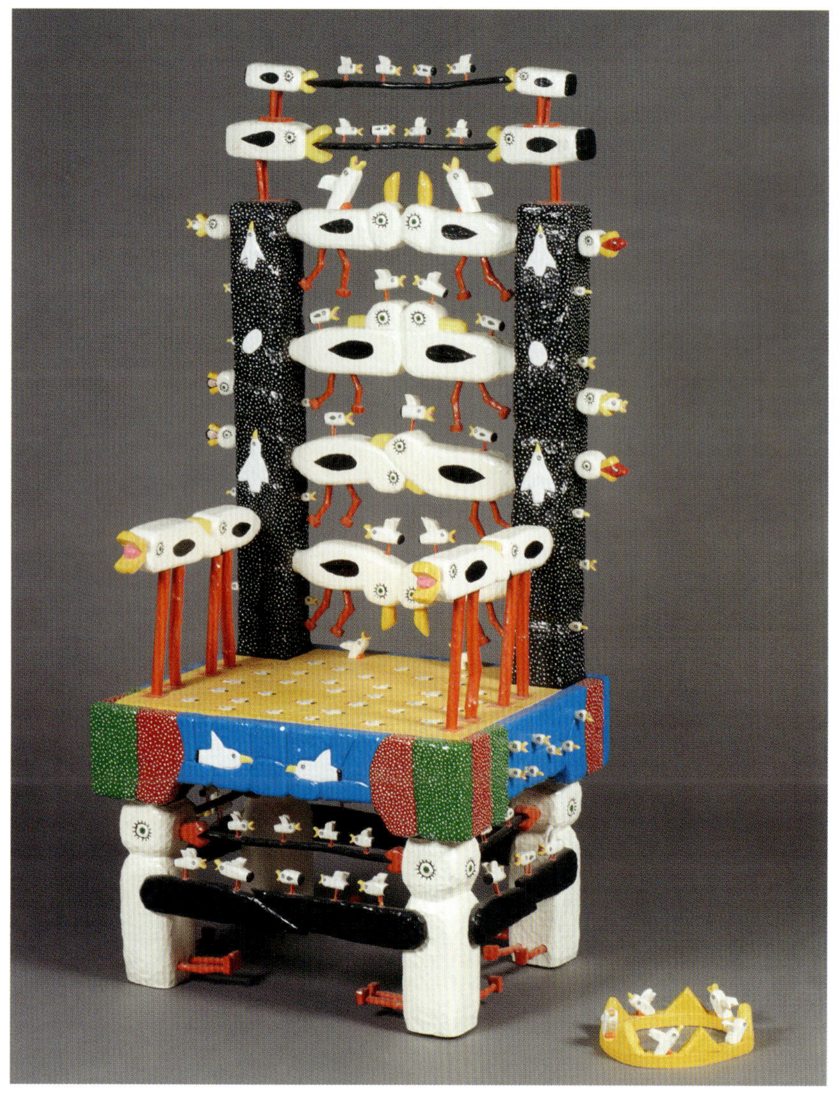

Seagull Throne, Barry Colpitts

(CANADIAN MUSEUM OF HISTORY, 2017.35.1 A-H, IMG2019-0043-0001)

"THE LONGER I DO IT, THE QUICKER they come, and the less good I am for anything else. Folk art is like the loaves and fishes, it keeps coming and coming."—Barry Colpitts[72]

After Maud Lewis's painted house, on permanent display at the Art Gallery of Nova Scotia in Halifax, the most famous decorated house in the province is Barry Colpitts's house in East Ship Harbour on the Eastern Shore. There are painted sculptures attached to the walls, fence, porch, shed—and even his truck. The house is more than a billboard for Colpitts's folk art business; it is a local landmark. Even the yoke for his oxen (from when he still used oxen to harvest wood) was decorated with whimsical carvings. Colpitts uses wood from his own woodlot for his carvings, choosing branches and logs that he feels can tell a story. "I use the trees in my backyard to make my carvings. I chop down the tree and look at the wood and branches to see what I might make."[73]

A regular at the Nova Scotia Folk Art Festival, Colpitts's work was included on the festival's poster in 2009. In the summer of 2014 the Acadia University Art Gallery mounted *Barry's World*, Colpitts's first solo exhibition at a public art gallery. His work is included in the permanent collections of the Nova Scotia Art Bank, the Beaverbrook Art Gallery, the Art Gallery of Nova Scotia, and the Canadian Museum of History, and in numerous private collections.

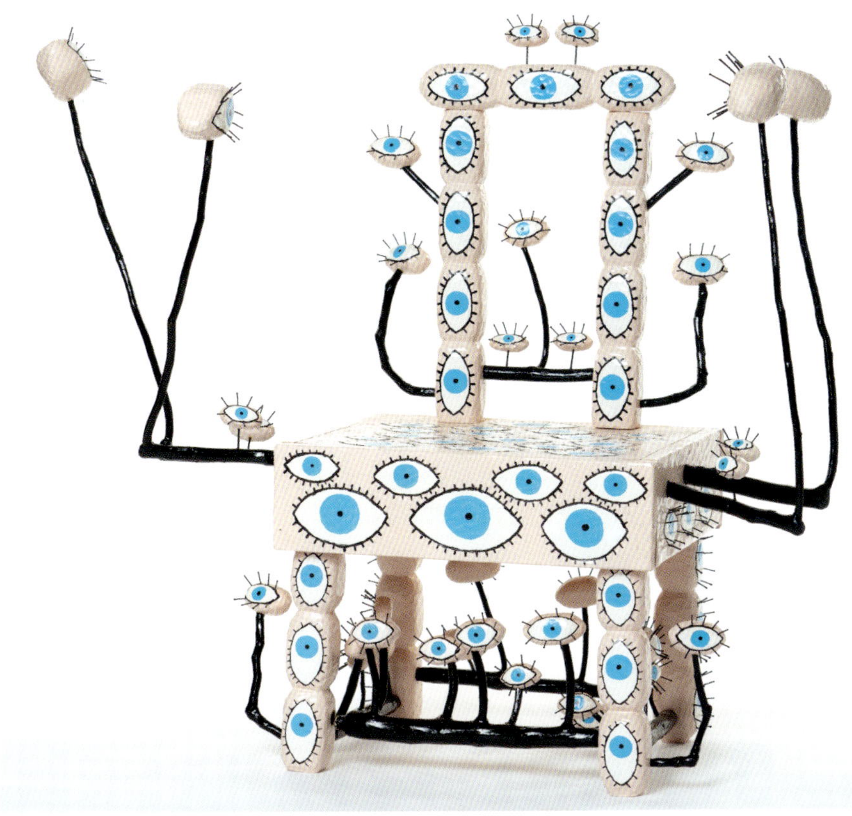

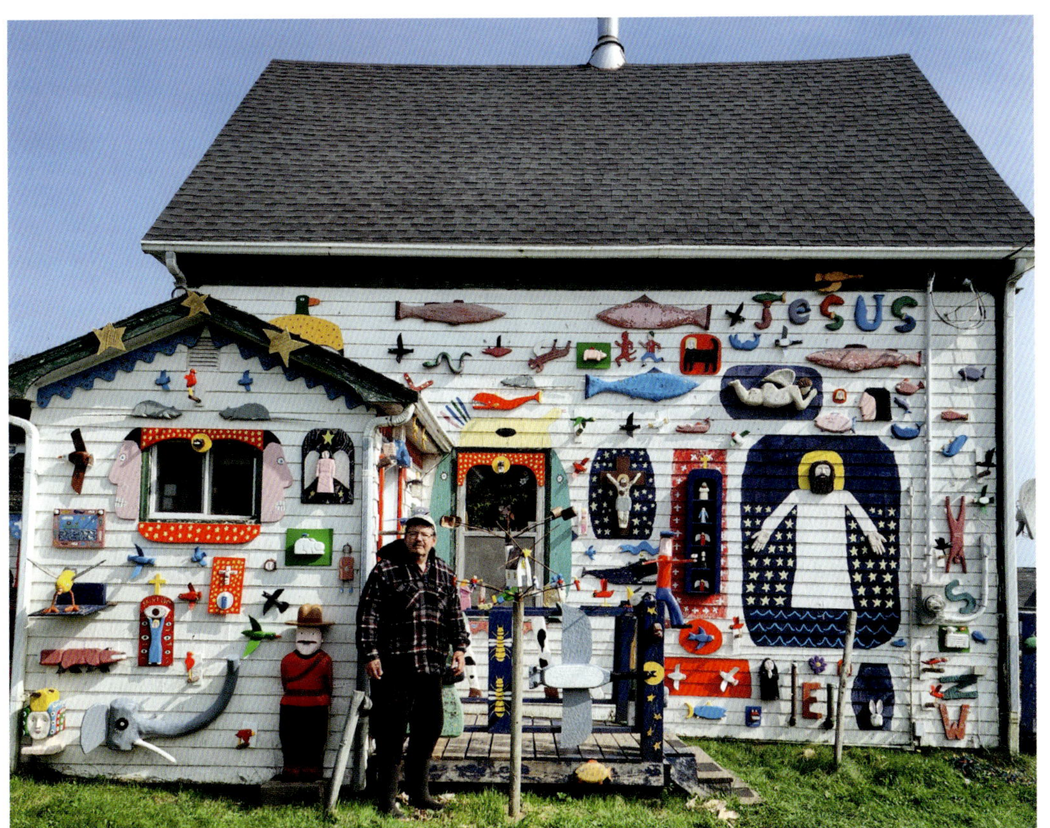

ABOVE: *Eyeball Chair*, Barry Colpitts

(MIKE TOMPKINS FOR AGNS)

BELOW: Barry Colpitts and his painted house

(BLACK SHEEP GALLERY)

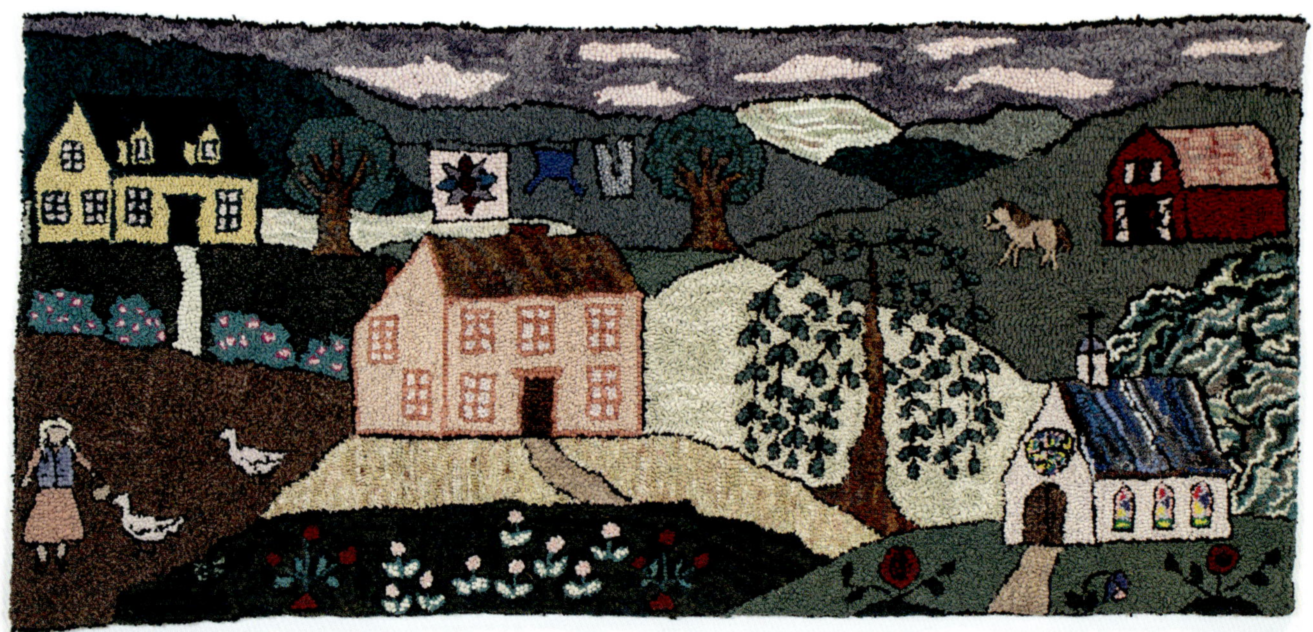

Village,
Deanne Fitzpatrick
(RAW PHOTOGRAPHY FOR AGNS)

DEANNE FITZPATRICK

(AMHERST, CUMBERLAND COUNTY)

b. 1965

"MY INFLUENCES ARE FOLK ART, BUT REALLY I THINK IT IS HARD TO call myself a folk artist. I am not outside the mainstream. I am well educated. I am a folk artist in that I am untrained artistically. I have never taken a fine art course."—Deanne Fitzpatrick[74]

Deanne Fitzpatrick was born in Freshwater, Newfoundland and Labrador, and moved to Nova Scotia for university, staying in Cumberland County where she worked as counsellor. She started to make hooked rugs, a form she remembered from her childhood in Newfoundland, but which she taught herself as an adult.

In 1992 her work was accepted for the Nova Scotia Folk Art Festival, and in 1993 she became a member of the Nova Scotia Folk Art Festival Society. As she herself acknowledges; however, she is hardly anyone's idea of a typical folk artist.

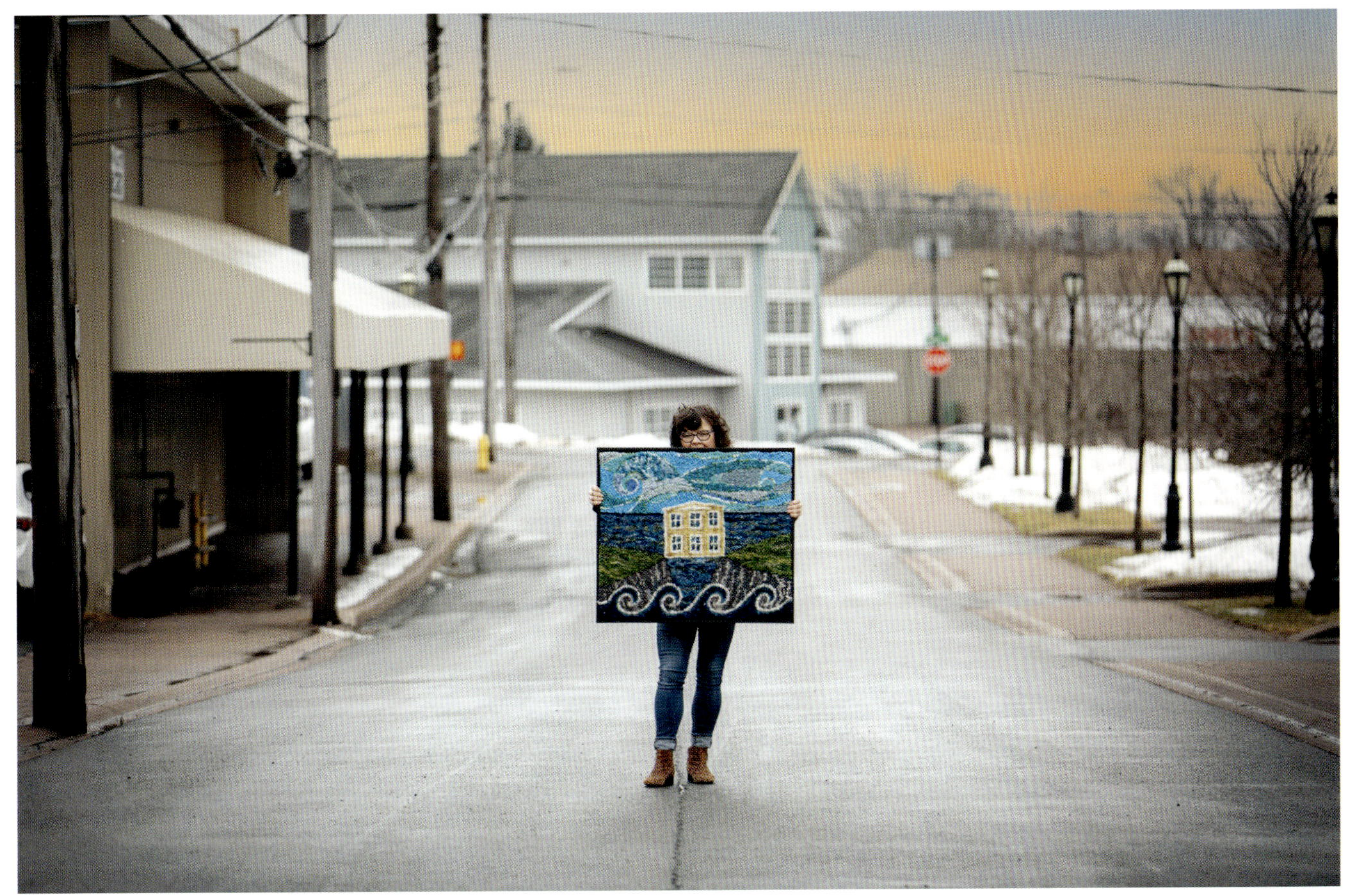

Deanne Fitzpatrick

(COURTESY DEANNE FITZPATRICK)

Like so many of the Nova Scotian artists working in a folk style today, her work crosses genres between fine craft, folk art, and fine art. Her work is included in the collections of the Canadian Museum of History, the Nova Scotia Art Bank, The Rooms, and the Art Gallery of Nova Scotia, which gave her a solo show in 1996. She now runs the Deanne Fitzpatrick Studio in Amherst and has written six books on rug-hooking.

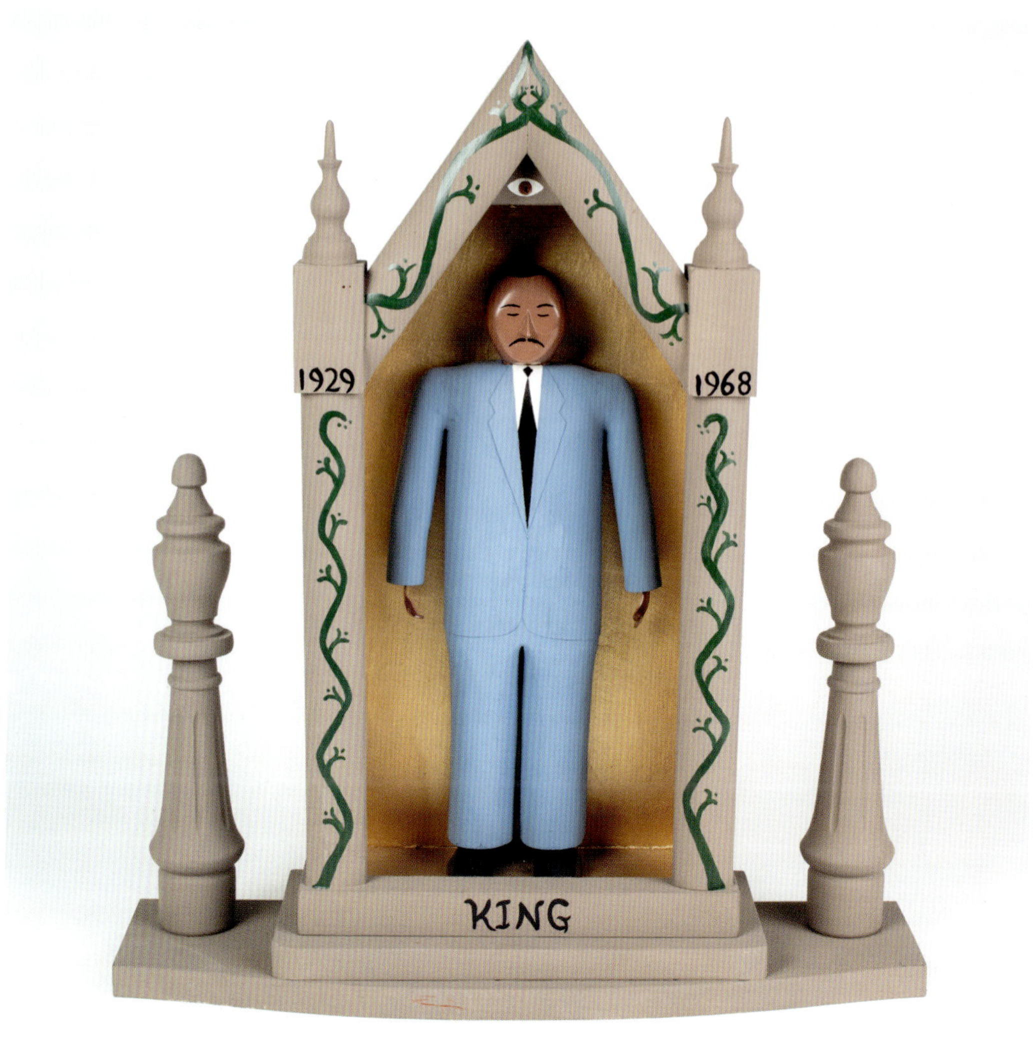

Martin,
Scott Higgins

(RAW PHOTOGRAPHY FOR AGNS)

SCOTT HIGGINS

(HARRIETSFIELD, HALIFAX COUNTY)

b. 1968

SCOTT HIGGINS BEGAN CARVING WHEN HE WAS EIGHTEEN. HE STARTED by carving duck decoys, but rapidly moved on to works that reflected on Nova Scotia's history and contemporary events. For seven years he showed at the

Houston North Gallery in Lunenburg, and was part of eleven shows there, including two solo exhibitions.

Higgins is not a typical folk artist in any way. After a burst of success beginning in 1987, he stopped making sculptures in the late 1990s. His last, and largest, sculpture, *Lord of the Flies*, was acquired by the AGNS in 2001. The gallery also acquired three of his paintings in 2002.

Higgins is no longer an active folk artist. Instead, after earning a degree in history at St. Mary's University, he completed a journalism degree at the University of King's College in Halifax (including a year in the school's renowned Foundation Program). Higgins has been a freelance writer and editor since 1995, writing for such publications as the *Chronicle Herald*, *Saltscapes* magazine, and *The Upper Canadian*. Among the many topics he has covered are a symposium on folk art and the Cape Breton folk artist David Stephens.

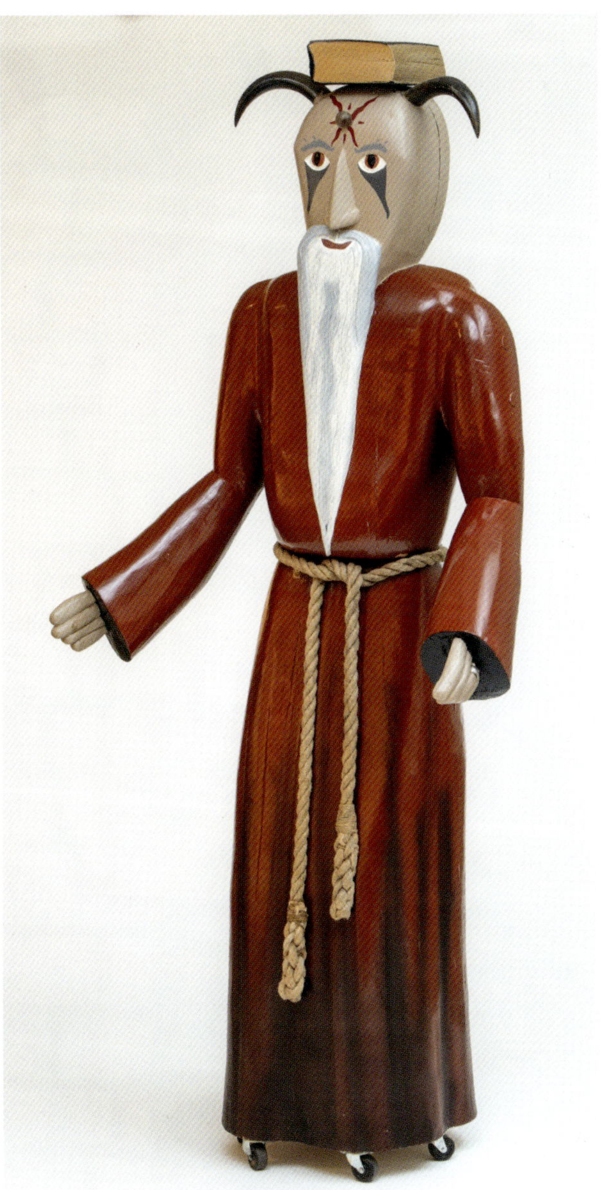

Lord of the Flies, Scott Higgins

(RAW PHOTOGRAPHY FOR AGNS)

Higgins's work is included in the collections of the Art Gallery of Nova Scotia, the Canadian Museum of History, the Canadian War Museum, and the Nova Scotia Art Bank, and in numerous public and private collections.

LAURA KENNEY

(TRURO, COLCHESTER COUNTY)

b. 1965

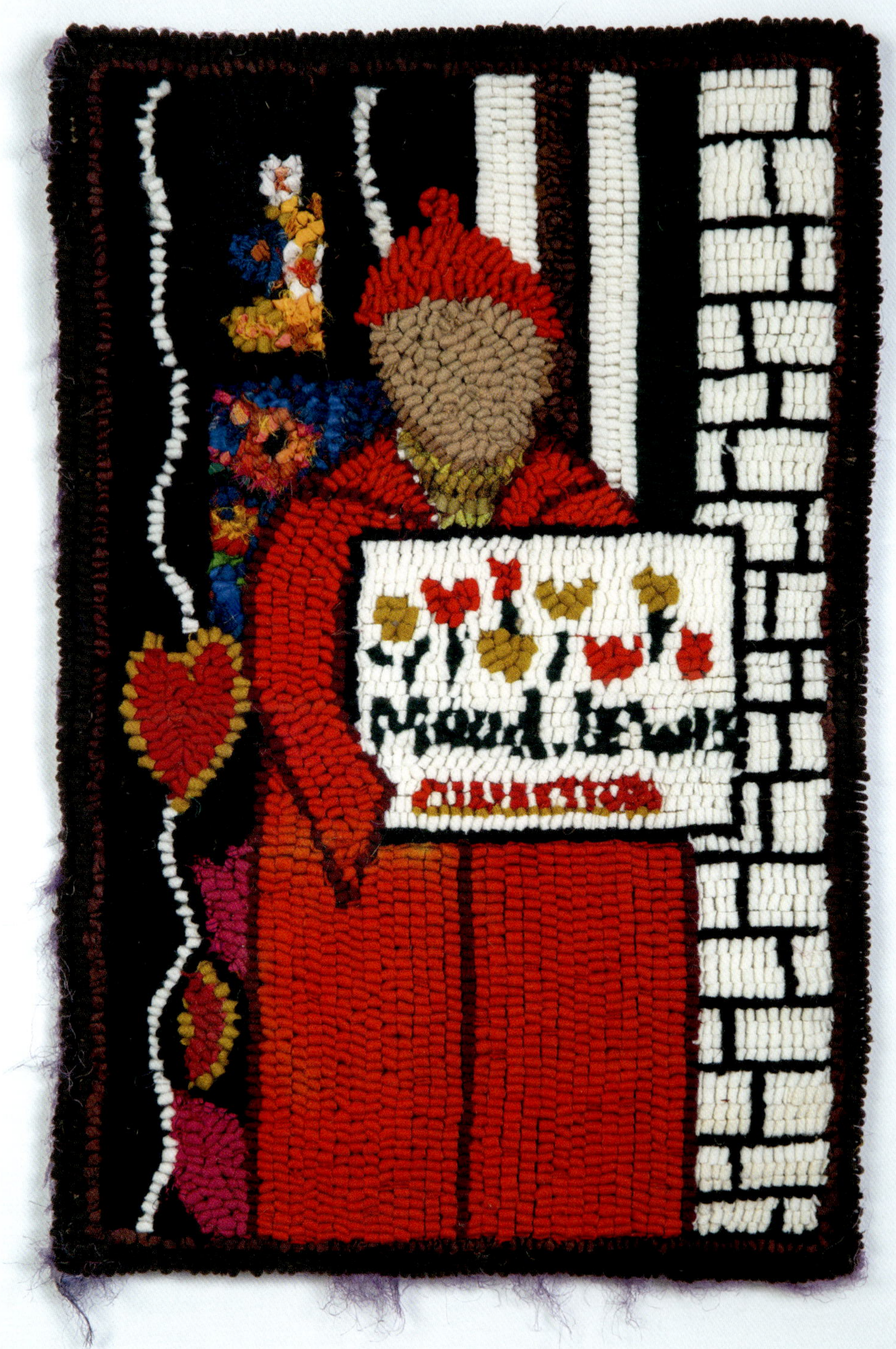

AGNS's Employee of the Month, Laura Kenney

(LAURA KENNEY)

LAURA KENNEY IS another folk artist who took a different route to the genre. Born in Moose Jaw, Saskatchewan, her family roots are in Nova Scotia. She moved to Truro in 1998 with her husband, and began rug-hooking that year, taking classes at the Rug Hooking Guild of Nova Scotia.

Her work is marked by its humour and its recurring characters, particularly Judy, who may be a sort of alter-ego for Kenney. "Judy can get overwhelmed by everyday tasks, yet she keeps her spirits up and with a sense of humour, Judy prevails; just as Maritimers do against all odds."[75]

Kenney started showing her rugs at the Nova Scotia Folk Art Festival in 2009 and has been an exhibitor every year since. In 2010 she was juried into the

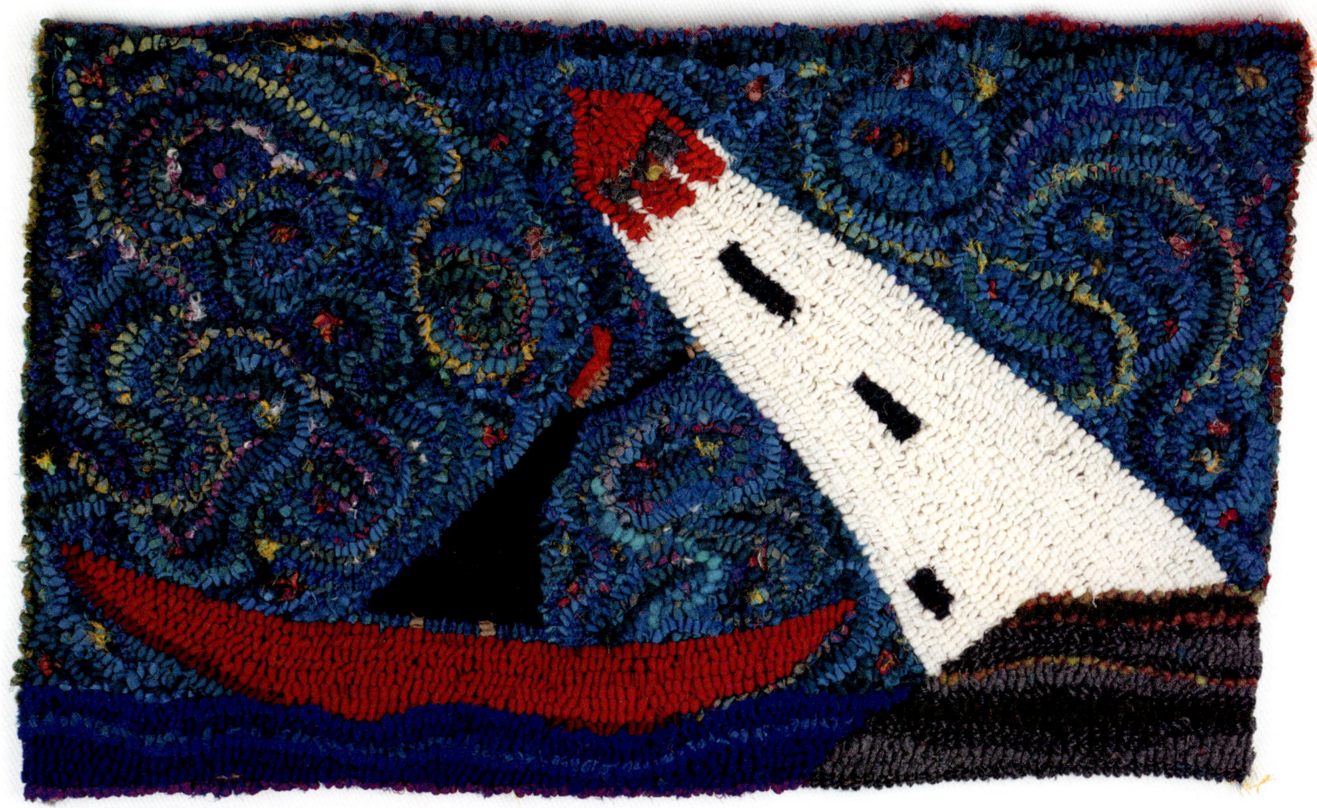

Judy...Saving the Lighthouse, Laura Kenney

(LAURA KENNEY)

Nova Scotia Craft Council, and two of her rugs have been purchased by the Nova Scotia Art Bank. In 2016 her work was included in an exhibition at the Art Gallery of Nova Scotia looking at the Nova Scotia fine art scene: *Terroir: A Nova Scotia Survey*.

Like other artists of her generation, folk art for Kenney is a style and an approach, but her work crosses genres depending on the context from which it is considered. In 2018 she and realist painter Steven Rhude mounted the two-person exhibition *Whose Maud?* at the Acadia University Art Gallery in Wolfville, a critical look at the industry that has grown up around folk artist Maud Lewis.

CRAIG NAUGLER

(BRIDGEWATER, LUNENBURG COUNTY)

b. 1973

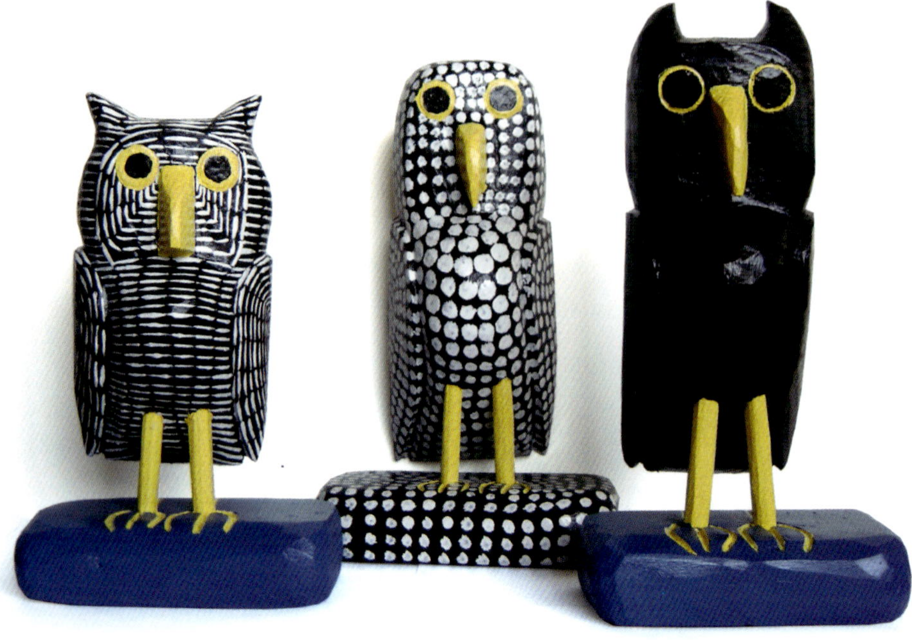

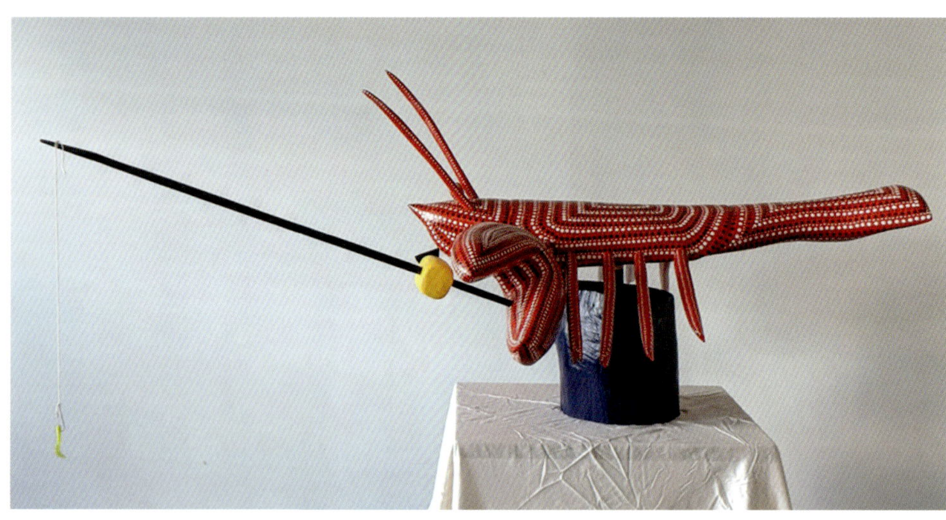

CRAIG NAUGLER IS THE son of folk artist Bradford Naugler; he has been making colourfully painted carvings since 1992. He began showing at the Nova Scotia Folk Art Festival in 1998, and his work can be found in galleries across Canada and the United States.

His carvings are primarily of birds and animals, though he makes figures and furniture as well. His spotted owls are probably his best-known works, many of which can be seen at Nova Scotia's White Point Beach Resort, where he has served as artist-in-residence.

ABOVE: *Owls*, Craig Naugler

(CRAIG NAUGLER AND BLACK SHEEP GALLERY)

BELOW: *Lobster Fishing*, Craig Naugler

(RITA VAN TASSEL, LUNENBURG HERITAGE SOCIETY)

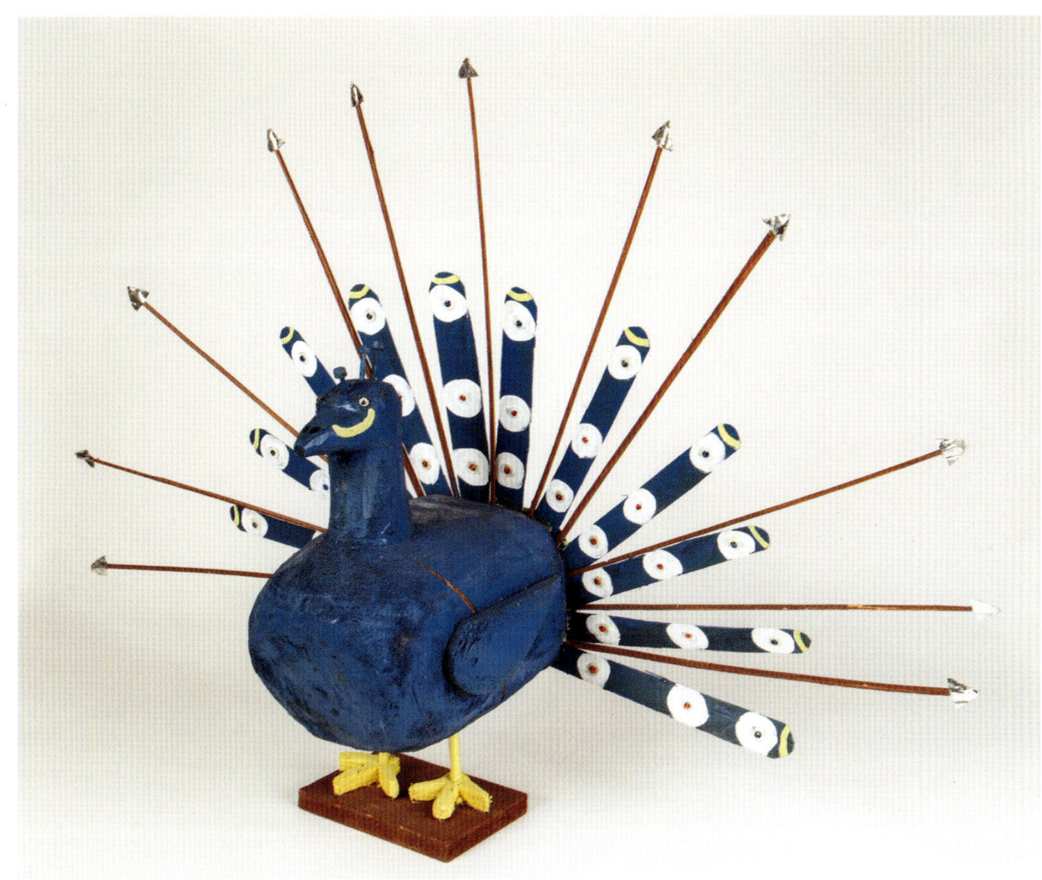

Peacock,
Peter Rafuse

(RAW PHOTOGRAPHY FOR AGNS)

PETER RAFUSE

(MELANSON, KINGS COUNTY)

b. 1949

A WOODSMAN WHO RUNS HIS OWN WOODLOT IN QUEENS COUNTY, PETER Rafuse started carving in 1991 with the encouragement of one of his neighbours. Rafuse's son, Blair, told the *Chronicle Herald*: "Garnet McPhail, actually, another folk artist down at the bottom of the mountain, he showed Dad, just to make a little extra money on the side, how to carve, and he picked it up."[76] McPhail helped Rafuse get his work into the Nova Scotia Folk Art Festival and he has been exhibiting there ever since.

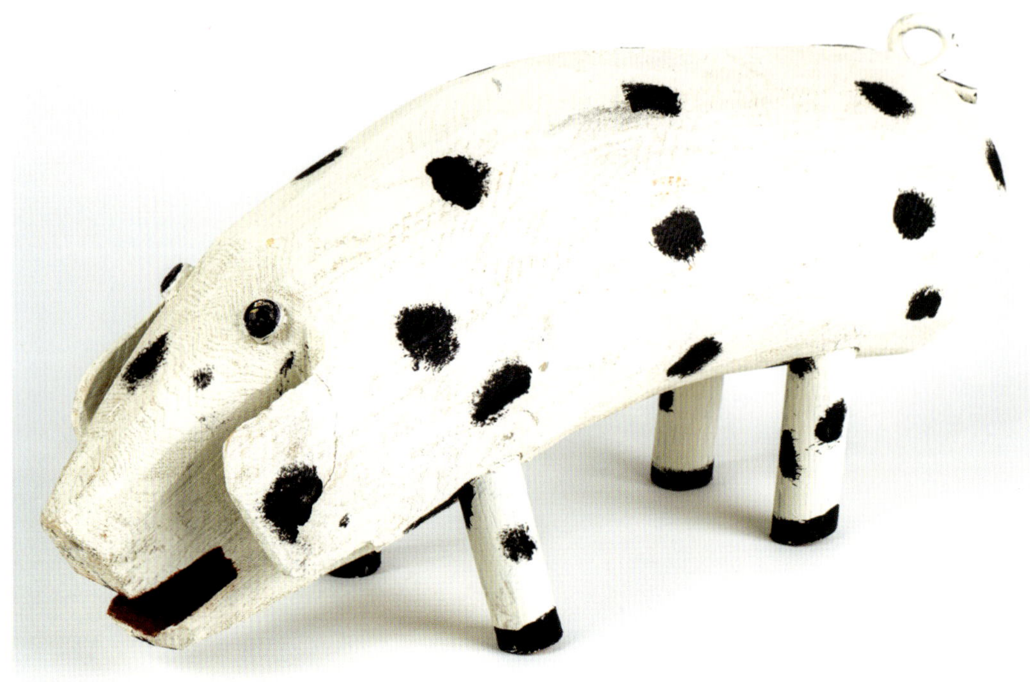

Pig,
Peter Rafuse
(RAW PHOTOGRAPHY FOR AGNS)

Rafuse carves his animal figures with a chainsaw before adding details such as legs and tails. His wife, Lisa, then takes over to do the painting. Peter Rafuse was the featured artist of the Nova Scotia Folk Festival in 2014, and his work is included in the permanent collection of the Art Gallery of Nova Scotia.

AFTERWORD

FOLK ART AS CONTEMPORARY ART?

IS IT SO STRANGE TO THINK OF NOVA SCOTIA FOLK ART BECOMING A genre of contemporary art? I don't think so. After all, folk art—at least the naïve or "outsider" sort of folk art—has always been related to fine art. Often a folk artist tries to emulate fine art, for instance, and the artist's lack of training, coupled with their own wit and skill, creates something new.

In Nova Scotia Folk Art we see several traditional fine art categories on display: landscapes, portraits and self-portraits, still-lifes, and nudes, for instance. Collins Eisenhauer did a portrait of Pierre Trudeau, and so did Walter Cook. Eisenhauer, Ralph Boutilier, Eddie Mandaggio, and Elmer Killen did self-portraits. Elmer Killen did a portrait of collector Chris Huntington, and Bill Roach did a portrait of folk artist Sidney Howard, who himself did portraits of Stompin' Tom Connors, Rita MacNeil, and John Diefenbaker, among others. Maud Lewis, Joe Norris, and Eddie Mandaggio took on the traditional painting genre of the still life, while Leo Naugler and Eli Whiteway made sculptures of traditional still life subjects. Collins Eisenhauer, Charles Tanner, and Murray Gallant made nudes. But it isn't just folk artists referencing fine art—the references also go the other way.

Gerald Ferguson, who along with Chris Huntington and Bernard Riordon did the most to bring Nova Scotia Folk Art into public collections, referenced traditional folk decoration in his stencil paintings of the 1990s.

As a major collector of folk art and country furniture, it was no coincidence that Ferguson was looking at the traditional decorative motifs stencilled on so many of the objects he was collecting. In his mixed-media works of the early 1970s, Eric Fischl, who was teaching at NSCAD at the time, referenced boats and fish, reflecting a contemporary take on traditional motifs. And Tim Zuck, known now as a realist painter, began painting in a manner heavily influenced by Nova Scotia Folk Art.

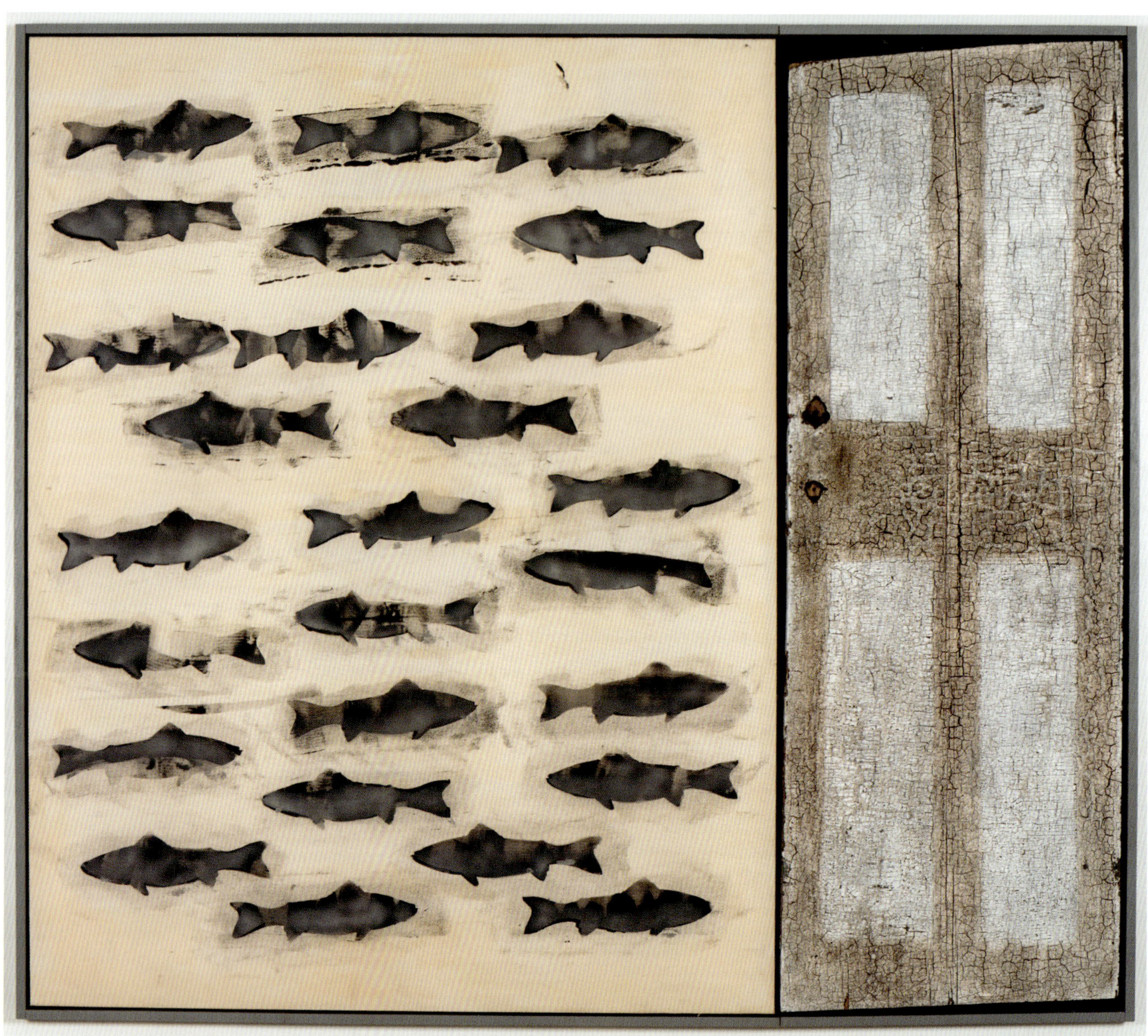

Fish and Door, Gerald Ferguson (AGNS)

In 1994 the Dalhousie Art Gallery mounted *Uses of the Vernacular in Nova Scotia Art*, an exhibition curated by Cliff Eyland and Susan Gibson Garvey that explored the relationships between folk art and forms of contemporary art that they felt adopted folk idioms. The exhibition included works by Nancy Edell, Gerald Ferguson, Kyle Jackson, Janice Leonard, Charlie Murphy, John Neville, Leslie Sampson, and Eric Walker. They also showed works by folk artists such as Collins Eisenhauer, Ellen Gould Sullivan, Maud Lewis, Leo Naugler, and Joe Sleep. Cliff Eyland, in his catalogue essay, was careful to point out how hard (and perhaps pointless) it was to cleanly differentiate between fine and folk art

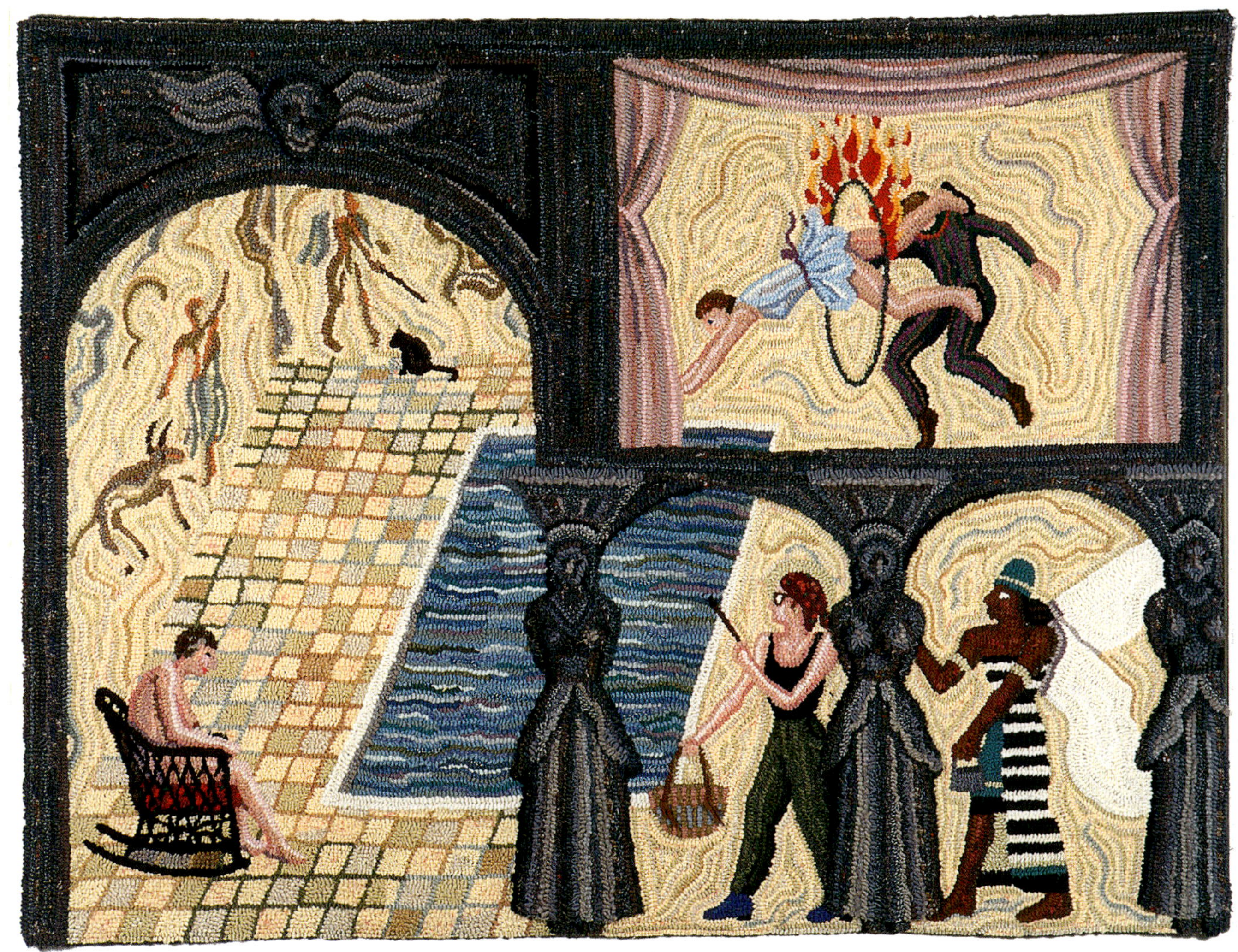

Waiting,
Nancy Edell
(AGNS)

in these cases. "Several of the art educated artists in this show are not simply making, as might be expected from their training, art historical references when they quote vernacular art," he wrote. "Conversely, the 'folk' artists in this exhibition make their work to professional standards, sometimes through the direct influence of art world professionals. Very often the professional and the primitive meet halfway."[77]

In that Dalhousie exhibition there were several instances of those meetings. Nancy Edell, for instance, whose work included intricate hooked rugs, did not study rug-hooking. She learned it the same way Laura Kenney and Deanne Fitzpatrick had—on her own and from seeking the advice of older women who knew the process.

Charlie Murphy never attended art school, but he was tutored by two famous artists—June Leaf and Robert Frank. Kyle Jackson studied at NSCAD before dropping out to become a folk artist. Decades later he returned to finish his degree and has mostly left the folk art designation behind.

In a world of smartphones and satellite television, what is a folk tradition anyway? Many of us are more familiar with the participants on *America's Got Talent* than we are with the flora and fauna of our own neighbourhoods, and we know more of the words to Ariana Grande tunes than to any folk songs taught to us by our grandmothers. There are exceptions to this of course, and Nova Scotia provides many of them. But the fact is that we have to work on our traditional cultures here as much as anywhere. We have to commit to it, and we have to live it. Kids in Mabou may still be learning the fiddle, but they also are learning Ariana Grande. Tradition adapts. That's how it survives.

Nova Scotia Folk Art has always been evidence of that ability to adapt. The first-wave folk artists were adapting to changes in work and the increased mechanization of logging, farming, and fishing that meant fewer labour jobs. They were adapting to newfound leisure time brought on by old-age pensions. After all, traditionally, the working class didn't retire—they worked until they died. These artists were adapting to visitors—tourists looking for souvenirs brought opportunities to earn money. And they were adapting to the market—to the tastes and expectation of galleries and collectors. The sum of those adaptations, works by Norris, Eisenhauer, Howard, and Boutilier, then became the standard to which other artists adapted, and so on.

Art, even folk art, is a conversation with peers, with history and with a vision of the future. Eddie Mandaggio was influenced by Collins Eisenhauer and Ralph Boutilier; the Naugler brothers by Mandaggio. And now Bradford's son Craig is making his own contribution to the conversation. Nova Scotia Folk Art is indeed a contemporary art, and, like every art form, it has practitioners that range from bad to good to great. Naïve, primitive, or folk—what matters is that those words define a style.

To return, finally, to the Oxford definition: "Sophisticated artists may also adopt a naïve style." The fact that an artist did not train at a university art school is no guarantee that they are unsophisticated. Professional and primitive can meet more than half way, and can easily be characteristics of the same artist.

Is folk art "all over" as the 1997 AGNS symposium asked? I think not, because there are still potential Charles Tanners (and Alex Colvilles) behind those weathered doors.

ACKNOWLEDGEMENTS

I WOULD LIKE TO ACKNOWLEDGE AND THANK ARTS NOVA SCOTIA, WHOSE support through a creation grant helped make this writing possible.

I would also like to thank the Art Gallery of Nova Scotia for their partnership and support in providing access to images of their collection, and for access to their folk art files. In particular, I would like to acknowledge the support of this project from Sarah Moore Fillmore (Chief Executive Officer) and Shannon Parker (Laufer Curator of Collections) and the research assistance of Troy Wagner (Assistant Registrar).

This book has benefitted greatly from the work of many other curators and authors. In particular, the work of Erin Morton, Chris Huntington, and Bernard Riordon was invaluable. I would also like to thank Audrey Sanford of Black Sheep Gallery for sharing her knowledge, and for all of her patience with my many questions and requests.

As always, I would like to thank my wife, Sarah Maloney, for her support during the research and writing of this book.

BIBLIOGRAPHY

Chilvers, Ian and Osborne, Harold. *The Oxford Dictionary of Art* (Oxford: Oxford University Press, 1988).

Crépeau, Pierre (editor). *From the Heart: Folk Art in Canada* (Toronto: McClelland and Stewart, 1983).

Cronin, Ray. *Gerald Ferguson: Thinking of Painting* (Kentville: Gaspereau Press, 2018).

———. *Our Maud: The Life, Art and Legacy of Maud Lewis* (Halifax: The Art Gallery of Nova Scotia, 2017).

Ferguson, Bruce. *Joe Sleep: Retrospective* (Halifax: The Art Gallery of Nova Scotia, 1981).

Ferguson, Gerald. *Folk Art from the Collection of Gerald Ferguson* (Halifax: Art Gallery of Nova Scotia, 2002).

Field, Richard Henning. *Spirit of Nova Scotia* (Toronto: Dundurn Press, 1985).

Fillmore, Sarah. *Terroir: A Nova Scotia Survey* (Halifax: Art Gallery of Nova Scotia, 2016).

Foshay, Susan M. *Hooked Mats: One for Sorrow, Two for Joy* (Halifax: The Art Gallery of Nova Scotia, 1996).

———. *Sidney Howard's Beacons and Strays* (Halifax: Art Gallery of Nova Scotia, 1998).

Huntington, Chris. *Charlie Tanner: Retrospective.* (Halifax: The Art Gallery of Nova Scotia, 1984).

———. *Joe Norris: Paintings and Furniture* (Halifax: Dalhousie Art Gallery, 1978).

Laurette, Patrick Condon. *Ellen Gould Sullivan: Hooked Mats* (Halifax: Art Gallery of Nova Scotia, 1979).

MacDonald, Frank. *William D. Roach: Folk Artist* (Sydney, University of Cape Breton Press, 2014).

Martin, Ken. *Chris Huntington and the Resurgence of Nova Scotia Folk Art 1975–1995* (Halifax: Art Gallery of Nova Scotia, 1997).

Morton, Erin. *For Folk's Sake: Art and Economy in Twentieth-Century Nova Scotia* (Montréal and Kingston: McGill-Queen's University Press, 2017).

Pearse, Harold. *Eva Comeau-Hersey: A Gift of Art* (Halifax: Art Gallery of Nova Scotia, 1998).

Sherman, Joseph (editor). *The AGNS Permanent Collection—Selected Works* (Halifax: Art Gallery of Nova Scotia, 2002).

Riordon, Bernard. *Folk Art of Nova Scotia* (Halifax: The Art Gallery of Nova Scotia, 1976).

———. *Joe Norris: Painted Visions of Nova Scotia* (Fredericton, Goose Lane Editions, 2000).

Nova Scotia Folk Art: Canada's Cultural Heritage (Halifax: The Art Gallery of Nova Scotia, 1995).

Stacey, Robert and Wylie, Liz. *Eighty Twenty: 100 Years of the Nova Scotia College of Art and Design* (Halifax: Art Gallery of Nova Scotia, 1998).

Woolaver, Lance. *The Illuminated Life of Maud Lewis* (Halifax: Nimbus Publishing, 1996).

Wyllie, Robin. *A Joyous Vision* (Lunenburg: Nova Scotia Folk Art Festival Society, 1996).

ENDNOTES

1 Erin Morton, *For Folk's Sake: Art and Economy in Twentieth-Century Nova Scotia* (Montréal and Kingston: McGill-Queens University Press, 2017), xvii.

2 Harold Pearse, "Nova Scotia Folk Art: Some Questions, Musings and Speculations," *A Joyous Vision: Contemporary Folk Art in Nova Scotia*, Nova Scotia Folk Art Festival Society, 1995.

3 Chris Huntington, *Charlie Tanner: Retrospective* (Halifax: Art Gallery of Nova Scotia, 1984), 4.

4 Ian Chilvers and Harold Osborne, *The Oxford Dictionary of Art* (Oxford: Oxford University Press, 1988), 182.

5 Ibid.

6 Riordon, *Folk Art of Nova Scotia*, 8.

7 Chilvers and Osborne, *The Oxford Dictionary*, 349.

8 Ibid.

9 Riordon, *Folk Art of Nova Scotia*, 8.

10 Ibid.

11 Morton, *For Folk's Sake*, 74.

12 Huntington, *Charlie Tanner*, 4.

13 Chris Huntington, "Folk Art is a Pillar of Nova Scotia's Cultural Expression," *Chronicle Herald*, April 14, 1997.

14 Scott Higgins, "Is Folk Art Dead," *Southender*, April 1999, 16.

15 Bradford Naugler, Artist File, Art Gallery of Nova Scotia.

16 Quoted in Bernard Riordon, *Folk Art of Nova Scotia* (Halifax: Art Gallery of Nova Scotia, 1976), 23.

17 Riordon, *Folk Art of Nova Scotia*, 24.

18 Samuel Bollivar, Artist file, Art Gallery of Nova Scotia.

19 Quoted in Riordon, *Folk Art of Nova Scotia*, 27.

20 Ibid, 26.

21 Ibid.

22 Ibid, 27.

23 Ralph Boutilier, Artist File, Art Gallery of Nova Scotia, interview by Sara Fraser.

24 Chris Huntington quoted in Erin Morton, *For Folk's Sake* (Montréal and Kingston: McGill Queen's University Press, 2016), 46.

25 Peter Crowell, e-mail to Art Gallery of Nova Scotia, July 2008.

26 Laura Clement, "Valley Quilter: Evelyn Dickie," *Valley Views*, 1977, 3.

27 James R. Nelson, "They Decorate a World They Want to Improve," *The Birmingham News*, April 15, 1979.

28 Quoted in Morton, *For Folk's Sake*, 106.

29 Quoted in Riordon, *Folk Art of Nova Scotia*, 32.

30 Ibid.

31 Sidney Howard, Artist File, Art Gallery of Nova Scotia, interview with Ted Rhodes.

32 Quoted in Peter Day, "Roadside Attractions," *Canadian Art*, Volume 2, Number 1, Spring 1985, 50.

33 Philip Brooks, "The Collector's Remembrances," in Susan McAlpine Foshay, *Sidney Howard's Beacons and Strays* (Halifax: Art Gallery of Nova Scotia, 1998), 4.

34 Karl MacKeeman, "Halifax: Folk Art of Nova Scotia," *Art Magazine* 30, Dec./Jan. 1976, 77.

35 Quoted in Riordon, *Folk Art of Nova Scotia*, 39.

36 Ibid.

37 Quoted in Riordon, *Folk Art of Nova Scotia*, 41.

38 Ibid.

39 Ibid.

40 Chris Huntington quoted in Ken Martin, *A Life of Its Own: Chris Huntington and the Resurgence of Nova Scotia Folk Art 1975–1995* (Halifax: Art Gallery of Nova Scotia, 1997), 14.

41 Harry Thurston, "Nova Scotia Traditions," *Equinox Magazine*, Number 39, May/June 1988, 55.

42 Chris Huntington, *Joe Norris: Paintings and Furniture* (Halifax: Dalhousie Art Gallery, 1978), 2.

43 Riordon, *Folk Art of Nova Scotia*, 47.

44 Quoted in Riordon, *Folk Art of Nova Scotia*, 49.

45 Bruce Ferguson, *Joe Sleep: Retrospective* (Halifax: Art Gallery of Nova Scotia, 1981), 6.

46 Ibid.

47 Riordon, *Folk Art of Nova Scotia*, 49.

48 Charlie Tanner quoted in Chris Huntington, *Charlie Tanner*, 4.

49 Donald Boudreau, Artist File, Art Gallery of Nova Scotia

50 Ibid.

51 David Woods, quoted in John DeMings, NovaNewsNow.com, posted March 31, 2008.

52 Harold Cromwell, Artist File, Art Gallery of Nova Scotia.

53 Woods, quoted in John DeMings.

54 Nikki Sullivan, "New Waterford Artist's Work to be Featured at Library, *Cape Breton Post*, Jan. 15, 2019.

55 Murray Gallant interview, *Folk Art Maritime*, Gallery Ramblings, folkart-maritime.com/extra_mile/page_n12.htm.

56 Quoted in Greg Stott, "Whimsical Whittlin', *Dofasco Illustrated News*, Spring 1995, 3.

57 Kyle Jackson, VANS Artist profile, visualarts.ns.ca kyle-jackson-artist-profile/.

58 Elmer Killen, Artist File, Art Gallery of Nova Scotia.

59 Alex Busby, *Folk Art Found Me,* National Film Board of Canada, 1994.

60 Quoted in Harry Thurston, "Nova Scotia Traditions," *Equinox Magazine,* Number 389, May/June 1988, 53.

61 Bradford Naugler, artist's statement on Nova Scotia Folk Art Festival website, nsfolkartfestival.com/bradford-naugler

62 Leo Naugler quoted in Alex Busby, *Folk Art Found Me.*

63 Stephen Outhouse interviewed in Michael J. Hennigan, "Non-Academic in Nova Scotia," *The Upper Canadian,* January/February 1993, 36.

64 Lorne Reid, quoted in Elissa Barnard, "Cape Breton Artist Reid Made his Mark Quickly," *Chronicle Herald*, March 28, 1991.

65 Stephen Godfrey, "Artist Searches for his True Colours," *Globe and Mail,* October 6, 1990, C1.

66 Ibid, C2.

67 Ibid.

68 Quoted in Elissa Bernard, "Cape Breton Artist Reid."

69 Quoted in Frank MacDonald, *William D. Roach: Folk Artist* (Sydney: Cape Breton University Press, 2014), 145.

70 Various authors, *From the Heart: Folk Art in Canada* (Toronto: McClelland and Stewart, 1983), 64.

71 David Stephens artist statement, davidpstephens.tripod.com/

72 Barry Colpitts interviewed by Hillary Nangle, mainetravelmaven.com/a-visit-with-nova-scotia-folk-artist-barry-colpitts/.

73 Barry Colpitts, Artist Statement, "Artisans of the Eastern Shore," seacoast-trailart.com/index.php/art/artist/16.

74 Deanne Fitzpatrick, interviewed by Hayley Perry, hookingrugs.com/pages/faq.

75 Quoted in Sarah Fillmore, *Terroir: A Nova Scotia Survey* (Halifax: The Art Gallery of Nova Scotia, 2016), 102.

76 Bill Spurr, "Folk Art is All in the Family for Peter Rafuse," *Chronicle Herald*, August 2, 2014.

77 Cliff Eyland, "Red Herrings, Clever Horses and the Benefits of Doubt," *Uses of the Vernacular in Nova Scotian Art* (Halifax: Dalhousie Art Gallery, 1994).